Praise for *Zoo*

"At last, the Baedeker to American zoos. These are the major portals to understanding our place in nature, and this book is a must for every home."

— DR. THOMAS E. LOVEJOY, assistant secretary for environmental and external affairs, Smithsonian Institution

"*Zoo* is an invaluable publication that will guide the interested public to this country's tremendously varied and exciting zoo experiences. Anthony Marshall has done a remarkable job of compiling a wealth of useful information, complete with penetrating comments and critiques. Clearly, if the public's interest in conserving the world's important and varied species of wildlife is to continue to grow, the importance of these zoological collections is paramount. To really become concerned at intellectual and emotional levels, one must be familiar with these endangered animals. Zoos, in all their great variety, provide that opportunity."

— LAURANCE S. ROCKEFELLER, past chairman, New York Zoological Society, and trustee emeritus, National Geographic Society

ZOO

ZOO

Profiles of
102 Zoos,
Aquariums, and
Wildlife Parks
in the
United States

ANTHONY D.
MARSHALL

Random House 🏛 New York

Library of Congress Cataloging-in-Publication Data
Marshall, Anthony D.
Zoo / by Anthony D. Marshall.
p.   cm.
Includes index.
ISBN 0-679-74687-0
1. Zoos—United States—Guidebooks.   2. Aquariums, Public—United
States—Guidebooks.   3. Ecotourism.   I. Title.
QL76.5.U6M37   1993
590'.74'473—dc20   93-33984

Manufactured in the United States of America on acid-free paper
2 4 6 8 9 7 5 3
First Edition

Book design by Victoria Wong

Contents

Preface

I am filled with the sense that life on this planet has meaning when I am with animals in their own natural habitat, whether it be observing primates in Africa, elephants in India, penguins in Antarctica, polar bears in the Arctic, horned guans in Guatemala, or swimming with sea lions in the Galápagos. While humans have attained greater intelligence than other species, man is but one of 1,392,485 identified animal species. This is a fact we must appreciate, and being in close proximity to other species can help us to better understand the interrelationship of living beings. When I visit a zoo my most memorable experiences are always close contacts with animals. While not all animals in captivity are approachable, many are. Walking among kangaroos at the Fort Wayne Children's Zoo, feeling a tarantula creep up one's arm, standing only feet away from the massive elk at Washington's Northwest Trek, and strolling through an aviary with free-flying birds, as well as petting domestic animals at zoos for children and using touch tanks at aquariums, are all experiences that bring humans in close contact with other species.

You too can experience this sense of meaning. When did you last visit a zoo? Why did you go? The zoo visit should have been entertaining for you and your family, but it could, should, have been more than that. Zoos are changing, and your expectations for them should change too. Good zoos today offer more than entertainment. They offer an opportunity to understand wildlife, wildlife habitats, and, most important, the need for conservation. Many animals at a zoo are representatives of species that are found in the wild, but some of them can now be found only at zoos; in the wild, they are extinct or becoming extinct as a result of man's destructive actions, including his destruction of wildlife's natural habitats.' Good zoos emphasize that if people care about the animals they see at the zoo, they can help save them in the wild by acting to preserve their habitats. The bottom line is that if habitats are not preserved, wildlife will be lost. By taking advantage of what zoos offer, visitors of all ages may learn how they can play a part in preserving, even improving, the environment of our planet.

The introduction to *Zoo* offers a brief overview of the historical development of zoos; some perspectives on zoos' and aquariums' education and conservation activities; and a "Zoo Visit Checklist" to help you in planning your zoo visit.

The main section of *Zoo* consists of in-depth profiles of 102 zoos and aquariums that offer both fun and education. The profiles contain practical information you need to visit a particular zoo or aquarium, such as how to get there and hours of operation, plus information on outstanding exhibits, special programs (including those for children), and other highlights. Also included are biographic sketches of a number of zoo directors, stories about zoos or animals, along with a sprinkling of my own experiences and reactions.

In the appendixes you will find some special listings including a selection of "Zoo Directors' Favorite Exhibits," "High- and Low-Profile Animals," and detailed information on organizers of wildlife-, conservation-, and nature-oriented tours and programs, for those interested in seeing animals in the wild.

In writing this book I have drawn on my past and ongoing association with animals. I have served on the Board of Trustees of the New York Zoological Society (renamed NYZS The Wildlife Conservation Society in 1992) since the 1960's; I serve on its Executive Committee, and am Chairman of the Education Committee. Since 1989 I have been a contributing editor for wildlife to *Condé Nast Traveler* magazine. I have been fortunate in having spent many years on business in Africa and a total of eight years as American ambassador in Madagascar, Trinidad and

Tobago, the Seychelles, and Kenya—countries with diverse and fascinating wildlife. These experiences form the basis of my interest and concern for animals. Furthermore, to obtain first-hand material on zoos for this book I visited 110 zoos and aquariums in the United States and interviewed more than 130 zoo/aquarium people.

It is my hope that *Zoo* will not only help readers get more out of a visit to a particular zoo, but will also give them a better understanding of what zoos are all about, why they exist, and what they are trying—or should be trying—to achieve. The role of zoos is no longer just to provide entertainment, as has been the case in the past, but to be an educational tool to increase public understanding of the ultimate goals of environmentalists: preserving the diversity of life on earth, saving habitats, and working for the survival of species, including *Homo sapiens*.

Acknowledgments

It would takes pages to list and individually acknowledge the directors of nearly all of the 110 zoos and aquariums I visited who kindly granted me interviews, plus the staff members I met, in addition to the many concerned environmentalists and zoological specialists I talked to. The dedication and interest of *all* of those I met was overwhelming. I have mentioned many in the text of this book, but thank them all for their help, concern, and assistance.

Introducing
the Zoo

Zoos Past, Present, and Future

The word *zoo* is derived from the Greek *zoion,* meaning
"living creature."

Background

Early humans, returning to their caves from the hunt or from
gathering foodstuffs, would pick up a sharp rock and, raising it
to the wall, make lines, images of animals. This was probably
humans' first effort to capture other species for collection—visual
collection. Collections of live animals date from as early as 4500
B.C. in what became Persia. Egyptians kept wild dogs, cats,
hyenas, leopards, and cheetah for hunting. About 1100 B.C. the
Chinese emperor Wen Wang built a 900-acre walled park in the
province of Ho Nan containing deer, goats, antelope, birds, and
fish. In sixth century B.C. Nebuchadnezzar created a zoo in Baby-
lon. The Greeks and Romans also had zoos, the largest, that of the
Roman emperor Trajan (A.D. 98–117) numbering 11,000 animals.
In France, Philip VI started a collection of animals at the Louvre
in 1333, and 300 years later Louis XIII kept animals at Versailles.
The Medici popes possessed a large menagerie in the Vatican. In
1100 Henry I of England put lions, leopards, and camels in a zoo
in Oxfordshire, which were transferred to the Tower of London

during the reign of Henry IV. They remained there until 1828, when London's Regent's Park Zoo opened as the first "scientific" (as opposed to purely entertaining) zoological park, launched by the newly formed (1826) Zoological Society of London.

Across the Atlantic, Aztec Emperor Montezuma created in Tenochtitlán (today's Mexico City) America's first botanical garden and zoological park. It was an extraordinary park staffed by more than 300 people. Its main purpose was ornamental, although it had a practical side as well, providing animals for hunting and sacrificial ceremonies, and skins and feathers for clothing and rugs. Don Hernando Cortés, in 1519, reported that in the emperor's zoo "lions, tigers, snakes and crocodiles were kept in barred cages along with 'strange people'—hunchbacks, albinos and dwarfs, for which the emperor paid high prices." Some parents, eager to make a profit, deformed their own children in order to take advantage of the emperor's appetite for the bizarre. Dogs were fed to reptiles, and tigers and leopards feasted on goats. Criminals were occasionally fed to carnivorous mammals.

In the United States, as in England, there were private menageries starting in the late 1700s, but the first modern zoos stem from the Victorian era. Several zoos vie politely for the title of America's first zoo. The Philadelphia Zoo dates from 1874, though its plan was approved in 1859. The Central Park Zoo in New York City opened earlier, in 1873, with a black bear, ducks, and pets in the basement of the Arsenal in Central Park, but its plan wasn't approved until 1861. Lincoln Park Zoo, in Chicago, gives 1868 as its founding date. In March 1887 the Smithsonian Institution in Washington, D.C., established a "little try-out zoo" for William Temple Hornaday, its first director, to "test the interest of the American public in collections of living animals." In 1890 Hornaday resigned and went to the New York Zoological Society, which opened in 1899. The first moated exhibit, a giant move away from the bare cement walls and bars of zoos' early era, was made in 1907 by Carl Hagenbeck at The Tierpark outside Hamburg for ungulates (hoofed animals), big cats, and flightless birds. Currently we are witnessing a move away from simple moated exhibits to natural-habitat exhibits.

What, Really, Is a Zoo?

Today the American Association of Zoological Parks and Aquariums (AAZPA)* has *accredited* 162 zoos and aquariums. All zoos and aquariums must obtain an exhibitor's license from the United States Department of Agriculture (USDA). In addition to the accredited institutions more than 1,250 organizations have received a USDA exhibitor's license, and up to 650 of these have collections of animals that could be classified as zoos and/or aquariums. The granting of an exhibitor's license guarantees the fulfillment of certain conditions. Yet the question remains: What do we expect of a genuine zoo?

Ivan is a 400-pound lowland gorilla who has lived behind bars for 28 years at the B&I Shopping Center in Tacoma, Washington. A visitor sees Ivan stretch his large frame, bend forward to gain balance, then stand up, hunching forward. He walks—it is more of a limp, though Ivan isn't lame—to the far wall of his concrete cell. His cell leads to two outdoor but equally restricted areas. He stops briefly, turns his hanging head sideways with a wistful look at daylight through the open door.

Ivan is well-fed, receives medical care, and is entertained by professionals who come to see him—a zoologist and two associates spend six hours daily with Ivan and he gets visits from anthropologists—and the general public, who come to gawk and conduct one-sided inane conversations. Ivan has been taught to paint, which he thoroughly enjoys. His paintings currently sell for $40 each. About 400 paintings (Ivan is a mass producer) have been bought by two interior decorators in San Francisco. The revenue goes to Ivan indirectly, through his owner, Ron Irwin, a respected local citizen and past president of the Tacoma Chamber

*7970 D Old Georgetown Rd., Bethesda, MD 20814. As this book went to press, the AAZPA changed its name to American Zoo and Aquarium Association, abbreviated AZA.

of Commerce. Ron claims it costs more than $60,000 a year to care for Ivan. Ron's father originally owned the sporting goods store at the B&I Shopping Center, which currently has monkeys, birds, and snakes. Ron's father initiated the idea of having a "zoo" in the store and applied for and was granted an exhibitor's license. The "zoo" is inspected by the USDA regularly and, Ron reports, "exceeds every regulation" in compliance with USDA requirements.

One part of the AAZPA's definition of a zoo is that it be open to the public at regular hours. But on its letterhead the AAZPA lists the aims of a zoo or aquarium as conservation, education, scientific study, and recreation—in that order. Ivan's home is not what a zoo should be; his life is not what a captive animal's should be. Humans took Ivan from his native habitat and put him in captivity for the purpose of letting people look at him. This is Ivan's sole purpose in being alive. Is this right? He is confined for humans' viewing pleasure. His incarceration serves no more important goal.

Animal rights activists look at cases like Ivan's and call for the abolition of all zoos. Wouldn't it be better to leave nature as it is, undisturbed? they ask. Of course it would. But unfortunately most of nature has not been and will not be left undisturbed. Humans, one of 244 primate and of perhaps 33 *million* plant and animal species, have already overpopulated many parts of the planet, exploiting and destroying. Humans have killed species for clothing and food, out of fear, and for fun. Furthermore, humans' activities have destroyed—and continue to destroy—habitat for hundreds and thousands of species. Wildlife is losing its struggle to survive in the wild. Humans must now act constructively. Zoos and aquariums do have a major constructive role to play in educating the public and in providing creative answers to some of the dilemmas of conservation. For most people zoos are the only place they will ever have a chance to see, smell, hear and, on occasion, touch an animal other than a house pet.

The Future: Zoos Are Our Conscience

In the summer 1991 issue of *Zoo Life*, David Lonsdale, assistant director of Chicago's John G. Shedd Aquarium, observed:

> Our urban population's understanding of how nature works has been lost. Zoos and aquariums can and must provide that understanding. We are part of the mosaic of information sources that attempt to demonstrate how and where man fits in the environment. Natural history museums, conservation organizations, documentary film makers and animal rights awareness groups all play a role in teaching the public about the living world. Every one of these organizations has a responsibility to disseminate accurate information about nature. Zoos and aquariums, however, find themselves in a unique position. They have the magic—living, breathing animals—the real thing.

One hundred and twenty million people visit zoos, aquariums, oceanariums, and wildlife parks in the United States and Canada each year. According to the AAZPA, "This is a greater attendance than at all football, baseball and hockey games combined." With an increasingly better educational focus by zoos all these people will have an opportunity to learn from their zoo experiences. Experience has shown that the more the public understands about animals and conservation issues, the more ready it is to support zoos as conservation organizations.

The question is: how? How should zoos and aquariums present the dilemma of conservation to the public for their understanding and positive reaction? The sections that follow on conservation, education, and ecotourism present not only the problem, but examples of what zoos and aquariums can and are doing to make their institutions places of learning as well as places of pleasure.

Conservation and Education

Conservation

WARNING!: One-half of all species of life since
The Beginning could vanish in the next ten years.

Alert!

The planet will lose one out
of five species currently alive
by 2002.

The planet will have lost two
thirds of its tropical rain
forests by 2000; 53 acres are
being destroyed every
minute by conversion to
agriculture or clear-cutting.

Facts

- Estimated total number of
  species: 33,526,024.

- Estimated number of
  animal species identified:
  1,392,485.

- Tropical rain forests
  cover 6% of the earth's
  surface and
  are home to 50–90% of
  all species.

- 40% of our prescription
  drugs are derived from
  plants and animals.

- 25% of our
  pharmaceutical drugs
  come from forest plants.

- Fewer than 1% of tropical
  plants have been screened
  for medical purposes.

- 75,000 plant species, many
  from the rain forest, are

Alert!	**Facts**
The planet may have no rain forests in 50 years.	edible; fewer than 20 species produce 90% of the world's food.
The planet is "losing 6,000 species each year from deforestation alone at a rate 10,000 times greater than before the appearance of humans on the planet." (estimates by E. O. Wilson*)	• Of the planet's known species 3,956 are endangered 3,647 are vulnerable 7,240 are considered rare.

*Frank B. Baird, Jr., Professor of Science, Harvard University.

The figures above make terrifyingly clear the need to conserve our natural habitats. A new breed of dedicated conservation explorers has come onto the scene to undertake wildlife research, many of them working with zoos, directly or indirectly. These men and women are providing the insight we need to save living things, our planet, and ourselves.

Zoologists' focus now is on biological diversity, which Kenton R. Miller, the director of the World Resources Institute's Forests and Biodiversity Program, defined as "the world's capital stock—the mix of plants, animals, and natural habitats that pro vide vital food, medicine, agricultural products, chemicals, and many other products."

Species Preservation

Scientists are attempting to identify more species, and are creating plans for species survival in which zoos play an important role.

In 1981, the AAZPA initiated a program to develop and implement Species Survival Plans (SSP's) in zoos around the country.

An SSP is directed toward saving a species from extinction. Some of the issues the zoologists drawing up the plans address are which species would benefit most from captive breeding in zoos, which have the greatest potential for habitat conservation and reintroduction, and which are "flagship" species, for whom a major conservation effort will benefit many other species that share the flagship species' habitat. The AAZPA is in the process of reevaluating its target of establishing 200 SSP's by the year 2000; currently 72 species are managed under 59 programs.

The emphasis of the 162 zoos accredited by the AAZPA (plus as many as 100 independent non-AAZPA-affiliated organizations) is breeding animals in captivity, not capturing more animals from the wild. However, where it is believed that an endangered species is unlikely to survive in the wild, a number of individuals of such species will be brought to zoos with the hope that through careful breeding (either natural or by artificial insemination), the species may be preserved and even reintroduced into its original habitat. Arabian oryx have been reintroduced to Oman (though they require armed guards to protect them); golden lion tamarin have been reintroduced to the rain forest of Brazil (where they have found it difficult to adapt to nature from their zoo life); Indonesian Balinese mynah and Californian and Andean condors have also been reinstated in their original habitats. Sumatran and Nepalese rhinos, highly endangered in their natural habitats, have been brought to the United States with the hope that they may be saved.

Habitat Preservation

Saving individual species is believed by some to be the ultimate objective of the SSP and other conservation efforts. The purpose of zoos is not to be living museums of species extinct in the wild, but most species bred in captivity are not returned to the wild. Gorillas and giant pandas, for instance, are two species we are unable to return to the wild because their native habitats cannot sustain them. They are, however, saved through SSP's as "flagship species," species that appeal to our more positive emotional human instincts. Gorillas are "like us"; pandas are cuddly. They are good PR for all nonhuman species. If we focus on saving them, the thinking goes, then we may become motivated to save others. The bottom line, though, is that species in the wild cannot be saved if their habitats are not preserved; thus habitat preservation should be the ultimate purpose of zoos and aquariums. The existence of zoos and aquariums is only acceptable if they support the process of educating the public to the desperate need to preserve natural habitat. Captive propagation should be a secondary objective.

The Wildlife Conservation Society International

The Wildlife Conservation Society International (WCSI), a division of NYZS The Wildlife Conservation Society (previously named the New York Zoological Society), headquartered at the Bronx Zoo, is in the forefront of conservation organizations and can serve as a model for conservation programs and action undertaken within the framework of a zoo or aquarium. WCSI has been dedicated to preserving the earth's wildlife and ecosystems since 1898. There are more than 70 endangered species at NYZS's various facilities. WCSI has 21 full-time conservation researchers on its staff as well as over 90 research and conservation fellows. Since 1897 the NYZS has undertaken more than 340 projects around the world. Currently WCSI is conducting 200 field projects in 46 countries throughout Central and South America, Asia, and Africa.

WCSI's strategy is to rely on long-term field studies to gather information on wildlife needs. WCSI depends on its familiarity with local conditions to translate results directly into conservation action and policy, to train local scientists in their own countries, and to build public awareness.

WCSI has played an important role in some notable conservation successes: saving the American bison and reintroducing it to the plains of Oklahoma, Montana, and South Dakota; undertaking the first study of the mountain gorilla in nature by George Schaller in 1958; undertaking an extensive study of rain-forest primates, their ecology and behavior as well as leading studies of African lions, Himalayan wild sheep and goats, and snow leopards. WCSI has made a major leadership contribution toward saving the panda in China, the Magellanic penguin in Patagonia (Argentina), the jaguar in Belize, and South American flamingos. Not only are there Przewalski's horses at the Bronx Zoo, but, more important, the NYZS has worked closely with the government of the Ukraine in Askania Nova, where 125 Przewalski's horses live on a 3,000-acre preserve.

WCSI has helped save the habitats of the okapis of the Ituri Forest in Zaire, the forest elephant of the Korup Forest in Cameroon, the spectacular savannah wildlife of Ngorongoro crater in Tanzania, wild antelope and asses in Chang Tang Reserve in Tibet, rain-forest birds in Papua, New Guinea, and the species that live in seven Central American countries covered by the regional Paseo Pandera project. WCSI has led the effort to preserve the African elephant and rhinos and to obtain legislation against the importation of bird plumage as well as the skins of spotted cats, crocodilians, and other endangered species, and has initiated protection for fur seals in Alaska.

WCSI has been instrumental in the establishment of 50 national parks and nature reserves in 20 countries, and in saving the habitats of threatened wildlife worldwide.

Education

Education is the tool of zoos and conservationists for getting the bad news out about what has happened to wildlife and habitats, to our environment on this planet. It also is the tool for telling what should be done and what is being done to halt the extinction process. Profiles in this book provide details on the kind of education programs conducted by and at zoos.

General information at zoo exhibits can be an effective way of describing the wildlife in the exhibit, interpreting aspects of the exhibits, and leading the visitor to seek further information. Signage should be clear, easy to read, and generally brief, and should contain a map showing the geographic location of the species' habitat. Back-lit glass and multicolored signage (as at the Primate World exhibit at the Fort Worth Zoo and in the Sea Cliffs exhibit at the New York Aquarium) are becoming more prevalent, as they attract attention and are easy to read. Many zoos now have interactive exhibits with buttons to push, wheels to turn, boards with questions on one side and answers on the other; small spades to scoop up particles of sand and insect life to be viewed under a microscope; "smart carts" (or biocarts) located at different points at a zoo where visitors can feel bones, skin, fur, and feathers and even have a live tarantula climb up their arms; videos to reinforce information; and touch tanks and eye-level peek holes for small tots at aquariums. Good zoos and aquariums capture the attention of the visitor at the exhibit.

The education experience at zoos and aquariums should go beyond specific animals to geography, ecosystems, and environmental concerns. A major focus should be placed on informing young children regarding animals and conservation. Most zoos have a corner for a children's zoo where domestic animals may be touched. More sophisticated children's zoos have audio and sensory exhibits to instill interest and appreciation. Increasingly common are organized overnight camping events at zoos, where children listen for the memorable roar of a lion, trumpeting of an elephant, hoot of an owl, or howl of a wolf.

Many school science programs contain little if any environmental and nature education. Zoos can help fill this gap. Students gathered together at a zoo or in their classrooms can experience the drama and wonder of nature, wrapped up in language and imagery that captures their interest and stimulates their dedication. The distant wildlife and habitats that students cannot see must be brought to them by means of lectures, photographs, and videos, and through visits to the captive ambassadors of species in zoos. In this manner the young (and old) will learn that education is the tool of conservation, and that they have a role to play.

Classes at a zoo vary from a few hours to an entire semester or whole academic course (as at the John Ball Zoo in Grand Rapids, Michigan); some even include computers and high-technology exhibits, as at the Living World at the St. Louis Zoo. Equally as important as reaching the minds of children is teaching teachers, and every zoo that has an education program should schedule courses for teachers if they can possibly do so. Some zoos, such as the Minnesota Zoo and the National Zoo's Conservation and Research Center at Front Royal, offer career programs for students. When you visit a zoo, ask about the education department's programs.

The emphasis and quality of zoo education programs varies considerably among zoos. The profiles in this book contain descriptions of zoos' and aquariums' educational activities. See also Appendix C for a more detailed description of some programs being pursued by NYZS The Wildlife Conservation Society's education department, the oldest in the United States, established in 1929.

Ecotourism, Ecotravel, and Eco-education

Increasingly, members of the public are interested in learning more about what they have seen at the zoo. They want answers to questions on migration, conservation, habitats, and the lives of animals. The more they see, the more questions they ask. They become involved; they begin to care; they want to do more than passively observe wildlife at a zoo or aquarium and then go home and forget the impact of what they saw.

They want to see wildlife in the wild, and once they have had this experience, they are more likely to want to *do* something to preserve wildlife and wildlife habitat. For such people, a growing range of ecotourism and ecotravel opportunities exist that focus on one or more aspects of wildlife conservation, from relatively traditional types of nature tours to hands-on conservation activities. Eco-education trips, as the name suggests, stress nature education.

Not everyone agrees on the meaning of the term *ecotourism*. The World Wildlife Fund defines it as "any kind of tourism that involves nature"—but I disagree with this definition. For example, nature-oriented travel is fun but not necessarily ecotourism.

In my view, ecotourism must be a conscious and calculated effort to provide tourism-generated income for the conservation of natural habitat. The local people should benefit from tourists' visits and thus be encouraged to preserve the natural surroundings in which they live. The habitat must be the ultimate beneficiary, not the tourist. Ecotourism is not a new concept: Amboseli National Park in Kenya is one excellent example of an area that developed along the lines of ecotourism long before the term was coined.

Appendix D contains further detailed information on organizations involved with ecotravel, ecotourism, and eco-education, including tour operators, environmental organizations, and zoos and aquariums themselves.

Zoo/Aquarium Visit Checklist

What to Find Out Before You Visit the Zoo

Confirm the hours the zoo is open.

Admission charges: Are there special rates for groups, seniors, children?

Try to avoid days when the zoo is likely to be crowded: holidays, weekends, free admission days.

Transportation to the zoo: If driving, confirm best route and the availability and cost of parking. If you are not driving, confirm time, location and cost of public transportation to and from the zoo.

What transport is there *at* the zoo (monorail, trains, bus, carts), how much does it cost, and what are the dropoff points?

Find out the times and locations of special demonstrations.

What are the feeding hours of, for example, seals, cats, penguins?

What lectures are being given on the day of your visit?

Are there guided tours? Self-guided tours?

Is there an annual photo contest by zoo visitors on wildlife subjects? The Los Angeles, Buffalo, and many others zoos have such contests.

Special events? Zoos have classical and jazz concerts, picnics, and lectures by visiting conservationists. Find out if there are special activities in the education center.

Are there programs for gifted children?

Are there career presentations?

Are there handicapped access limits? If you need a wheelchair, ask for one in advance.

Are strollers allowed? Available for rental?

Is there a family center or are there changing facilities for infants available in restrooms?

Are there picnic areas at the zoo besides the restaurants? Is a reservation necessary?

Some zoos have walking trails starting from the zoo. Investigate.

Is there a family night, or other evening activity, at the zoo?

If English is not your language, does the zoo provide assistance?

Ask the zoo to send you a brochure.

What to Take

Camera: Decide on what kind of a camera you want, video, still, or both? A zoom, wide-angle, or telephoto lens produces impressive results. A panoramic camera (Kodak, Fuji) can be most effective in photographing exhibits, but use only if there is full light. Don't use indoors.

Film: Zoo gift shops usually sell film, but it may be more expensive than you expect or may not be the right type.

At the Gate

Get a map at the ticket booth.

Decide what animals or exhibits interest you most. Check them out on the map. Decide on the best way to see them.

Any new births?

Are there animal rides—elephant? camel? Where? Cost?

Locate restrooms, particularly if with children. Restrooms are usually located at the entrance and near restaurants or snack stops; at larger zoos also at other locations.

Are there trained volunteers or others at the zoo who can answer your questions?

Is it okay to feed the animals? If so, which ones? Some zoos have feeder machines; if so, bring change. Most zoos prohibit feeding, but some allow feeding of some animals.

Some zoos have tape players and cassettes for rent.

At the Zoo

Emergencies: Locate telephone or a guard or zoo employee.

Don't try to see too many exhibits during one visit.

Look at the gift shop at any time but buy on your way out.

Enjoy the planting. Zoos are taking greater interest in plants.

If you do take transportation *at* the zoo, get off to look at the animals!

Identify some of the endangered species at the zoo. Your children may be glad you did!

Don't throw anything into an animal exhibit. Coins can kill, either by choking the animals or through zinc poisoning.

After Your Zoo Visit

Visit a natural history museum, keeping in mind what you have seen at the zoo.

Attend a workshop class of the education department at your zoo.

Become a docent (tour guide).

Find out what you can do for species and habitat conservation.

102 Zoos
and
Aquariums

☛ ARIZONA–SONORA DESERT MUSEUM

2021 North Kinney Road
Tucson, Arizona 85743
(602) 883-2702
Open: 7:30–6; call for winter
hours
Best for: Small cats; Mexican
wolves

Year opened: 1952
Acres: 186.5
Animal population: 4,792
(3,778 fish); 289 species
Director: David Hancocks

Getting there: A 30-minute drive west of Tucson: Take Interstate 10 west to West Anklam Road (scenic). Museum located in a cactus forest in Tucson Mountain Park.

Conservation: Breeding successes: Mexican wolf, Harris's hawk, pallid bat, kit fox, margay, golden eagle, caracara, Inca dove, cactus wren, Albert's towhee.

Education: Interpretation of the Sonora Desert region. Creation of "Desert Discovery" kits; collaboration with Pima Community College on teacher workshops. Strong docent program. Field trips in Arizona and New Mexico.

Special attractions: Hummingbirds. Earth Sciences exhibit (cave).

Gift shop: Small with regional touch.

Food: Restaurant, light meals.

The Arizona–Sonora Desert Museum is situated on 186 acres 14 miles west of Tucson. Driving there from the city, you go over a low mountain, through Gates Pass. Looking west at the pass, you can see the Tucson Mountain Park, a forest of saguaro cactus, below you. A saguaro cactus is a monument of nature unto itself, reaching a height of 50 feet and weighing as much as six tons. On average it lives to be more than 200 years old. The road winds down to the Arizona–Sonora Desert Museum, which sits among the cactus. But this museum is really a zoo with a number of regionally oriented open-air exhibits. In the Small Mammals exhibit are black-tailed prairie dogs, javelinas, coatis, mule deer, kit foxes, and coyotes. The Mountain Habitats exhibit has mountain lions, difficult-to-handle black bears, white-tailed deer, and Mexican wolves, which are probably extinct in the wild. In the Small Cat Grotto are ocelots, margays, jaguarundis, and bobcats. Bighorn sheep have a mound of their own, and the desert tortoise, a threatened species (for which there is an adoption program to private custodians in southern Arizona) and chuckwallas are near the aviary. Fish, amphibians, reptiles, scorpions, and insects are kept near the entrance. The underwater viewing site for otters and beavers is a favorite; visitors easily spend an hour there watching the animals cavorting.

A very well-executed and, for a zoo, unusual exhibit is Earth Sciences, opened in 1988. Situated in a simulated cave, the exhibit consists of a collection of 127 mineral specimens, all from Arizona. The Earth Sciences staff presents programs on copper mining, desert plant evolution, comets, rocks, and the geology of Arizona. An interpretive kit for docents with 14 fossil specimens is a useful educational tool to represent the four eras of geological time. Director David Hancocks explained the museum as "a meld between exhibits and nature, a holistic approach, replicating habitats at altitudes of 4,500 to 7,000 feet. Visitors should receive an experience; they should not be told all they should know from their visit."

EDUCATION

The Arizona–Sonora Desert Museum attributes its success in education to the 150 volunteers and the 60,000 hours they put in per year, much of it spent in one-on-one contact with the public—visitors to the museum as well as participants in outreach programs.

The museum has developed desert kits, which contain teaching materials and information on various themes related to desert ecology: the saguaro, predator-prey relationships, riparian habitats, and reptiles and amphibians. The kits are available on loan to teachers, having been funded by the Burlington Northern Foundation.

The Tortoise Adoption Program provides for the placement of

surplus captive tortoises. The Venomous Animal Education Program gives information on identification, precautions, and first aid.

The museum's 40-foot square open-air walk-in hummingbird exhibit is not much larger than the San Diego Zoo's, and is brightly lit by the Arizona sun, reflecting the light of the cactus-covered desert. The exhibit was opened in 1988 with 21 hummingbirds of eight species (at least 15 hummingbird species can be seen in southeastern Arizona). You stand among the fast-winged birds, watching them flit from branch to branch and feed. Animal keepers who clean the enclosure also spend at least four hours daily replenishing feeders with a superior nectar stock from Germany, plus fruit flies for protein. No matter how close you may feel physically and in spirit to the hummingbirds, remember that they are distance fliers, many species moving from one continent to another. The reason these hummingbirds are trapped is to better humans' understanding of these magnificent, powerful little creatures. Hummingbirds can also be viewed at Wild Animal Habitat (Kings Island), Ohio, and the San Diego Zoo.

THE DESERT ENVIRONMENT

The word *desert* suggests the ultimate in dryness; perhaps an image of thirsty volunteers of the French Foreign Legion, caps askew, perspiration caking the sand on their faces as they hold the fort (or attack it) appears in your mind's eye. Or perhaps your thoughts on the desert lead you to Lawrence of Arabia swaying atop a camel as he heads doggedly toward a mirage over a plateau void of life. In sum: emptiness and suffering.

But such images are deceptive. The desert is selectively alive. It comes to life when there is water. After the rains in the Kalahari, the landscape is colored with blooming flowers; fish that have been waiting buried in the sand come to life in a pool of fresh water; wildlife that has been patient suddenly reappears.

It is critical that the world's population understand the desert: how it came about, what it is, how it is presently being formed and why, and what lives in it. Man is creating desert by destroying vegetation. Twenty-five percent of the Tai Forest National Park in the Ivory Coast has been lost over the past 30 years. A decline in rainfall over the past 25 years in Africa, particularly in the Sahel, is the result of the loss of trees, which attract precipitation. Five hundred thousand square miles, or one seventh of the United States, is desert; that's an area more than three times the size of California. Understanding the desert leads to insights regarding the essential importance of biodiversity in deserts as well as rainforests. The Arizona–Sonora Desert Museum vividly demonstrates that a desert is not lifeless.

🐾 OUT OF AFRICA

P.O. Box 17928
#2 Fort McDowell Road
Fountain Hills, Arizona 85269
(602) 837-7779, 837-7677

Open: Tues.–Sun., 10:30–5

Shows: Daily and Fri. and Sat. evenings

Best for: Cats, cats, cats

Year opened: 1988

Acres: 8

Animal population: 71; 14 species

Directors: Dean Harrison (president) and Bobbi Harrison

Getting there: Located 40 minutes northeast of Phoenix on McDowell Road to U.S. Highway 87. Follow signs.

Special attractions: Daily cat shows; call to check times.

Gift shop: Outstanding, different.

Food: Excellent, super fast food.

Dean Harrison of Out of Africa, on the outskirts of Phoenix, thinks animals "teach their young to cope with their environment better than humans do." Out of Africa is a zoo with a twist. Not accredited by the AAZPA, it is situated on land leased from the Fort McDowell Indian Reservation. Out of Africa is a wonderful kind of wildlife park where people and animals live and work together. Cohabitation and cooperation are the principle themes. Owners Dean and Bobbi Harrison's premise for dealing with animals is the "need for fulfillment, which is a lifelong process." Out of Africa began as a research project to determine the basic needs of big cats. After opening Tigerville USA in southern Oregon in 1986 the Harrisons discovered "what has always been missing at traditional zoos, circuses, and wild animal parks, which is to see and experience an actual relationship with a truly wild-by-nature animal, such as a lion or tiger." The Harrisons pioneered what they call "relationship training," which "promotes man's association with his fellow creatures rather than keeping them at academic arm's distance." Out of Africa has a number of other animals besides cats, including an 18-foot Burmese python named Colossus and a color-changing panther chameleon from Madagascar.

The Harrisons' approach to their work and their animals is steeped in philosophy ("Learn to play to earn a living"); insight ("Lions are guided by instinct and reason; they are educated, but not literate"); and perception ("The difference between cats and man is emotion"). To make their points, the Harrisons enter a cage with an African lion (named Sahara), Siberian tiger (named Saginaw), African-Chinese leopard (Saja), and black leopard (Eclipse). They are all in the same cage at the same time. "They can learn to live together," Dean Harrison commented to me, "which man cannot. They will even protect another species of cat that has normally been an enemy," he added, "for environment is stronger than heredity."

In the cage there was no question of who was in charge: the cats. The Harrisons have never carried weapons into a cage. "A weapon is a sign of fear. Love is togetherness—working for others more than for yourself. *We* have something to learn from *them.* You cannot demonstrate love and fear at the same time." The Harrisons work on the principle of love. As a result, they claim, the cats have never harmed them.

Out of Africa is a fascinating experience, though criticized by some for being "off-track." I found the Harrisons' approach to wildlife different, refreshing, and definitely educational. Besides watching the Harrisons communicate with the cats, the public has an opportunity to touch the animals, which are held by competent, qualified associates of the Harrisons. I would not advocate the type of education found at Out of Africa for all zoos, but the Harrisons' approach to humans' relationship with animals does provide a special insight, and understanding animals should certainly be one of *our* major aims.

♞ THE PHOENIX ZOO

455 North Galvin Parkway
Papago Park
Phoenix, Arizona 85008
(602) 273-1341

Open: 7–4; call for winter hours

Best for: Monkeys and lemurs

Year opened: 1962

Acres: 125

Animal population: 1,264; 342 species

Director: Warren Iliff

Note: The zoo is privately owned; no public funding.

Getting there: If approaching the zoo from the west, from Route I-17 take McDowell Road to Galvin Parkway. If coming from the east, take Scottsdale Road, north, turn west on McDowell Road, then turn off onto Galvin Parkway, which leads to the zoo. A 30-minute safari train ride on zoo grounds.

Conservation: Oryx reintroduced to Saudi Arabia and Oman.

Education: Family education emphasized at the zoo. Puppet shows for grades K–1; junior Zoofari, grades 1–3; desert animals, grades 3–5; native species, grades 4–8; wildlife adaptations, grades 5–8; speakers program, grades 4–8. Traveling bird of prey shows; naturalist tours; endangered species tour; morning bird walk.

Special attractions: Arizona Trail, African Veldt.

Gift shop: Excellent. Get a painting by Rudy the elephant, born in Thailand in 1973. Originals and numbered lithographs of Rudy's originals are available.

Food: Many choices. Three snack bars: Rhino, Mill House, Gator. Plaza, Crossroads, and children's zoo have snacks as well.

Warren Iliff, director of the Phoenix Zoo, graduated from Harvard, majoring in government, and spent time at the National Zoo in Washington, D.C., and the zoo in Portland, Oregon. He's a Marine, runs a good zoo, looks into the future, and is interested in education and conservation. He is also a council member of the Jersey (Channel Islands) Wildlife Preservation Trust and a board member of the Jane Goodall Institute. Before coming to Phoenix he was director of the Dallas Zoo.

Iliff told me he had three objectives for the Phoenix Zoo. At the national level, to become the zoo with the best education program in the country. At the state level, to be the best conservation organization in the state. At the zoo itself, to treat the members of the public as though they were coming for a class. He believes that the monorail ride should be an educational tour. An endangered species two-hour walking tour answers such questions as: How much meat does a tiger eat in a day and what are the requirements to be a zookeeper. The Phoenix Zoo also organizes naturalist tours to explore wildlife and nature in areas around Phoenix.

Iliff plans to make the zoo a five-habitat zoo, in addition to the Arizona Trail and the children's zoo: (1) desert, (2) tropics (the image of the Phoenix Zoo as an oasis in the desert), (3) woodland (perhaps), (4) savannah (again, perhaps), and (5) aquatic. Iliff firmly believes that education, which should be a family affair, can be fun without being frivolous and serious without being somber and boring. "We can get across some vitally important messages while visitors are enjoying themselves," he observes.

The zoo is appealing and invites exploration. The hilly landscape, much of it rock, has been well used in exhibit construction. The Nubian ibex exhibit, which the public views from a distance, makes particularly good use of the rocky terrain. Cheetah have trees and bushes on their grounds, with a good running area. Iliff's favorite exhibit at his zoo is the African Veldt. The children's zoo is very attractive with a waterfall, 16 exhibits, a nursery, and hands-on activities, including a Poultry House, Mouse House, and raccoon, tamarin, prairie dog, and monkey exhibits, plus numerous birds and a Brooder House. A petting zoo is located near the puppet theater. In January 1993 a new natural habitat exhibit with termite mounds opened with meerkats, aardwolves, and African crested porcupines.

⅃ REID PARK ZOO

1100 South Randolph Way
Tucson, Arizona 85716
(602) 791-3204

Open: 8:30–3:30; call for winter hours

Best for: Anteaters; tigers; ostriches

Year opened: 1967

Acres: 17

Animal population: 994; 147 species

Director: J. Stephen McCusker

Membership: Tucson Zoological Society
(602) 881-4753

Getting there: Located in Reid Park, adjacent to Randolph Park and golf course, all of which are bounded by East Broadway, Alvernon Way, Country Club Road, and East 22nd Street. Easiest approach is from East 22nd Street, turning onto Lake Shore Drive (between Alvernon Way and Country Club Road).

Conservation: Breeding threatened and endangered species: Grevy's zebra, lion-tailed macaque, Bali mynah, ruffed lemur, white rhinoceros, small-clawed otter.

Education: Reid-Me-a-Story on weekends for children; roving interpretative stations; zoomobile visits libraries, nursing homes, schools throughout Tucson (for information, call 791-4475).

Special attractions: Polar bear exhibit reopened December 1989, with underwater viewing; use of water in exhibits.

Gift shop: Modest. Needs beefing up.

Food: Snack bar at entrance, or picnic in the park.

The Reid Park Zoo is primarily an educational facility with strong support from docents. On Saturdays, docents abound, most making use of artifacts. One, next to the lion exhibit, had a lioness skull in her hand for visitor examination. Another docent, standing next to the giraffe exhibit, held a giraffe tooth. Still another docent was allowing a tarantula to scuttle across his palm and up his wrist. Zoo signage is excellent, with birth dates of animals shown.

The zoo is proud of its giant anteater breeding program. The anteater is the zoo's mascot, and so it is no great surprise that the anteater exhibit is very effective. Its simplicity is its strong point. Additionally, the zoo visitor may have close contact: the anteater's vacuum-cleaner snout nuzzles up to within inches of you along the simple wooden fence. You may feel the blow of its breath against your hand—or face. An anteater once made an unauthorized exit from its enclosure and wandered casually down the tarred path only a few feet away into the restrooms. They love toes. The long-snouted creature snuck up, unnoticed and unheard, lashed out its four-foot-long tongue into a stranger's shoe, and wrapped it solidly around a toe or two. Needless to say, the person who had sought a moment of privacy was considerably surprised by this unexpected ablution. The fence has been strengthened since this happened.

Two ostriches decided to mate on the day of my visit. First they performed a balletlike chase, ending with a graceful flapping of their giant wings, and the male's twisting back and forth of his long neck. One never knows what surprises await one at a zoo.

The Reid Zoo makes good use of plantings and water. A particular turn in the path brings you to a pond for black-billed swans and a sense of privacy and intimacy for both human and animal. The adjacent aviary is a pleasant place to walk, with ducks, pigeons, and parrots. Tucson is surrounded by desert and cacti, so this spot of green is a refreshing sight.

ᚼ WORLD WILDLIFE ZOO

16501 West Northern Avenue   **Open:** 9–5; July 15–Sept. 15
Litchfield Park, Arizona 85340   9–3
(602) 935-WILD

Best for: Kangaroos; ungulates; lory parrots

Year opened: 1984

Acres: 45

Animal population: 1,484; 311 species

Director: Mickey Ollson (owner/manager)

Getting there: Located a half-hour haul west of Phoenix. Traveling north on I-17, take Exit 206 west on Northern Avenue, past Litchfield Road and Luke Air Force Base. The zoo is three miles west of Litchfield Park.

Conservation: Breeding of endangered species for zoo populations. Started with birds. Received 1982 AAZPA award for breeding the caracara, a vulturelike hawk (nine different species to three generations). Also more than 100 Stanley cranes.

Education: With the financial support of two local businesses, World Wildlife Zoo began its first education program at the start of 1993. An educational theater puts on three performances daily with mammals such as a tenerec, boas, and birds. Also an outreach program with a donated Ford van. A curator position has been established to run the programs.

Special attractions: Four ostrich species, five oryx species, some bird species not displayed at other zoos. Parrot feeding at 11:00 and 1:30—check when you enter the zoo.

Gift shop: No.

Food: Minor snacks.

World Wildlife Zoo is classified as a zoo, but it doesn't look like a modern zoo with natural habitats. World Wildlife Zoo is a breeding farm, owned and managed by the director. The exhibits are pens on zoo streets. The animals you see here today you may see at your zoo tomorrow. The lory parrots are a riot of color and are fed three times daily. Don't miss feeding time. There is a Tropics Exhibit and an aquarium, both of some interest. The Small Mammals building contains forty-five species, including dwarf and black-and-white ruffed lemurs, agoutis, meerkats, and four species of marmosets. Ring-tailed lemurs can be found out-of-doors. Owner-manager Mickey Ollson told me that Earl Wells, the director of the Fort Wayne (Indiana) Children's Zoo, is drawing up a plan for a new eight-acre area for red kangaroos, wallabies, and emus that visitors will be able to walk through at World Wildlife Zoo. Very few zoos (in Fort Wayne; Oklahoma City; and Prospect Park, Brooklyn, N.Y.) have created kangaroo or wallaby walk-throughs. It is fun for people, and the animals don't seem to mind, as long as you leave them alone.

𝕋 CHAFFEE ZOOLOGICAL GARDENS OF FRESNO

894 West Belmont Avenue
Fresno, California 93728
(209) 498-2671

Open: 10–6:30; call for winter hours

Best for: Aruba Island rattlesnakes; butterflies; Reptile House

Year opened: 1929

Acres: 24

Animal population: 576; 195 species

Director: Ralph Waterhouse

Membership: Fresno Zoological Society, (209) 264-5988

Getting there: Located one block east of U.S. 99, between Olive and Belmont avenues, in Roeding Park ($1 car entry fee).

Conservation: Recognized for captive breeding of the rattleless rattlesnake, New Zealand North green gecko, Madagascar ground boa, and Aruba Island rattlesnake.

Education: Education center with on-site and school programs; zoomobile that visits more than 530 classrooms; entomology classes in schools; zoo camp.

Special attractions: Rain-forest walk-through, education programs, Rain Forest, Reptile House.

Gift shop: Modest; plans for two, one with an elephant conservation theme.

Food: Snacks only, but there are plans for improvement.

In 1990, the Fresno Zoo was renamed the Chaffee Zoological Garden of Fresno in recognition of the 25 years Dr. Paul S.

Chaffee, D.V.M. (Doctor of Veterinary Medicine), known as "Doc," served as director of the zoo and as a president of the AAZPA. Through his efforts the zoo changed from one of small barred cages to one of natural habitats. The Reptile House, built in 1979, has individually computerized, climate-controlled environmental chambers. The collection of reptiles and amphibians places the emphasis on rare and endangered species from the Indian Ocean region and the South Pacific islands.

The zoo has a small one-acre Asian elephant exhibit and five elephants. The master plan calls for an area five times the present size which will retain the present recirculating waterfall, providing water for an elephant bathing pool. However, it may be 10 years before this plan is a reality.

In 1988 a half-acre walk-through rain forest was opened with over 100 tropical birds, turtles, a South American anteater, green iguanas, and lizards, along with a bird house that has been converted into a small-bird and butterfly exhibit. Among the birds are a pair of bleeding heart doves and five red-throated parrot finches. The current exhibit has a population of 250 butterflies representing 20 species. Butterflies' life span is from a few days to several weeks; the specimens are currently obtained from Georgia, the United Kingdom, and San Diego, but eventually Chaffee Zoo intends to breed butterflies itself.

The most significant recent conservation event was the successful birth of Aruba Island rattlesnakes. Ten snakes that had been collected from populated areas were given to five U.S. zoos in 1990. The Chaffee Zoo has been the first to succeed with a birth of this species.

The zoo camp, which is held in the education building at the zoo, has proved to be increasingly popular over the past few years. Certified teachers take K–6 students on field trips for a week of fun and learning. Better stewardship of the earth's resources is the main message. In 1993 a mountain camp was established near Yosemite Park.

♦ LOS ANGELES ZOO

5333 Zoo Drive
Los Angeles, California 90027
(213) 666-4650
Open: 10–6; call for winter hours
Best for: Sifakas; gerenuk; Sumatran rhino
Year opened: 1966
Acres: 113

Animal population: 1,610; 508 species
Director: Mark Goldstein
Membership: Greater Los Angeles Zoo Association (213) 664-1100
Sister zoo: Nagoya Zoo, Nagoya, Japan

Getting there: Take Route 5 toward Glendale; zoo is in Griffith Park, near junction of Ventura and Golden State freeways in Glendale (northwest Los Angeles).

Conservation: Some breeding successes: Arabian oryx, bongo, golden lion tamarin, gorilla, California condor, Pesquet's parrot, shingle-back and prehensile-tailed skink.

Education: Call the education department, ext. 5, for the schedule of programs, including teacher workshops and classes.

Special attractions: Adventure Island (see comments below); animals noted under conservation (above).

Gift shop: Several good shops at the zoo.

Food: Several snack stands.

The Los Angeles Zoo is on the rebound, taking positive steps toward a productive future. Thirty years ago the Los Angeles municipal government made an initial mistake when it passed a bond issue to build a new zoo with instructions that it be modeled after European zoos. The result is a zoo that still has the remnants of moats. The zoo would like to ready itself for the twenty-first century with the creation of an education visitors' village, a new animal health center (off zoo property) and a water environment exhibit. Whether the city (i.e., the voters) will financially support this three-pronged major expansion program is still undecided, but the future looks promising. The cost? Twenty-five million dollars.

The Los Angeles Zoo's four-year-old 2.5-acre Adventure Island, at the entrance, allows children to get personal contact with animals—it features animals of America. Activities include petting domestic animals and other hands-on experiences: touch a wall, "zooputer," pond microscopes, slime wall, sculptured animal masks, bat imaging, animal identification. It all sounds terrific, and children have fun running around, pushing, pulling, poking, touching, yelling. But are they learning? Adventure Island is a good concept but inadequately designed, misusing some high technology, and failing to get all of its messages across. One presentation that did impress me was a path containing metal animal-footprints that when stepped on emitted animal sounds from hidden speakers. The dramatic hi-tech holographic "Pepper's Ghost," used in the owl exhibit, is less impressive. It projects an image of Betty White, actress and board member, flitting about the exhibit, with unclear audio. It is out of place, is not made to relate to the exhibit, and is badly done. Looking up it was possible to see the cameras in the ceiling that project the image. The "secret" of how the image appears is lost. The Los Angeles Zoo should keep Pepper's Ghost, but bring him to life.

The Los Angeles Zoo Discovery Program, launched in the spring of 1991 by the education department, is more successful. The program presents abstract concepts on a level that five-year-olds can enjoy and relate to. The program is a hands-on adventure. Flamingos, alligators, seals, capybaras, kangaroos, gorillas, rhinoceroes, anteaters, and elephants are the focus of this imaginative program. Have you ever wondered why an anteater sticks out her tongue, or how far a kangaroo hops? Children are asked to guess how many ants an anteater could eat in a day (the answer: 30,000). Teachers can attend Zoo Discovery weekend workshops, after which they can prepare their students for a trip to the zoo for a nine-exhibit visit. The teachers bring their Zoo Discovery kits, which contain touchable materials such as fur, molted flamingo feathers, hair from an elephant's tail (like leathery wire), scales, a plastic rhino footprint. Children are asked to look at the picture of a rhinoceros horn and then feel a rhino fingernail, which gives them a greater sense of rhino identity than simply seeing a picture. The program has become enormously popular with students and teachers.

The Los Angeles Zoo received six baby gorillas in 1965. The zoo was still under construction and conditions were inadequate for the gorillas—tragedy resulted. All six baby gorillas were infected with a parasite through contact with a pair of South American bush dogs, with the resultant death of all but one gorilla, Kay.

In 1983 the AAZPA initiated an SSP for the gorilla, and forty-seven zoos in the United States, with a gorilla population of 322, participate in the program. Many gorillas have lived at the Los Angeles Zoo since the first six: Cleo, born in L.A. in 1978; Kay, caught in the wild; Chris, caught in the wild, a visitor to Los Angeles from Sacramento; Sandy, wild caught, on loan from the Rio Grande Zoo in Albuquerque, New Mexico; Evelyn, born in L.A. in 1976; Lina, born in L.A. in 1973; Tzambo, wild caught; Rapunzel, on a visit from the Cincinnati Zoo; Caesar, born in L.A. in 1977; and more.

Long-necked gerenuk (also known as Waller's gazelle and in Swahili called *swala twiga*, "giraffe gazelle") are often on their hindlegs searching for a tender shoot on a tree. The gerenuk may also be seen at the North Carolina, St. Louis, and San Diego zoos.

A particularly pleasant retreat at the zoo is to be found at the Treetops Terrace, where the planting suggests a secret meeting place. An attractive waterfall adds to the serenity. On my visit, an African crested crane stood at the top of the waterfall, appearing to believe it was his.

Don't miss seeing the Sumatran rhino. Sumatran rhinos are the smallest of five species of rhinos and the most primitive, having changed little in physical appearance over the past 30 million years, and are covered with hair.

At the Los Angeles Zoo many exhibits are merely functional and look barren, but the zoo is doing something about this. A program has been established in which volunteers "make over" an exhibit on weekends. Kathy, a leopard, had her cage remodeled by volunteers. So did drills, who in the wild are surrounded by a jungle habitat. Drills are a species of baboon found in West Africa from the Cross River in southeastern Nigeria to the Sanaga River in Cameroon. Volunteers brought driftwood into the exhibit and arranged it in steplike fashion, placing rocks into what had been a plain concrete pool, and arranging tree stumps and logs in which to hide food. Dirt and woodchips were added as well as leaf litter where worms and crickets could be hidden.

Dr. Michael Wallace, curator of conservation and science at the Los Angeles Zoo, is SSP coordinator of both the Andean and California condors. The Los Angeles Zoo has played a major part, along with the San Diego Zoo, in saving and rehabilitating the California condor, which, with a wingspan of nine and a half feet, is the largest North American bird. In 1800 there were estimated to be 2000 California condors. By 1987 there were no condors flying free, though 27 were lodged in zoos. After 15 years of trying, two chicks from San Diego's Wild Animal Park and Los Angeles Zoo were released on January 14, 1992 into the rugged mountainous sanctuary in Los Padres National Forest, some 60 miles north of Los Angeles. There have, however, been problems, including 3 deaths, 2 as a result of high-tension wires. It became apparent that a more remote area had to be found. By December 1993, with 71 in zoos, 11 more condors had been released, including 5 in Canyon, 50 miles northwest of Los Padres. Meanwhile, 37 Andean condors, born in captivity in the U.S., have been released in South America. These birds, living relics of the age of mastodons and mammoths, have been saved by man. The cost is estimated at $17,000,000 for the California condor. The price of salvation is high.

Zoo Director Mark Goldstein, who will lead the zoo through its 1992–2002 master plan, is particularly proud of the zoo's conservation record. In 1992 the first drill was born at the zoo—the first to be born in North America in 10 years. A few days later Zoo Atlanta announced the birth of a drill, and both youngsters are doing well. On February 14, 1992, the first birth of a sifaka in the United States occurred—at the Los Angeles Zoo. The sifaka, a lemur from Madagascar, came to Los Angeles on loan from Duke University. The Los Angeles Zoo participates in the Madagascar

Fauna Group, which hopes to bring into the United States additional populations and other species of lemurs.

🦙 THE LIVING DESERT

The Living Desert
470900 Portola Avenue
Palm Desert, California 92260
(619) 346-5694
Open: 9–5; closed June 1 to Sept. 1
Best for: Total desert habitat
Year opened: 1970

Acres: 1,200
Animal population: 850; 125 species
Plants: 7,000 individuals, 1,500 desert species
Director: Karen Sausman

Getting there: From Palm Springs take Ramon Road east to I-10 (or Route 111 to Monterey Avenue [Route 74]), then turn south. Signs shortly on your left.

Conservation: Whole zoo preserves desert ecosystem. SSP success with addax, Arabian oryx.

Education: Docent-led classes and tours, speakers, special exhibitions, trips; providing of supplemental science curricula in local schools and colleges.

Special attractions: Aviary featuring birds from the Sonoran Desert. Botanical gardens of 10 major North American desert regions.

Gift shop: Jewelry, history books, cactus plants, nice postcards.

Food: Ice cream, soft drinks; *no* food.

The Living Desert, established in 1970, is partly a zoo and also has 1,500 species of desert plants, from the Joshua tree to the hedgehog cactus. There are exhibits of miniature displays of 10 different North American deserts, interspersed with wildlife including bats, snakes, lizards, screech owls, coyotes, and the world's smallest fox; an aviary of Sonoran desert birds, including thick-billed parrots, Beechey jays, and burrowing owls, which is well done. The North American botanical displays, or "living dioramas," explain such things as how plants are used for food, medicine, and clothing by the local Cahuilla Indians. Found in the gardens are smoke trees, saguaros, myriad cacti, and palo verde. Jon Stewart, Living Desert's botanist, creates and cares for a watering system that helps plants that would expect moisture at a different time of year in their own habitat. He also is responsible for the excellent signage, which he wants to improve by spotlighting ecosystems, not only identifying individual plants. Stewart is also responsible for the botanical aspects of the Eagle Canyon exhibit (where large animals are on exhibit), but laments that "visitors don't see the plants," as they are looking for animals.

The Living Desert's literature states: "One of Living Desert's major objectives is to foster, through interpretive exhibits, programs and publications, an awareness of, and an appreciation for, the variety of plants and animals in worldwide desert ecosystems." (Fully one-seventh of the earth's surface is classified as desert.) Fulfilling this objective is the Education Department's number one job. Each year the Living Desert provides to more than 17,000 children in school groups a free introduction to the desert. The Discovery Room, open on all weekends and holidays, offers hands-on natural history activities designed for family interaction. Children are especially fond of "critter close-ups," a chance to see and touch small desert animals such as tortoises, snakes, and birds.

The Living Desert's Master Plan for the Year 2000 includes interpretive desert exhibits of four continents (North America, South America, Australia, and Africa) on a 200-acre site. North America is already complete and Africa has been started. Each area will have live animals in full-scale botanical reconstructions.

Desert plants are available for sale at the nursery. The excellent education center and discovery room is housed in an attractive building with a modest library, where you can find copies of the *National Geographic* going back to 1923. In the discovery room visitors can touch live and dead exhibits. The Living Desert is the starting point for six miles of nature trails, for which guide books are available.

➤ MONTEREY BAY AQUARIUM

886 Cannery Row
Monterey, California 93940
(408) 648-4800
Open: 9:30–6; call for winter
hours (375-3333)
Best for: Kelp; sharks; reefs
Year opened: 1984

Acres: 2.2
Animal population: 124,064
(includes over 120,000
invertebrates); 410 species
Director: Julie Packard
Sister aquarium: Tokyo Sealife
Park, Tokyo, Japan

Getting there: A short drive or 10-minute walk from downtown Monterey to Cannery Row, on Monterey Bay.

Education: LIVELINK program; Aquaravan, wetlab, internships; a 273-seat auditorium; two classrooms and a research laboratory. Courses for teachers and students. Summer courses and workshops (for further information write to the education department or call 648-4850).

Special attractions: Monterey Aquarium is the only place in the U.S. where jellyfish are bred and remain on display. The kelp tank is spectacular. Feeding shows daily at the Sea Otter (11:00, 2:00, and 4:30), Kelp Forest (11:30 and 4:00 [diver hand feeding]), and Monterey Bay Habitats exhibits. Free, self-guided tour scripts with maps in Japanese, German, French, and Spanish.

Gift shop: Very good book selection.

Food: Portola Café: self-service buffet or full-service luncheon (10:00–5:00). Great view of bay.

There is little question that Monterey Bay Aquarium is one of the two or three outstanding aquariums of America—some say it's number one. It is intended to be an extension of Monterey Bay, which is home to 27 species of sea mammals.* Many professionals say that the 335,000-gallon, three-story-high forest of *Macrocystis pyrifera* kelp, with eight-inch-high waves to keep the kelp moving and alive, is the best of all aquarium exhibits. At 28 feet it is the tallest aquarium exhibit in the world; its acrylic window

*See *National Geographic* magazine, February 1990, "Between Monterey Tides," which besides the highly informative text also has excellent graphics and superb photographs.

panels are 15 feet high, 8 feet wide, and 7¼ inches thick, and weigh 2½ tons each. Fresh seawater is recycled every 79 minutes.

The Monterey Canyon exhibit is also outstanding. It provides a look at the bay's 10,000-foot depths and the life forms that live at that depth. It is the only aquarium where jellyfish, difficult to keep alive in a confined exhibit space, are raised and on continuous display. Sea nettles, and moon, purple-striped, peach-blossom, crystal, and Paulau jellies (the latter three being the first of their species to reproduce in the United States) are among those on permanent exhibit at the Planet of the Jellies. By March 1993, 10 of 17 species of jellyfish were breeding. A giant octopus that sucks the glass of its exhibit with little gripper cups pleases viewers to no end. The Monterey Bay Habitats exhibit is a 336,000-gallon, 90-foot-long hourglass-shaped exhibit containing large sharks, bat rays, ocean sunfish, salmon, mackerel, striped bass, and other species. The Great Tide Pool exhibit displays the bay's intertidal life: sea stars, anemones, crabs, as well as fish. The pool serves as a release point for sea otters in Monterey's sea otter rescue and care program.

The aquarium's design concept is that when you enter the aquarium building you are meant to feel that you are on the periphery of the bay. You enter what was once the Hovden Cannery, where sardines and squid were packed from 1916 until 1972. It's a little like entering a well-lit bus terminal: noisy and too bright. A 43-foot model of a gray whale looms overhead, accompanied by a calf and a convoy of orcas, dolphins, seals, and sea lion models. You may go left or right to view aquarium exhibits, and if you go straight you'll walk onto a wooden terrace (an oyster bar is a few feet away) from which you may well see seals on a rock and an otter swimming on its back—in the open ocean. Roughly 1,700 sea otters live along the bay's coast. A close-up look at otters is possible at the indoor aquarium exhibit, where they dive, turn, swim and play in their two-story exhibit.

Monterey's aquarium is spectacular and very educational. A guided tour of the aquarium is conducted Monday through Friday at 9:30. Fifty-minute discovery labs are available to teachers and no more than 30 students at a time on Kelp Forest Ecology and Marine Mammal Life-styles. In addition, teachers may have access to a lab with their students, with previsit orientation for the teacher. For reservations, call (408) 649-3133. Touch pools are well supplied with sealife, such as a decorator crab or bat star, and microscopes, magnifiers, and telescopes are available for a closer look.

Some fascinating new educational programs are being planned. LIVELINK, scheduled to begin operation in 1996, will bring offshore Monterey Bay (whose resources have been declared a marine sanctuary) into the aquarium. In its research of Monterey Bay the aquarium has been using an ROV (remote operated vehicle) equipped with cameras, sensors, and sampling devices such as suction tubes to retrieve marine creatures. Using LIVELINK, the aquarium will have an Open Ocean exhibit for the public showing scientists at work. LIVELINK will provide live broadcasts of images to the aquarium's auditorium from an ROV operating to depths of 3,300 feet on a 4,000-foot-long tether cable accompanied by an optic cable. The ROV will go out into the bay three to four times each week for a day to collect video images, which will be sent to a surface vessel and then microwaved up to 70 miles from the ship to relay stations, from which the signal will be relayed live to the auditorium. Eventually satellite capability could bring LIVELINK to an even broader audience.

🐾 SACRAMENTO ZOO

3930 West Land Park Drive
Sacramento, California 95822
(916) 264-5166

Open: 10–5; call for winter hours

Best for: Cats; orangutans; flamingos; hippos

Year opened: 1927

Acres: 15

Animal population: 351; 124 species

Director: Maria Baker

Membership: Sacramento Zoological Society
(916) 264-5888

Getting there: In William Land Park, east of I-5 and south of Route 50. Exit I-5 at William Land Park, take Sutterville Road east to Land Park Drive for zoo entrance.

Conservation: Rare Feline Breeding Center.

Education: Zoomobile tied into interpretative centers. Zoo works with California State University, Sacramento, for teaching credit. Teacher workshops for the Elk Grove Unified School District and California Science Teachers Association. Overnight "safaris" in the zoo for children. Call 264-5889.

Special attractions: The Cactus and African gardens. Camel and elephant rides in the summer.

Gift shop: Modest.

Food: Two food stands.

Most zoos have some sort of river theme presentation, but only a few *highlight* rivers. The Sacramento Zoo is one of them. In 1988 the Sacramento City Council established rivers as the theme for the zoo. While the zoo currently emphasizes the importance of water at its waterfowl, hippo, alligator and snapping turtle exhibits, the 20-year Master Plan, which started in 1989, highlights the value of water to animals. The hippopotamus, crocodile, beaver, and otter exhibits will show how these animals all live underwater. Grizzly bears will be found in the Sacramento/American River theme area of the zoo. The need for water conservation on our planet is stressed both by the graphics used on signs and in education programs including the zoomobile. Zoo visitors are encouraged to develop their power of observation, and thus to learn.

The Sacramento Zoo's education department places considerable emphasis on graphics to educate the public at exhibit sites. The zoomobiles, run by the zoo's Interpretive Center, visit schools, and 66,000 children visit the zoo annually. The zoo also works with student teachers and universities, offering a teacher workshop where students receive teaching credit for their work.

The zoo's orangutans, Josephine and Baldy, have posed for postcards for Hallmark Greeting Cards.

The zoo's master plan calls for a lake in the center of the zoo that will simulate Africa's Lake Victoria with flamingos, marabou storks, white-faced tree ducks, cranes, and more ducks. At water's edge will be located the Rivers Interpretative Center. The savannah and cats exhibits will also have interpretative centers, and there will be a reptile education center. Currently, the animal group that receives the greatest attention at the Sacramento Zoo is the cats: there are 14 species of felines at the zoo, including eight endangered ones, such as the Asian lion, Siberian tiger, clouded leopard, and cheetah. The zoo has bred jaguars, margays, Geoffroy's cats, Siberian tigers (there are approximately 750 Siberian tigers in captivity and 300 in the wild), and Asian lions, as well as clouded leopards and cheetahs. A new facility for the cats, the Rare Feline Breeding Center, opened in May 1992 and houses twelve species of exotic cats.

♀ SAN DIEGO ZOO

P.O. Box 551
San Diego, California 92112
(619) 231-1515
(619) 234-3153 (recorded information)

Open: 9–4 (summer), grounds close at 7 P.M.; call for winter hours

Best for: Apes; tigers; Malayan sun bears

Year opened: 1916

Acres: 125

Animal population: 4,034; 820 species

Director: Douglas Myers

Membership: Zoological Society of San Diego
(619) 231-0251

Sister zoo: Chengdu Zoo, Sichuan Province, China

Getting there: Located in Balboa Park, near juncture of I-5 and Route 163. From I-5, exit on Park Boulevard, continue north to Zoo Drive. At the zoo, double-decker bus; "Skyfari" aerial tram.

Conservation: CRES program. Excellent medical facility, programs and staff. Breeding of Przewalski's horse, Eurasian bison, Siberian tiger, rhino, Bali mynah, bonobo.

Education: Zoo Institute has classes, Koala Club for young. Teachers can attend a Saturday workshop, receive a free kit on loan, and return with their class for a zoo visit. Animals taken into city classrooms. Wildlife Treks into the local countryside with experts. Two zoo tours of special note: (1) "Discovering Diversity," a two-hour rain-forest rendez-vous, meeting rain-forest animals and learning what you can do to save the rain forest; (2) "Inside Story," a three-hour visit, arriving at the zoo before it opens to see animals let into their enclosures and operations of the zoo. "E" symbols throughout the zoo indicate that the animal is endangered. For full details on educational programs, call (619) 557-3962 or 557-3969.

Special attractions: Hummingbird House small but good. Wegeforth National Park, where animals are used in presentation on recycling and avoiding environmental pollution. Notice orchids, ferns, palms, vines, bananas, eucalyptus throughout the zoo.

Gift shop: Excellent. For those who have a computer with a CD-ROM drive, the zoo has a package for either Windows or DOS on the zoo's animals and plants, with 1,300 color photographs and 2,500 pages of articles. For information on mail orders (Visa or MasterCard), call (619) 451-1792 or (800) 628-3179.

Food: Fast food galore at the plaza on entry. Stands elsewhere.

In the 1940's when I was stationed near San Diego at the Marine Corps's Greens Farm (no farm!) at Camp Elliott, and later at Camp Pendleton, the San Diego Zoo was a pleasant little place to visit, quiet and even remote. Now, it is one of the largest and certainly one of the most publicized zoos in the world, with an annual advertising/public relations budget of $5 million.

The climate is kind to San Diego and to the zoo. Things grow, and the result is magnificent, with very effective flora.

The zoo has a multi-million-dollar strategic long-range plan for restructuring the zoo into nine climatic zones: the tropical rain forest, savannah, desert, grassland, temperate forest, taiga, tundra, montane, and island. Phase II, the Heart of the Zoo, costing $16 million, includes the new 2½-acre, $3.6 million gorilla exhibit and more than 3,000 cuttings and seedlings imported from Africa. Gorilla Jimmy now has a $250,000 waterfall to splash in, and Samantha, who loves to climb, has a $75,000 play area. Remote TV cameras allow keepers to observe the gorillas and monitor the well-being of newborns. Visitors, as a zoo report notes, "go ape over babies."

People like gorillas because they seem to be like us. But I was more impressed by Jimmy's waterfall than by the rest of the Gorilla Tropics exhibit, which didn't live up to its rain-forest label. The gorilla exhibit is structurally sound with interesting natural habitat touches such as a log over water, and viewing areas are good. The second phase of Gorilla Tropics, which opened in 1993, added a dimension to the exhibit by including bonobos (pygmy chimpanzees), Angolan colobus monkeys, crowned eagles, Jackson's chameleons, and African pythons. Nevertheless, the exhibit fails to create involvement with gorillas. Humans are looking at a captive animal on exhibit, even though his cage is now dressed up in "natural habitat." The signage could be more educational.

Flamingos are placed at the zoo entrance, and their color is magnificent. However, more educational signs could relate the flamingos' beauty to how spectacular they are in their natural habitat.

The three-acre Tiger River achieves this objective. A path leads downward from near the entrance to the zoo, past artificial boulders in a misty, tropical flora atmosphere, to the tigers. In the nearby Kroc Family Tropical Rain Forest are tapirs, pythons, crocodiles, and water dragons as well as birds. From behind glass at the bottom of the path you may get a clear close-up view of the orange-and-black Sumatran tigers descending from what appears to be a limitless beyond, behind a cliff. A fallen log provides footing for the thirsty tigers and a close-up view for the visitor behind glass. This is without doubt an effective exhibit. It is comfortable for the tigers (who are otherwise penned up in concrete and barred cages "backstage"), and creates a wilderness image in the minds of the watchers.

Siberian tigers are helpless when they are born. Their eyes usually don't open until they are two weeks old, and they can't focus until the third week. At six weeks the cubs drink water but are not interested in eating until the eighth week. Furthermore, Siberian tigers love to swim, but they must learn to do so, and introducing cubs to a full pool at too early an age could be catastrophic. Not surprisingly, when Siberian tiger cubs Misha, Boris, and Raisa were born on May 17, 1990, they were kept off exhibit with their mother until August 17, allowing them to prepare for life out-of-doors.

I found the zoo's hummingbird exhibit particularly appealing; it is very small and off the beaten zoo-track, in a corner of the zoo, to the left as you enter. On entering you find yourself very close to the birds, which presented a problem to the zoo that has been rectified. Theft-minded admirers reached out and pocketed a bird to take home. The word got out that the zoo was losing birds because of ill-care, which was not the case. The slow-moving birds were replaced with quick thinkers and losses have been reduced to near zero. (Also see hummingbirds in the Wild Animal Park profile.)

The San Diego Zoo provides the visitor with a good look at—and education on—bears. Of the six genera and eight species of bears, bear biologists report that only the polar bear and American black bear populations are currently stable. Visit the Malayan sun bear exhibit which opened in 1989; sun bears chew holes in solid cement, so the construction of their exhibit was a challenge.

Koalas are a major attraction at San Diego and the other six zoos in the United States that have them: Chicago's Lincoln Park, San Antonio, Los Angeles, Minnesota (Minneapolis), and San Francisco. In 1925 the first koalas ever to be exhibited at a zoo were brought from Australia (where they are considered a "flagship" species) to San Diego; they had been named Cuddlepie and Snugglepot by the children of Sydney, after characters in a children's book by May Gibbs. The San Diego Zoo has received 26 koalas from Australia since 1925, and has bred 61. The zoo lends its koalas to other zoos in the United States, and even abroad. At the San Diego Zoo the koalas' eucalyptus leaves (their only diet) come from the zoo grounds and three fresh browse farms, and the zoo is attempting to obtain 300 more acres at a former Marine

Corps base to grow more eucalyptus. The zoo works with the Queensland National Parks and Wildlife Service on the issue of saving koalas habitats in Australia.

At the time of writing the San Diego Zoo had been denied its request to the U.S. Fish and Wildlife Service for a permit to import two pandas from China on breeding loan for three years (see profile of the Columbus (Ohio) zoo for a more detailed account of panda visits).

Exhibits and animals that should not be missed include:

- the new (1993) Australasia rain-forest complex, which highlights lories, a nectar-feeding family of parrots, and includes more than twenty aviaries
- the two-humped Bactrian camel from Chinese Turkestan and Mongolia, shorter than the one-humped dromedary camel
- the sloth bear from India and Sri Lanka, whose diet is mainly insects, honey, eggs and carrion
- red-beaked, blue-, yellow-, and brown-feathered stork-billed kingfishers from the Asian tropics
- the orangutan, a disheveled red furry mass that lumbers across the grass and climbs to a perch, and sometimes will come up to the glass and stare at you with eyes that seem to be asking a question
- the cold-blooded naked mole rat
- the Sumatran hairy rhinoceros.

The aviary is a must, and new exhibits are planned for colobus monkeys, African crowned eagles, Jackson's chameleons, and African pythons.

The Center for the Reproduction of Endangered Species (CRES) is a vital component of San Diego Zoo's conservation program. CRES is noted for its achievement in having created the first frozen zoo (cryopreserved sperm) toward the preservation of more than 300 species and subspecies. CRES has programs on behavior, comparative physiology, reproductive physiology, endocrinology, genetics, infectious disease, pathology, virology, and immunology. CRES supports a number of international programs. In Papua New Guinea CRES has 10 people to educate the government there on conservation. In Namibia, Dr. John Phillips conducted a two-year field study on the monitor lizard toward understanding the physiological processes controlling the release and reception of chemical signals. Since 1987 CRES has been working in Costa Rica capturing birds, primarily hummingbirds, from the rain forest and training Costa Rican zoo personnel in captive-husbandry techniques. CRES reintroductions have included Guam rails to the island of Rota, in the Marianas; thick-billed parrots to Arizona; Arabian oryx to Oman (to which 140 oryx have been reintroduced); and Numbian ibex to Jordan. In Paraguay CRES has conducted a breeding program of peccaries. CRES is studying viruses that affect koalas and helping the Vietnamese try to save the remnants of a rare and primitive species of Asian cattle, the kouprey.

CRES has also supported the Charles Darwin Research Station tortoise programs in the Galápagos. A San Diego tortoise played an interesting role in the success of a tortoise breeding program. The Hood Island tortoise is one of the more seriously endangered subspecies of Galápagos tortoises, and all surviving animals are housed at the Charles Darwin Research Center there (*galápagos* is Spanish for "tortoise"). The breeding program resulted in a dozen eggs by the mid-seventies, but the gene pool was limited as there were only two males. When the director of the Darwin Center visited San Diego in 1976 he saw a tortoise that looked very much like a Hood Island subspecies—and so it was. The tortoise, numbered "21," was put on a plane and sent to the Galápagos. Three years later "21" became a father.

🐘 SAN DIEGO WILD ANIMAL PARK

15500 San Pasqual Valley Road
Escondido, California 92027
(619) 234-6541

Open: 9–4, grounds close at 5; call for summer hours

Best for: Nairobi Village; Insect House

Year opened: 1972

Acres: 2,200

Animal population: 3,438; 440 species

Director: Douglas Myers

Membership: Zoological Society of San Diego

(619) 231-0251

Getting there: Take I-15 thirty miles north of San Diego, then go south to Via Rancho Parkway. Follow signs.

Conservation: SSP animals, including California condor, barasingha, clouded leopard, oryx.

Education: Guided zoo tours: three-mile bus tours; animal shows featuring free-flying birds, elephants; rare and wild animal show. Excellent graphics and signs at exhibits. Offers education programs of the San Diego Zoo. Insect show (summer only), Thursday through Sunday at 8:15 P.M. and 9:15 P.M.

Special attractions: 50-minute monorail tour and 1 hr. 45 min. photo caravan in trucks. Call (619) 747-8702, ext. 5022 for reservations. Animal shows (check times). Three thousand plant species throughout the Wild Animal Park (WAP): at the Australian Rain Forest, Fuchsia House, Baja California Garden, Conifer Arboretum, and Bonsai Pavilion. Herb garden tour Saturday at 10:00 A.M. (summer). Tour the Hidden Jungle to discover biodiversity before the WAP opens, for ages 10 and up, at 8–10 A.M. in the summer. For reservations call (619) 738-5057.

Gift shop: Take-homes and gifts galore. African carvings.

Food: Breakfast, lunch, dinner at Thorn Tree Terrace, Mombasa Cooker, and Samburu Terrace.

The San Diego Wild Animal Park is located on 1,800 acres in Escondido, a 45-minute drive north of the San Diego Zoo, and was opened on May 9, 1972. Both the zoo and the park operate under the policies and supervision of the Zoological Society of San Diego. The Wild Animal Park offers a unique opportunity for the public to view wildlife in the open, while at the same time providing the animals freedom within a confined space large enough to contain the number of the species that encourages reproduction. It has worked, and more than a million visit the park annually. The Wild Animal Park was the result of an initiative of former San Diego Zoo director Dr. Charles Schroeder. There are more than 3,400 animals on display representing 440 species.

A 50-minute WGASA monorail ride provides a guided tour and view of many of the 2,500 animals on the simulated veldts and plains. The monorail begins and ends at Nairobi Village, passing the Asian waterhole, the Asian plain and Mongolian steppe, the trans-Asian highlands, the Arabian desert and Australian rain forest, traveling past Sumatran tigers, okapis, baboons, cheetahs, and Asian lions, through African territory, and passing gorillas, cheetahs, rhinoceroses, camels, zebras, baboons, and okapis. The Wild Animal Park wanted a Swahili-sounding name for its monorail. However, WGASA is not a Swahili word. The fact of the matter (I have it from a very good source) is that the board of directors of the San Diego Zoo had spent some time considering what the monorail should be called, everyone offering his or her own suggestion. Finally one member pounded the table with his hand in total exasperation, and exclaimed, "Who gives a shit anyway." So, that's what they called it, WGASA.

Photo caravans via fancy open-air truck offer an opportunity to motor through the exhibits seen from the monorail, with occasional petting of an animal. And close-up photography produces satisfying results.

Don't miss the 1.25-mile footpath, the Kilimanjaro Trail, which passes through an Australian (how did that get in there?) rain forest with emus, kangaroos, and wallabies. Then go to Pumzika Point for an East African view. The trail twists past hornbills, cheetahs, Sumatran tigers, Asian lions, African and Asian elephants, and lowland nyalas. Kilimanjaro was never like that . . . must be zooetic license.

Such is also the case in Nairobi Village. When I first visited Nairobi, Kenya, in 1954 it was a small town. That was some 50 years after the railroad reached a swamp at Nairobi on its way from Mombasa to Uganda. Today Kenya's capital is overcrowded with people and jammed with cars, but before 1900 Nairobi was surrounded by African wildlife. WAP's Nairobi Village fantasy is inhabited by animals and visited by people. Western lowland gorillas have an attractive grassy knoll near the monorail (for their entertainment? to watch the people go by?). Ring-tailed lemurs leap on the ground and into three rubber trees on a small island. Golden lion tamarins, koalas, Kirk's dik-diks (the smallest species of antelope), and exotic waterfowl, to which you may feed grain from a coin-generated dispenser, are all residents of Nairobi Village. Around them are scattered commercial ventures, including food stops for people and shops.

One of the park's greatest achievements is its captive breeding program; it has succeeded with such animals as the white rhino, the California condor, the cheetah, the Sumatran tiger, the langur, the southern white rhinoceros, the addax, and the oryx. The park participates in a reintroduction program, and 35 Arabian oryx of the 130 born at the park have been reintroduced to Saudi Arabia and 16 to Oman, although they must be constantly guarded by Bedouins lest they be poached. Jim Dolan, general curator, has said, "We believe that places like the Wild Animal Park, working together with other zoos, offer the best hope of safeguarding these animals."

In 1992 a new exhibit opened, containing 14 species—the 4,400-square-foot Hummingbird Pavilion in a glass building (formerly housing butterflies) behind the lagoon and next to the Tropical American Walkthru. The Hidden Jungle exhibit, which opened in 1993, has a second greenhouse of mixed species, including butterflies, hummingbirds, bugs (of course), poison dart frogs, iguanas, chameleons, and even a two-toed sloth. Butterflies, bought as cocoons from Costa Rica, New Guinea, and South America, are placed in the hummingbird exhibit at the rate of 500 butterflies each week and live from three days to three weeks. The Wild Animal Park is pleased to have established a rain forest–friendly commerce whereby the natives harvest the cocoons from the forest without damaging the ecosystem.

Other zoo activities include visiting the aviary and petting *kraal*, watching langurs swing from trees, or being entertained by a bird show, elephant rides, and animal antics shows.

The Wild Animal Park isn't really a zoo and it isn't "the wild." But for those who have not seen animals in the wild, the Wild Animal Park's vistas and contact with animals will be a thrill.

🐻 SAN FRANCISCO ZOOLOGICAL GARDENS

One Zoo Road
San Francisco, California 94132
(415) 753-7080
Open: 10–5
Best for: Cats; gorillas; lemurs
Year opened: 1928

Acres: 75
Animal population: 6,859
(5,972 invertebrates); 343
species
Director: David Anderson

Getting there: From central San Francisco, go west on Herbst Road toward coast (to South Gate entrance), or on Sloat Boulevard (to main entrance). Parking at both entrances.

Conservation: SSP: snow leopard, black rhinoceros, gorilla, orangutan, lemur.

Education: Emphasis on teacher training. Nature trail.

Special attractions: Primates and penguins. Insect zoo (one of six in United States).

Gift shop: Excellent.

Food: Restaurant.

Birds get special attention at the San Francisco Zoo. The San Francisco Zoological Society supports a program of avian flight demonstrations as well as the breeding and release of peregrine falcons and Harris' hawks into the countryside in places where they are likely to join members of their own species. More than one hundred peregrine falcons have been released to date by the zoo.

Bald eagles have also been raised at the San Francisco Zoo and reintroduced into the wild. In 1992 a male bald eagle was flown down to Catalina Island and left there with wishes for a happy future—but it flapped its wings and set out to sea, got tired, and landed on a shrimp boat. A man with attention to detail saw that the bird had an identification tag. The zoo was informed and the eagle brought back to the zoo for a rest and then returned to Catalina. This time an acclimation period was arranged, so when he was re-released he was content on the island. But he may still be watching for an opportunity to board a eco-cruise ship headed west.

Another bird that is getting special treatment is the Andean condor. One of the zoo's birds produced eggs in 1992 and the chicks will be taken to South America where they will be released. I once saw an Andean condor in flight near Cotapaxi, an extinct volcano in Ecuador. It was wonderful to see the condor soaring at a great height against the backdrop of the snow-capped peak. What we learn about the Andean condor may help us save the endangered California condor.

A further highlight of the zoo is the lemurs. The zoo's director, David Anderson, was at Duke University for eight years, where he was involved with the Primate Center, which has a lemur population of over 700 as well as other prosimians. Prosimians are the more primitive of the two branches of the primate order and include lemurs, lorises, galagos, pottos, indris and aye-ayes. Anderson is on the Primate Center Scientific Advisory Committee and is also chairman of the Madagascar Fauna Group, whose intention is to save the habitats of lemurs in Madagascar by declaring reserves as protected areas and seeing that their protection is enforced. There are about 36 species and subspecies of lemur, 33 of them found only in Madagascar. (I have a special fondness for lemurs, for while living in Madagascar I made a friend of a ring-tailed lemur named Sebastian, or Basti. He had been caught by villagers on the southern part of the island. They had a tight rope about him, strangling him, but for a few francs they gave him up. He lived with me at the American Embassy residence for about a year, then went to the zoo in Antananarivo, the capital, where he mated and produced twins.) The fourth-largest island in the world, Madagascar has unique wildlife; more than 6,000 species of flowering plants, 233 species of reptiles, 230 species of birds, and 142 species of frogs are all *unique* to Madagascar. Because there have never been predators on the island such as lions or even hyenas, smaller wildlife like the lemur have been able to survive, even though humans have destroyed much of their habitats. Some species populations have become extinct already or are probably too decimated to save. But Anderson's work and the attention that is now being given to Madagascar, which is described as "the naturalist's promised land," may help the lemur and other species survive.

A small but very dedicated education department is headed by Diane Demee-Benoit. She started as a docent on the nature trail at the zoo when it first opened in 1976, when she was 13. The zoo feels that adults are sometimes embarrassed to ask other adults a question, so they station young people along the trail's 18 stops. Demee-Benoit trained as a field biologist, only to find that if she was to "accomplish something" it would be through public education. Her greatest push at the San Francisco Zoo is for elementary- and secondary-school teacher training. She has found that elementary-school teachers in particular are scared of teaching science and rush to the zoo for help. When exposed to zoo science, many become enthralled with what they learn; they become leaders among other teachers in passing on Benoit's message: Look beyond the zoo walls toward the goal of conservation, and become environmental activists.

A $25 million program has been launched for the construction of a new leopard complex, a new orangutan exhibit, minor restorations throughout the zoo, and the construction of an African savannah and forest. The gorillas will remain in their present early-1980's exhibit.

♀ CHEYENNE MOUNTAIN ZOOLOGICAL PARK

4250 Cheyenne Mountain Zoo
Road
Colorado Springs, Colorado
80906
(719) 633-9917

Open: 9–6; call for winter
hours

Best for: Giraffes; apes

Year opened: 1926

Acres: 150

Animal population: 508;
139 species

Director: Susan Engfer

Getting there: From Route 115 south of Colorado Springs turn west onto Cheyenne Mountain Boulevard. Follow road past Broadmoor Hotel. Signs indicate Will Rogers Shrine of the Sun and Cheyenne Zoo.

Conservation: Primates, black-footed ferret, endangered Wyoming toads.

Education: More than 30,000 schoolchildren toured the zoo in 1993. Two-week summer ecology camp.

Special attractions: Great Ape House; marmosets, who came to the zoo because they kept tunneling into a bank.

Gift shop: Modest.

Food: Light snacks; there are plans for a restaurant that serves meals.

The Cheyenne Zoo sits atop a rocky mountain with a magnificent view (underground is a NORAD defense installation). The zoo was built in 1926 by the nearby Broadmoor Hotel, and was supported by the hotel for many years. By 1980 the Broadmoor didn't want the zoo anymore, and it then had to shift for itself. Now restructured, the zoo is financially independent. It launched a $13 million capital fund campaign, making possible the construction of a new entry plaza and the creation of an exhibit of giraffes that can be fed by visitors; in 1991 the Ape House was opened. The giraffes are discovered by the visitor immediately on entering the zoo; they are lined up with their necks stretched out for Ry-Krisps. It is fun to feed them, but the exhibit somewhat lacks an educational touch. The Ape House, with orangutans, gorillas, colobuses, and small primates, has been a great success. Tropical rain-forest and *kopje* exhibits are to be built when funds become available through the work of the Cheyenne Mountain Zoological Society.

One hundred and thirty-five docents conduct 20,000 school tours annually. An animal puppet program initiated in 1991 has been a great success in teaching children about wildlife. I heard first-graders using words like *camouflage* at a puppet show. Jane Goodall, who worked closely with Dr. Louis S. B. Leakey for many years when she lived at the Gombe Reserve in Tanzania studying chimpanzees, started her chimpanzee program at the zoo in Colorado Springs; the program now has 16 participant zoos.

The Cheyenne Mountain Zoological Park is one of six institutions involved in a breeding program for the black-footed ferret, labeled as one of the most endangered species in North America. In 1986 the only fifteen black-footed ferrets known to be in the wild were captured and put into the breeding program. By the fall of 1993 there were 500 black-footed ferrets, plus 139 animals which have been released in Wyoming.

♟ DENVER ZOOLOGICAL GARDENS

City Park
Denver, Colorado 80205
(303) 331-4100

Open: 10–6; call for winter hours

Best for: Beavers; primates

Year opened: 1896

Acres: 73.5

Animal population: 2,500; 548 species

Director: Clayton Freiheit

Getting there: A short drive from downtown, in the City Park.

Conservation: Conservation programs for nearly 20 species, including Grevy's zebra, snow leopard, Andean condor, golden lion tamarin, scimitar-horned oryx. Reintroduction programs for the latter two.

Education: One out of every five Colorado elementary-school students studies at the zoo. Teacher training. College students study animal behavior at the zoo. For further information, call 331-4118.

Special attractions: Primate Panorama, Northern Shores, Bear Mountain.

Gift shop: The main gift shop has three areas: (1) clothing (hats, shirts, ties); (2) specialty (handcrafted items from around the world, including American Indians crafts); (3) books, cards, and a huge collection of stuffed animals and toys.

Food: The main restaurant is the Hungry Elephant (specialty food, pastas, deli sandwiches); for snacks there are the North Shore Café (sandwiches, hot dogs, drinks), Brown Bear (sandwiches, drinks), and an ice-cream stand at the zebra exhibit.

Denver's new Primate Panorama, to open in 1996 at a cost of $9.5 million, will include five acres for chimpanzees, orangutans, and mandrills (blue-faced, red-nosed, thick-maned primates), an aviary, cranes, and a lemur island. The gorillas' share of this real estate will be 29,500 square feet; having been lodged in a simple glassed-in exhibit, they will undoubtedly be happy to move into new quarters with companions.

I find the beaver exhibit very appealing. They have an island in a water-filled moat, which they share with two pelicans. The beavers have made their lodge, with the help of zookeepers, from concrete blocks, branches, and logs, and they continue to modify it as they are regularly given additional branches. In 1990 three beavers were born—thoroughly delightful.

Bear Mountain was the first naturalistic exhibit in America, built in 1918, at the then high cost of $50,000, out of cast rock and plaster of Paris reinforced with burlap. It was restored in 1989 using rubber and latex, and now houses grizzlies and Himalayan black bears. The background looks like natural rock and is accentuated by a high waterfall and pond. A log sits in the water for the bears' sport.

Northern Shores, with water that flows through three exhibits, presents animals native to cold coasts and definitely should not be missed. You can see polar bears (including underwater viewing), plus a snowy owl (with a feather and egg exhibit at the site), Arctic fox, and river otter. I also liked exhibits of the river hippo; a mist-filled Bird World building with hummingbirds, hornbills (Director Clayton Freiheit's favorite exhibit), aquatic birds, and penguins. You may get a good, close look at American bison and camels. Tropical Discovery, opened November 1993, is a 22,000-square-foot $7.5 million exhibit that Freiheit describes as "tropical habitats and what is in them—a generic jungle." It highlights endangered species, including the golden lion tamarin and scimitar-horned oryx. An invertebrate exhibit includes leaf-cutter ants, Madagascar hissing cockroaches, a wolf spider, Mexican red-legged tarantulas, and marine invertebrates.

Freiheit sees the real mission of a zoo as education, and a $2.5 million education facility is being built there. One out of every five Colorado elementary students studied at the zoo in 1987; if, say, a student has to write a term paper on wolves the zoo will provide ideas and even help.

The greatest challenge Freiheit faced at the Denver Zoo had less to do with animals than with people and money. The city of Denver withdrew much of its financial support in the late 1970's and early 1980's. One year the city government told Freiheit that the zoo's funds would be cut by 55 percent. The zoo took the only action it could: It made up its budget shortfall by doubling the admissions fee, and in 1983 it started to market and advertise itself. The net result was to place the zoo in a sound financial position from which it could move forward on developing new exhibits.

🐾 BEARDSLEY ZOOLOGICAL GARDENS

1875 Noble Avenue
Bridgeport, Connecticut 06610
(203) 576-8126
Open: 9–4
Best for: Siberian tiger; red wolf; golden lion tamarins
Year opened: 1922

Acres: 36
Animal population: 274; 117 species
Director: Gregg Dancho
Membership: Connecticut Zoological Society
(203) 331-1557

Getting there: From I-95 take Exit 27A to Route 8/25 north, then take Exit 5 east to Boston Avenue. At the fourth traffic light turn north onto Noble Avenue, to Beardsley Park entrance. There is a $5-per-car fee for entrance to the park.

Education: Focus on rain-forest animals. Zoomobile: Prekindergarten through high school.

Special attractions: New World Tropics Building, New England farmyard.

Gift shop: Has items with conservation message: books, bluebird houses, microscope kits.

Food: Snacks.

Beardsley's main exhibit is the New World Tropics Building, opened on July 15, 1992. It is a rain forest containing a forest stream, small tributaries, and three-tiered waterfall and populated by caimans, several species of turtles, woolly monkeys, ocelots, sloths, agoutis, keel-billed toucans, and golden lion tamarins. Planned for the near future are four wall exhibits: insects, venomous creatures, orchids, and endangered amphibians of the tropics.

ZooLab, an interactive educational facility with microscopes and other learning tools, will be opening in the near future.

The zoo displays with pride two endangered species, the red wolf and Siberian tiger, and participates in the red wolf SSP. The red wolf's zoo territory is lightly wooded, and a sign alerts the visitor to the fact that the animal is a "shy, elusive predator." Not quite true here. This one moves furtively about, pausing to watch the swish of traffic on Routes 25 and 8.

A greenhouse, half of which is open to the public, is botanically diverse and pleasing and is managed completely on a volunteer basis by the Men's Garden Club of Bridgeport.

Beardsley Zoo also has a New England farmyard with sheep, rabbits, a Jersey cow, waterfowl, a raccoon, a caracara falcon, and—somewhat incongruously for New England—a llama, a Scottish highland cow, and African pygmy goats. An instructive sign notes that "people began keeping wild animals as sources of meat, milk and hides over ten thousand years ago."

➤ MYSTIC MARINELIFE AQUARIUM

55 Coogan Boulevard
Mystic, Connecticut 06355
(203) 536-9631

Open: 9–5:30; call for winter hours

Best for: Dolphins; sharks; seals

Year opened: 1973

Acres: 36

Animal population: 4,448; 141 species

Director: President/CEO: Hugh Connell

Getting there: From I-95 take Exit 90 and follow signs (about three hours from New York City and two hours from Boston).

Conservation: Whales.

Education: In-house and traveling programs. Programs in four school systems.

Special attractions: Shark tank; outdoor exhibits.

Gift shop: Book and gift shop with innovative marine animal items.

Food: Restaurants and snack stops abound in the immediate environs. Why not visit Mystic Seaport, too. Eat at their excellent restaurant. Lunch (oyster stew recommended) at the Inn at Mystic Museum.

The Mystic Aquarium is a popular public attraction. Droves of people turn off I-95 east of Mystic Seaport and pour into the wayside marine exhibit to see Atlantic bottle-nosed dolphins, beluga whales, California sea lions, and northern fur seals. There are 48 indoor exhibits, including "The Open Sea," a cylindrical 35,000-gallon display with 16 windows to view six sharks. Five species of seals are displayed in a 2.5-acre outdoor exhibit; during the summer the water is cooled for them. In the 30-minute demonstrations in the 1,400-seat Marine Theater, marine biologists explain the anatomy and abilities of beluga whale and bottle-nosed dolphin. Mystic Aquarium also has a number of very good small exhibits; for example, one may view brine shrimp under a microscope. There is also an exhibit of the protective egg cases (also known as mermaid purses) of chain dogfish, a type of shark. After mating the female lays eggs in cases, each containing a single embryo with a yoke sack for nourishment. The eggs remain in the cases for six months, then the shark is born. The Audubon Institute's aquarium in New Orleans also has a mermaid's purse exhibit.

One reason I particularly like the Mystic Marinelife Aquarium is Hank, the elephant seal (the elephant seal is the world's largest pinniped). Watching Hank reminds me of a morning I spent sitting on a rock on San Benito Island off the west coast of Baja California, observing a huge male elephant seal, weighing close to 8,000 pounds, wallowing in the pleasure of his surrounding harem. He made a pass at one, mounted another; there were grunts and squeaks. At Mystic, Hank has no harem, but he has scores of admirers as he raises his snoot into the air, wobbles it about, and snorts.

♀ NATIONAL ZOOLOGICAL PARK

3000 Connecticut Avenue, N.W.
Washington, D.C. 20008
(202) 673-4721

Open: 8–8; call for winter hours

Best for: Panda; invertebrates

Year opened: 1889

Acres: 163

Animal population: 2,659; 531 species

Director: Michael Robinson

Membership: Friends of the National Zoo, (202) 673-4950

Getting there: By subway: Metro Red Line, Woodley Park–Zoo stop is four blocks from zoo. By bus: Metrobuses L2 and L4 on Connecticut Avenue. By car: From Rock Creek and Potomac parkway, take first turn-off east of Connecticut Avenue, follow signs to zoo parking area.

Conservation: Research, breeding, at the National Zoo and at its Conservation and Research Center in Front Royal, Virginia (is *not* open to the public; see profile on Front Royal). Strong SSP emphasis, and particular pride in its participation in the golden lion tamarin reintroduction program in Brazil.

Education: Classes for children and adults; breakfast at the zoo to observe early-morning feedings; animal information carts; films; symposiums; lectures on subjects such as "how we look at animals," genetics, the environment, "the natural history of water"; nature photography trips; free weekend tours; and zoo-sponsored trips abroad. For information: 357-3030. Teacher education and education of foreigners at Front Royal center.

Special attractions: Amazonia rain forest exhibit (opened Nov. '92).

Gift shop: Three shops. The one in the Education Building is outstanding, especially for books. The Cub Shop at the Mane Restaurant near Amazonia has a particularly good selection of small animal stick-on figures. The gift shop in Amazonia (on exiting the exhibit) is small but concentrates on the rain forest and the Amazon in particular, with good books on animals found in the rain forest and on biodiversity.

Food: Mane Restaurant (fast food); Panda Plaza; Pop Stop ice cream shops.

The National Zoological Park was the creation of William Temple Hornaday, who proposed in 1887 that the Smithsonian Institution create a zoo in Washington, D.C. Soon, an exhibit of live animals was opened on the Mall—a "little tryout zoo to test the interest of the American public in collections of living animals." People donated animals and the collection grew. Hornaday suggested a larger facility, and ultimately President Grover Cleveland signed an appropriation bill on March 2, 1889, to establish a zoo in Rock Creek Park. Hornaday became the zoo's director and remained so until 1890, when he left to become director of the New York Zoological Society.

Director Michael Robinson came to the National Zoo as its director in 1984, when he left his post as deputy director of the Smithsonian Tropical Research Institute in Panama. He has a mandate from the Smithsonian to bring the zoo into the twenty-first century with an emphasis on education and conservation. It is also clear that he is putting his own imprint on the zoo.

For example, Robinson believes that "education is a more important function of zoos than captive breeding." Many zoo directors would argue that without captive breeding there can be no education role. (The Conservation and Research Center at Front Royal, Virginia, is the conservation arm of the National Zoo.) Robinson calls the zoo a "biopark," and *that's* also controversial. As a part of the biopark theme, Robinson opened an Elephant Museum in December 1986, which tells the story of elephants throughout history as they appeared in art, religion, war, and circuses. Robinson's efforts are considerably assisted in having the Smithsonian Institute as his "boss" and the U.S. taxpayer as his patron.

The current number one attraction at the National Zoo is undoubtedly the giant panda Hsing-Hsing, partly because pandas are such gentle-looking animals, and partly because there are no other resident pandas in the United States. China is promoting a rent-a-panda program, but the AAZPA disapproves and will take action against any zoo that has a panda on loan from China (see the Columbus [Ohio] Zoo and San Diego Zoo profiles). Unsuccessful attempts were made to breed Ling-Ling and Hsing-Hsing, who were both received from the Chinese government in 1972 as a gift, and Ling-Ling died on December 30, 1992.

Primates, particularly gorillas, are always a top-interest exhibit at a zoo. The National Zoo has 18 species of primates, ranging from the two-ounce mouse lemur to the 350-pound gorilla. The National Zoo's gorillas have very simple indoor exhibit areas behind glass. Director Michael Robinson believes that gorillas in zoos don't need a natural habitat exhibit; real trees are not necessary. A mattress, he believes, might be better for a gorilla than leaves. "We assume," he berates, "that animals are as sophisticated in their needs as Man, and they may not be." Here, gorillas watch TV in their exhibit area.

The National Zoo participates in a reintroduction program for golden lion tamarins that, thus far, has proved of questionable success. The tamarins that have been residents of the zoo since 1986 are the spokes-animals for the approximately 400 remaining golden lion tamarins in the wild in Brazil. More than 100 have been born at the zoo's Conservation and Research Center in Front Royal, Virginia.

The zoo's invertebrate exhibit, in a basement off Olmstead Walk and adjacent to the Reptile House, opened in 1987. It has a laboratory atmosphere and more than 150 invertebrate species in exhibits that trace the path of invertebrate evolution. A curious eye will find sponges (there are about 5,000 species in the oceans), octopus, live brain corals, three types of sea urchin and anemones, giant squid, and butterflies. A Japanese spider crab flexes its feelers. Starfish, sea cucumbers, and serpent stars are waiting to be seen, as are clams, oysters, snails, and slugs. Leaf-cutter ants are at work toting their green burdens into their tunnels and sequestered chambers. Doyenne of the basement is a 20-pound lobster that may be 50 years old. A large sandbox at the far end of the space contains wiggly things invisible to the eye that can be scooped up by a child and placed under a microscope. It is this type of hands-on experience that makes a zoo an institution of instruction and not an entertainment center. Robinson sees the invertebrate exhibit as another step toward transforming the zoo into the biopark he envisions.

The world's rain forests are virtually *the* top current priority of zoos. Two-fifths of the world's rain forests have already been destroyed, mostly during the past fifty years, and at the present rate of destruction the rain forest will have disappeared in another fifty. Hence, the emphasis by concerned zoos.

The National Zoo focuses its interest on the rain forest of the Amazon, the largest river system in the world. Amazonia, a 12,000-square-foot exhibit that opened in November 1992, places a nearly equal emphasis on plants and animals, and 60 percent of the latter are aquatic species. One enters Amazonia at ground level and sees a wall of three separate aquarium tanks that appear to be a single tank. Signs are excellent here as throughout Amazonia, and occupants of the aquarium are clearly and informatively identified. Around the corner from the aquarium is a field workshop with workbenches, tables with reading material, a microscope, a magnifying glass, and tanks with fish and turtles. A staff member, "Dr. Brasil," is on hand to answer questions on the rain forest, the exhibit, and animals. Upstairs is "The Forest," the main exhibit, running the length of the building and skillfully arranged with a winding dirt-colored cement path (imprinted with leaf "fossils"), where one is immediately confronted with the base of a huge "kapok tree," its roots extending in every direction. Hummingbirds flit by your face, and a four-ounce pygmy marmoset, the smallest of the true monkeys, sits on a branch above your head in the thick foliage. The atmosphere is lush, mist falls and rises, you hear the sound of the waterfall and the dripping of water from rocks. All the trees (papaya, rubber, sandbox, balsa, cocoa), vines, and other plants are labeled, and there are plastic-covered notebooks identifying birds and giving information on medicine in the forest.

The education department has used the Amazonia exhibit as a

framework for classes, seminars, and briefings, as well as for a film series viewed by school groups and world leaders. Expected to open in 1994 is the Amazonia Gallery with a "Jewels of the Forest" collection of 22 exhibits, which will present an opportunity to see a colony of army ants inside the thorn of a bush. A camera will show what an orchid looks like to a bee; touch-screen computers will demonstrate how a giant water bug catches a fish, how a spider weaves a web, and how birds hatch from eggs. The message is: Learn about innovative programs to save the rain forest, a treasure of biodiversity. The National Zoo has also established a working relationship with NASA to obtain satellite photographs of the Amazon Basin over the past 20 years. Michael Robinson, who sees nature in vivid terms, described Amazonia to me as a "Breughel not a Constable."

With its Amazonia exhibit the National Zoo is part of a trend to emphasize not only natural habitats (such as the rain forest) but larger conservation issues. This, says Robinson, is the aim of the comprehensive presentation possible in a biopark.

♱ MIAMI METROZOO

12400 S.W. 152nd Street
Miami, Florida 33177
(305) 251-0401

Open: 9:30–5:30

Year opened: 1972

Acres: 740

Animal population: 3,080; 281 species (before Hurricane

Andrew, August 1992)
As of January 1994:
population: 12,000; 250 species

Director: Robert Yokel

Membership: Zoological Society of Florida
(305) 255-5551

Getting there: Located about 10 miles southwest of Miami International Airport, south of the junction of the Homestead Extension Turnpike and Route 94. From Route 1, take S.W. 152nd Street exit west 3 miles to zoo. From Homestead Extension, take S.W. 152nd Street exit west ¼ mile to the zoo.

Conservation: On SSP and other conservation programs.

Education: Programs curtailed after the hurricane. Education programs started up again in the summer of 1993.

Special attractions: The determination and spirit of the people who work at the zoo.

Gift shop: Imaginative T-shirts and books, African wood and soapstone carvings, video- and audiotapes.

Food: Good fast food; restaurant will take time to reestablish.

After sustaining $50 million worth of damage during Hurricane Andrew (August 1992), Miami Metrozoo has made a valiant recovery. Six primates died and 127 birds were listed as dead, missing, or unrecoverable; the elevated monorail, the koala building, the aviary, and the restaurant (which was leveled) were casualties, but the zoo reopened on December 18, 1992. The monorail was back on track in time for summer 1993 crowds.

Director Robert Yokel described his zoo as a cageless zoo. It is a flat 290 acres effectively accentuated by rocks and decorated by planting. The zoo site was originally occupied by the Richmond Naval Air Station. Before the hurricane, a favorite exhibit was "Wings of Asia," a delightful 1½-acre, 65-foot-high aviary containing more than 300 bird specimens representing 80 species. When I visited it the keeper was giving personal care to the flora. Sheltered from the Florida sun by a canopy of trees that included numerous palms and hardwoods were miniature islands and hillsides banking a pleasing brook and waterfall; a meandering path took the visitor across a hanging bridge to an observation deck. A sense of isolation enveloped the visitor to this miniature Asian forest as an orange-bellied leafbird was sighted on a branch and a purple swamp hen was seen fording the stream. On a peninsula at the center of the aviary was a cluster of seats across from a tropic wetland marsh, where a visitor could melt into the scenery for a moment of escape. The hurricane totally destroyed the aviary, but it will be rebuilt in the same location, this time with far greater protections for the birds from the weather, particularly winds. Among the other exhibits that appealed to me at the zoo were the white-banded gibbons swinging gracefully on their artificial banyan tree branches on an artificial moated island adjacent to the siamangs; a white tiger prowling past a highly photogenic replica of thirteenth-century Angkor Wat. Three koalas were supplied with seven species of eucalyptus leaves from five zoo acres. The Cat House has been restored, but the Koala House will take longer.

Miami Metrozoo was a good zoo and will be again; Robert Yokel is to be congratulated for doing an extraordinary job in pulling the zoo together after the hurricane—though when asked what his "dream zoo" would be, he replies without hesitation, "No zoo at all."

🐾 ZOO ATLANTA

800 Cherokee Avenue, S.E.
Atlanta, Georgia 30315
(404) 624-5600

Open: 10–6:30; call for winter hours

Best for: Gorillas; reptiles; orangutans

Year opened: 1889

Acres: 39

Animal population: 874; 234 species

Director: Terry Maple

Membership: Friends of Zoo Atlanta (Second largest in the United States), 624-1235

Getting there: Zoo is in Grant Park adjacent to Cyclorama. By bus: Number 31 or 32 from downtown at the Five Points rail station. By car: Take I-20 east from downtown, go south at Exit 26 ("Boulevard Rd.").

Conservation: SSP programs, participation in various international conservation and research programs.

Education: Teacher workshops; half days at zoo for preschoolers.

Special attractions: African Rain Forest. For information on special events: 624-5600. Zoo events: 624-5678. Group (15+) reservations: 624-5639.

Gift shop: Very good.

Food: Excellent at Okefenokee Café; snack stops abound.

When Director Terry Maple arrived at Zoo Atlanta from the San Diego Zoo in 1975, he found the zoo in deplorable shape and the press on the attack. He turned the situation around, privatizing the zoo in 1984 and placing 12 business leaders on the board of directors.* The Ford Motor Company sped to help as a major donor, and Zoo Atlanta was on its way to becoming a natural habitat zoo, with an eventual projected animal population of 1,500 to 2,000.

Zoo Atlanta's Ford African Rain Forest and the gorilla exhibit are outstanding. The gorillas are on 3.1 acres in three areas separated by wide and deep moats. Willie B., who arrived at the zoo in 1961 from Cameroon (he was named after a former mayor of Atlanta, William B. Hartsfield), weighs 459 pounds, is six feet high, and has an arm span of 8 feet 4 inches, a 40-inch-diameter neck, and a 62-inch chest. Gorillas at zoos tend to put on much more weight than in the wild, owing to a lack of exercise and a different diet. In 1989, Willie B. at the age of 31 astonished everyone and in particular his lead keeper, L. Charles Horton, by deciding to mate with six-year-old Kinyani. Willie B. had lived a solitary life for 27 years and hadn't had an opportunity to socialize with other gorillas, much less fall in love. Horton states that in his early days as a keeper it was believed that "It's too late, he's been alone too long. He hasn't learned to be a gorilla, and besides, most of them are sterile anyway." Horton had cared for Willie B. for 15 years, and was elated to see him become involved in family life and interact with other gorillas.

Adjacent to the gorilla exhibit is what I consider the best orangutan exhibit in the United States, designed in 1981, featuring a 55-foot-high tree (orangutans like heights). One particular animal heads for the high tree first thing in the morning, climbs it, and remains perched atop it for most of the day.

The Reptile House, with taped sounds of the Amazon, has a grand collection with 600 inhabitants, but its atmosphere is some-

*Zoo Man: Inside the Zoo Revolution, by Terry L. Maple and Erika F. Archibald; Longstreet Press, Marietta, Georgia, 1993.

what clinical. There one can see three gharials, an endangered species of crocodile with a slender snout that lives a solitary life in Himalayan rivers. The slender snout makes gharials easy to distinguish from other crocodiles. They are fed live trout every Wednesday. (The bald eagles, located near the African Plains exhibit, are also fond of trout.)

Within spitting distance of the Elder's Tree, a small amphitheater, and a stone's throw from the Swahili Market may be seen the lion, who has a heated, gunnite *kopje* (rock) to stretch out on.

Director Maple says that the zoo places "a priority emphasis on education and research," which may explain the 65 percent increase in student group visits between 1988 and 1989. The curator for education credits the big jump to teachers' changing perception of the zoo as a teaching tool rather than just a break from classroom routine. Conservation, including support of and participation in field activities, has involved Zoo Atlanta in the gorilla program in Rwanda, Cynthia Moss's elephant research program in Amboseli National Park in Kenya, the Madagascar Fauna Group's efforts to establish parks in that country and save lemurs, the Sumatran Tiger Group, the Black Rhino Group, and SSP programs for the radiated tortoise, orangutan, gorilla, and drill.

▶ THE CECIL B. DAY BUTTERFLY CENTER/CALLAWAY GARDENS

Pine Mountain, Georgia 31822
(706) 663-5154
Open: 9–5
Best for: Butterflies
Acres: 12,000 (Day Center:
4½)

Year opened: 1988
Animal population: 1,000; over 50 butterfly species

Getting there: Seventy miles south of Atlanta and 30 miles north of Columbus, on U.S. Highway 27 in Pine Mountain. From I-185 take Exit 13 or 14.

Special attractions: The five-acre John A. Sibley Horticultural Center: exotic and native plants. Includes a Tropical Conservatory, Rock Wall Garden (focus on azaleas, ferns, citrus, and camelias, many plants native to China and Japan), the Sculpture Garden, The Grotto (ferns, rainbow moss, wandering jew), Floral Conservatory (large beds of flowering plants, 18 major themes), and the Outdoor Garden (lawns and flower beds, nature trails, birdwalks).

Sports facilities: Golf: 63 holes. Tennis: 17 lighted tennis courts. Racquetball: Two indoor courts. Swimming, boating, water skiing, hiking, biking, jogging. Twenty-three miles of roads and dedicated paths.

Accommodations (at Callaway): Mountain Creek Villas (luxurious); The Inn (350 rooms/suites); Country Cottages (155 rooms/suites with fully equipped kitchens). For reservations at The Inn, Cottages, Villas, or lodge: (800) 282-8181. For information: (706) 663-2281.

Food: Georgia Room (deluxe), Gardens Restaurant (casual), The Veranda (Italian), Plantation Room (Southern buffets), Flower Mill (burgers and pizza), Country Kitchen (casual breakfast or lunch).

Some collections are highly specialized, exhibiting only cats, lemurs, raptors, birds, monkeys, or reptiles. One institution, the Cecil B. Day Butterfly Center, specializes in butterflies. In fact, the center supplies many of the butterflies seen in zoo and wildlife center exhibits, including those at the San Diego Zoo, the North Carolina Zoological Park, the Cincinnati Zoo, the Chaffee Zoo (Fresno, California), Marineworld Africa U.S.A. (Vallejo, California), and Wings of Wonder at Busch Gardens, Florida. The Day Center obtains its butterflies (and breeds them when they arrive) from Malaysia and Taiwan as well as other countries.

The Butterfly Center is a part of Callaway Gardens, a public, educational, horticultural, and charitable organization, owned and operated by the nonprofit Ida Cason Callaway Foundation. Callaway Gardens is the creation of Cason J. Callaway and his wife, Virginia Hand Callaway, "to provide a wholesome family environment where all may find beauty, relaxation, inspiration and a better understanding of the living world." After-tax proceeds go to the foundation to support its efforts. The Day Center is a zoo of wings in a glorious setting of other enticements of nature.

Local wildlife includes 230 species of birds and 50 species of other wildlife. At the Day Center's octagonal conservatory, enclosed by 854 panes of glass, a visitor may walk among 1,000 tropical butterflies of 50 species, and 50 species of tropical plants. Waterfalls cascade 12 feet into the 275-square-foot pool. Directly outside the Day Center is a garden created with plants intended to attract many of the 70 local species of butterflies.

The Lepidoptera are a very large and important order of insects that includes the moths and butterflies, of which 13,700 species may be found in the United States and Canada. Endangered butterflies include the El Segundo blue, Lange's metalmark, Lotis blue, Mission blue, Mitchell's satyr, Palos Verdes blue, Queen Alexander's birdwing, San Bruno elfin, Achaus swallowtail, Smith's blue, and the Uncompahgre fritillary.

A butterfly metamorphoses from egg to larva (caterpillar) to pupa to butterfly. A caterpillar, a crawling, furry creature chewing its way from leaf to leaf, will turn into a pupa, an ugly object hanging from a branch that gives no forecast of the beauty it will become: a striking butterfly that awes us with its color, movement, and delicate shape. The beauty of butterflies does not make them simply an ornament of nature, however. Frank Elia, manager of the Day Butterfly Center, explained that a large *population* of butterflies is not an indication of plant diversity, but species diversity of butterflies in a habitat is a good indicator of plant diversity in the area. Since the life of a butterfly is short, butterflies' presence in a habitat confirms that plants on which they feed still exist there. In pointing out the ecological utility of butterflies, Elia made the point that the often maligned collector of butterflies only catches and kills one butterfly, leaving the eggs and caterpillars behind, whereas a bulldozer doesn't kill the adult butterflies but destroys eggs, caterpillars, and their habitat.

➤ SEA LIFE PARK HAWAII

Makapuu Point, Oahu
Hawaii 96795
(808) 259-7933, 923-1531
Open: 9:30–5, Fri. until 10
P.M.
Best for: Reef tank
Year opened: 1964

Acres: 22
Animal population: 19,113
(4,000 fish, 15,000
invertebrates); 252 species
Director: Robert Moore
Membership: No (privately
owned)

Want to get married? In the evening, the park may be yours, with catering by the Sea Lion Café. The ceremony may even be aboard the refurbished whaling ship, the *Essex*. Sea Life Park will provide a non-denominational minister, leis for bride and groom, chilled bottle of champagne, photographer, park admission for up to 10 people (if you have more than 10 friends it will cost you more), a limousine for four hours, and the services of a wedding coordinator (who will arrange for witnesses, flowers, video, and information on license, and hotel accommodations). Telephone: 1-800-SOS-8046.

Getting there: Located on Oahu island. Take Route 63 or 61 north of Honolulu.

Conservation: Focus on Hawaiian sealife, but also birds, plants. Humboldt penguins bred at the park.

Education: Behind-the-scenes tours, maximum of 16 people per tour. Minilectures.

Special attractions: A "wholphin," whose father was a false killer whale and whose mother was an Atlantic bottle-nosed dolphin hybrid; Whaler's Cove; Pacific Whaling Museum, including scrimshaw toys, dolls, figurines, sticks.

Gift shop: Sealife specialties; muumuus; jewelry; whale items.

Food: Sea Lion Café specializes in island favorites; Rabbit Island Bar and Grill for the view, relaxation, and a mai tai; snack bars.

Can you pronounce the name of Hawaii's state fish? *Humuhumunukunukuapua*. Or an even longer Hawaiian fish name? *Lauwiliwilinukunukuoioi*. You'll see both at Sea Life Park. The behind-the-scenes tours are 40 minutes long and well worth doing. You may learn much you didn't know about marine life; for instance, that:

- Hermit crabs have one large pincer, the crusher, and one small pincer, the shredder. The right pincer normally is the crusher, but Hawaii's hermit crabs have their crushers on the left, making them the only "left-handed" hermit crabs in the world.
- A dominant female wrasse (a type of spiny fish) can metamorphose into a male if one is needed.

One "must-see" at the Sea Life Park is Whaler's Cove, a ⅝ replica of the whaling ship *Essex*, where you can go below deck and look out of the acrylic portholes at dolphins and the wholphin. Another "must-see" is the endangered Hawaiian Monk Seal Care Center, where stranded or injured seals and their pups stay until they are well enough to be returned to their native habitat in the northwestern Hawaiian Islands. The Hawaiian reef tank contains 4,000 specimens, including sharks, rays, and a moray eel. Dolphins perform on a daily schedule at the enclosed 400-seat Hawaii Ocean Theater, and sea lions perform by surfing on a boogie board and playing a game of volleyball. Don't miss the red-footed and brown-footed boobies, the albatross, and the iwa (or great frigate) birds. The Turtle Lagoon contains three of the seven known sea turtle species: loggerhead, hawksbill, and green sea turtle.

BROOKFIELD ZOO (CHICAGO ZOOLOGICAL PARK)

3300 Golf Road
Brookfield, Illinois 60513
(708) 485-0263

Open: 9:30–6; call for winter hours

Best for: Snow leopards; dolphins; okapis

Year opened: 1934

Acres: 200

Animal population: 2,516; 419 species

Director: George Rabb

Sister zoo: Zoological Society, Victoria, Australia

Getting there: By car: From Chicago drive west on I-290 to 1st Avenue, turn south to 31st Street, turn west (right) to reach zoo. Extensive parking available. By train: Take Burlington-Meta train to Hollywood station; for information, call (312) 322-6777. By bus: For information call The Rapid Transit Authority: (800) 972-7000.

Conservation: Leading-edge programs in behavioral studies, genetic diversity; focus on Australia's platypus.

Education: A full range of education programs. The Discovery Center is a highlight. For information, call ext. 361.

Special attractions: Dolphinarium. Fragile Kingdom contains an African desert and an Asian rain forest. New $8 million Habitat Africa exhibit is a five-acre naturalistic savannah, highlighting the African savannah's diverse wildlife, habitats, and conservation issues.

Gift shop: Very good; special Brookfield Zoo items.

Food: Wide choice of restaurants and snack bars.

Brookfield Zoo's cable address is a giveaway to Brookfield's opinion of itself: THE BEST ZOO. *Best* is always a bit strong, but unquestionably Brookfield is one of the very best.

George Rabb joined the Brookfield Zoo as a curator of research in 1956 and has been director and president of the Chicago Zoological Society since 1976. He is chairman of the American Committee for Institutional Conservation and deputy chairman of the Species Survival Commission (SSC) of the International Union for the Conservation of Nature (IUCN). He is also species coordinator for the SSP on the okapi, an African mammal related to the giraffe. Rabb is a strong supporter of International Species Inventory System (ISIS), which has 320 participant institutions from 34 countries and currently tracks 100,000 species (the aim is three to four times that). Rabb's vision of exhibits in the future is that technology will include the audio component using the digitalized capacity of the compact disc (CD). Incorporating this technology into new exhibits will bring an addition dimension to natural habitats.

Rabb takes pride in Brookfield's accomplishments in conservation. The zoo bred the first black rhinoceros, okapi, Dall sheep, and addax in America. In Australia, Brookfield acquired 14,000 acres and gave it to the Australian government's national park system for the protection of emus, wombats, and kangaroos.

Brookfield describes its Tropic World as a large naturalistic grotto, with a waterfall, river, cement-gunnite trees, and epoxy-covered vines; it is the pride of Director Rabb. The three-sectioned exhibit—South America, Asia, and Africa—contains much to see. In South America one encounters the dusty titi monkey in a duet with its mate, the South American tapir (which is related to the horse and rhinoceros), the spider monkey (the last four inches of tail are hairless so that it can get a good swinging grip), as well as the golden lion tamarin, giant anteater, and two-toed sloth. In the Asia exhibit are the orangutan, tonkeana macaque, gibbon, and siamang. In the Africa exhibit are the glorious black-and-white colobus, mandrill, sooty mangabey (who are grooming experts), pygmy hippopotamus (whose hairless skin secretes a clear fluid to keep its body moist), and gorilla. Two groups of four gorillas each will ultimately be joined into one group. Birds inhabit all three exhibits. Dr. Rabb is pleased to make the point that the mangrove exhibit of the Bronx Zoo's renowned Jungle World profited from Brookfield's Tropic World.

Brookfield's Australian Walkabout was built in the 1960's and represents an early use of gunnite, a synthetic composition material used in making rocks for natural-habitat exhibits. The Walkabout houses bats and other mammals. It is now somewhat run-down but is a good example of a certain stage in the development of exhibition techniques.

The Seven Seas Panorama's 800,000-gallon, 2000-seat dolphinarium is a delight—by far the best of its kind. Opened in May 1987, it has two holding pools of 100,000 and 35,000 gallons for the eight dolphins and excellent natural light. The show *is* entertaining and is also educational. There are eight underwater viewing windows to see the dolphins performing their antics, apparently smiling as they swim by. Careful monitoring of the water's bacteria count is undertaken by the zoo's animal hospital—which is important, as one dolphin can produce 20 pounds of organic waste daily. Considerable behavioral study is under-taken during the dolphins' off hours, when they are quietly ob-served. Another exhibit at Seven Seas Panorama is home to the walrus and seals. One million of the $12 million construction cost of the Seven Seas Panorama was raised from peanut sales at the zoo!

The children's zoo has a variety of horses, including a 34-inch-high miniature steed and a 2,000-pound Clydesdale, along with hawks, owls, ravens, a bald eagle, a turkey vulture, pigs, and—a collie! A dog show in the children's zoo makes the point that dogs and humans have been friends and working partners for thou-sands of years. There are demonstrations of obedience exercises, retrieving, cart pulling, sheep herding, and canine skills that help deaf people focus on different aspects of this relationship. The "Pet and Learn," "Sensory Corner," and "Domestic Animals" areas are attractive and educational.

Other children's activities include a "Be a Bird" exhibit in-stalled in the aquatic-bird house, where children may test their abilities on a flying strength machine that electronically measures a child's arm strength to "fly"; a flying walk, which guides chil-dren through flight motions as they walk over an aerial panorama; and a "peek" board, providing a form of X-ray vision to compare the bones of a human skeleton with those of a bird.

In the reptile house is a regiment of 2,000 Brazilian cock-roaches all maneuvering around each other, which reminded me of one incident that occurred in Madagascar. As American ambas-sador I dutifully and with great pleasure traveled throughout the country. At that time one trip took me to a barren stretch on the southwestern coast of the island, to a town called Morandavo. My deputy chief of mission, Peter Walker, and his wife, Pamela, joined me and my wife on the trip. Accommodations were diffi-cult to obtain anywhere outside of Antananarivo, the capital, and I ended up staying at most unusual places. A minister in the government whose home town was Morandavo generously lent us his bungalow, for which we expressed our deep appreciation. Until we got there. While we were settling in before going to a goat barbecue on the beach, Pam Walker, in the bathroom, cried out, "Peter, come, right away!" Peter replied, "I can't." He was producing a hard slapping noise against the wall of their bedroom, which grew louder and more intense. "But, Peter, I need help. There's a cockroach in here and he's bigger than both of us." Peter finally came to Pam's rescue in the standoff with "the-most-enormous-cockroach-I-have-ever-seen." When a battle between the species is taking place, it is rather hard to think conservation.

George Rabb believes that zoos and aquariums must be more effective in conveying the urgent call for involvement and action in both conservation and education, not just presenting a gloom-and-doom picture. Like some other zoo directors, including L. Patricia Simmons of Akron, Ohio, and Y. Sherry Sheng of the Metro Washington Park Zoo, Portland, Oregon, Rabb has instituted a recycling program at Brookfield Zoo geared toward both visitors and employees.

🐾 LINCOLN PARK ZOOLOGICAL GARDENS

2200 North Cannon Drive
Chicago, Illinois 60614
(312) 294-4664
Open: 9–5
Best for: Apes; lions; koalas
Year opened: 1869
Acres: 35

Animal population: 1,592; 337 species
Director: Kevin Bell
Membership: Lincoln Park Zoological Society
(312) 935-6700

Getting there: By car: From downtown Chicago, take Lake Shore Drive north to Fullerton Street, turn left to Stockton Drive. By public transport call the Rapid Transit Authority: (312) 836-7000.

Conservation: Extensive commitment. Programs in Mexico (forest habitat), Indonesia (reintroduction of the Bali mynah bird, where only 50 birds are left in the wild), Colombia (spectacled bear), Paraguay (peccary), and Belize (river turtle). Release of peregrine falcons from Illinois Beach State Park in Zion. Breeding gorillas.

Education: Symposiums on conservation issues. Science literacy and environmental education programs for schoolchildren; teacher and parent workshops.

Special attractions: Small Mammal House, Sea Lion Pool, Farm at the Zoo, children's zoo. Feeding times: Dairy cows, 11:00; elephants, 1:15; sea lions, 2:00; apes, 3:00.

Gift shop: Two locations, at large mammal area and at the Lion House.

Food: Snacks and popcorn.

The philosophies of recently retired director Lester Fisher still guide the Lincoln Park Zoo; he took over the directorship in 1962. Fisher initiated a number of new exhibits—the Farm at the Zoo, the sea lion pool, outdoor areas for tigers and lions, and a small-mammal house—and in the 1989 annual report articulated his zoo philosophy: "During this century, . . . humankind has become the principal agent of rates of extinction among animals and plant life that are at the highest levels in world history. . . . Lincoln Park Zoo is a center for conservation, education and recreation. These activities are interrelated. Some of us have a hard time getting concerned about the future of an animal or plant many thousands of miles away. . . . Yet, it is becoming more and more obvious that as the earth becomes uninhabitable for a variety of exotic or unfamiliar species, the future of our own species is gravely compromised." Fisher is a strong advocate of the SSP and cites its influence in the reintroduction of the Bali mynah through the cooperation of the Lincoln Park Zoo, the International Council for Bird Preservation, the government of Indonesia, Java's Surabaya Zoo, and the AAZPA. In 1987 10 American zoos, after successful captive propagation, were able to send 39 birds to the Surabaya Zoo in Java. Their offspring have been released into the wild, their native habitat.

In 1976 the Great Ape House was built at the Lincoln Park Zoo for lowland gorillas. Today's exhibits generally offer gorillas more space and touches of natural habitat than the 20 gorillas who occupy this underground facility appear to have, but Fisher claims, "it works, and the animals do well." The exhibit certainly allows a close-up look at the animals, though they have little or no privacy.

The gorillas that first arrived in the United States at the turn of the century didn't live long. In the 1930's and 1940's two gorillas were well known, Gargantua, a circus gorilla, and Bushman, who resided at the Lincoln Park Zoo in Chicago and died in 1951 at the age of 21. His death was attributed to old age, but he was actually in his prime, and the cause of his death was possibly his heart. The advances made by medical research on gorillas in the past 40 years might well have extended his life by many years. From 1958 to 1968, 41 infant gorillas were imported legally from Equatorial Guinea; their mothers had been killed in order to obtain the infant. Many of those who survived capture didn't survive long at the zoo, since the zoos didn't know how to care for the baby gorillas.

The Kovler Lion House, one of the oldest (1912) buildings at the zoo, was renovated in 1989–90 to create 10 naturalistic interior and exterior habitats for lions, tigers, leopards, cheetahs, and jaguars. In August 1990 four cheetah cubs were the first cheetahs to be born at the Lincoln Park Zoo.

The Lincoln Park Zoo is one of seven zoos in the United States that exhibit koala bears. One of the difficulties in maintaining a koala on exhibit is that it eats only eucalyptus leaves. Lincoln Park and the San Antonio and Miami zoos solved the problem: They get their supply from a farm with five acres of eucalyptus of seven different species.

The Farm at the Zoo has interactive displays and teacher workshops; and a second exhibit for children, Pritzker Children's Zoo, emphasizes wildlife observation and problem solving. The education department at Lincoln Park Zoo places great emphasis on environmental education and the development of science literacy curricula. Its purpose is to change attitudes in a positive way toward science.

One of the education department's success stories is the Green Team, a science literacy program on environmental education for fourth-, fifth-, and sixth-graders, made possible by a grant from the State of Illinois. The zoo asked parents and teachers from underserved school constituencies for input as to what the zoo could do to help them teach science. An advisory board, with four teachers participating, oversaw the creation of curriculum material and health science kits (about animals) for students to take home. Parents' workshops were also established. The program's first year, 1992, was considered an enormous success.

Another project is Chicago Science Explorers, in which 12 other institutions in the Chicago area participated; it was funded by the U.S. Department of Energy. The program is centered around a video program featuring Bill Curtis (CBS) in action-adventure stories that present various scientific concepts.

➤ JOHN G. SHEDD AQUARIUM

1200 South Lake Drive
Chicago, Illinois 60605
(312) 939-2426
Open: 9–6
Best for: "Marine Jewels"; penguins

Year opened: 1930
Acres: 4
Animal population: 7,095; 712 species
Director: Ted Beattie

Getting there: Buses, or nice walk from downtown.

Conservation: Working relationship with other aquariums.

Education: Programs include scientific courses, excursions, hands-on workshops; aquatic science center. Library open to the public 1–6, Wed.–Sat.

Special attractions: Oceanarium, "Marine Jewels."

Gift shop: Two Sea Shops; very water-related materials.

Food: View with the food at Soundings restaurant or the Bubble Net family restaurant.

The Shedd Aquarium doubled its size when it decided to build its $43 million oceanarium for Pacific black whales, beluga whales, sea otters, white-sided dolphins, penguins, and seals. The rocky coastlines of the Pacific Northwest and southeast Alaska

are re-created with fir trees, lichen, and barnacled rocks surrounding the five cold saltwater pools.

Synthetic seawater is made by the aquarium for its three gallery displays of ocean habitats: shallow coasts (sea otters), tropical
coral reef, and cold-water habitats (penguins). Three freshwater
galleries present cold northern waters, temperate North American rivers, and lakes and other tropical freshwater habitats of
Australia, Asia, Africa, and South America. While somewhat
overwhelming as a global, all-encompassing aquatic presentation,
it is extremely impressive and well presented.

The aquarium has done well on education with films, classrooms and an Aquatic Science Center, gallery tours, a library,
workshops and special classes, and a Wet Pet Program.

During the main presentation in the oceanarium, a docile,
cooperative beluga whale lies on her back while she receives an
injection against infection by a handler. A fish is the reward for
her cooperation. To do in public what would be expected to be
done backstage is a magnum leap forward in public education.

The penguins' aquarium habitat on the lower level in the
section called "Interpretative Exhibits" simulates their native
habitat, the Falkland Islands. In the "old" part of the aquarium
are exhibits that should not be missed, even though they're a bit
old-fashioned. Of particular interest are the venomous fishes (sail-
fish, tang, and spotted scorpion fish); the "river tributaries"
exhibits with a Chinese pagoda motif and small tanks, excellent
signs, and abundant vegetation in the tanks; and the "Marine
Jewels," cowries and banded coral shrimp. Don't miss the center
circular tank, and note the architecture.

◀ FORT WAYNE CHILDREN'S ZOO

3411 Sherman Boulevard
Fort Wayne, Indiana 46808
(219) 482-4610

Open: 9–5; closed mid-Oct. to
late April except Halloween,
Christmas

Best for: Bats; Africa
Year opened: 1965
Acres: 38

Animal population: 812; 199 species
Director: Earl Wells

Getting there: From Route 24 turn south onto Sherman Boulevard to Franke Park.

Conservation: Indonesia project support of the snub-nosed langur for captive propagation.

Education: Emphasis is on children.

Special attractions: You can have close contact with bouncing kangaroos.

Gift shop: Excellent.

Food: Excellent. Plan to eat here.

Fort Wayne is one of the two best smaller zoos in the country (the other is Caldwell Zoo, in Tyler, Texas). The setting is attractive, well maintained, varied. The plants and flowers are magnificent. Some exhibits found at Fort Wayne are different from or better than those at other zoos. Everywhere there is an educational message presented in an understandable, interesting way. In 1992 the name of the education department was changed to the Communications Department, making the point that the education effort must be broadened. This zoo is absolutely tops!

According to Director Earl Wells, Fort Wayne calls itself "Children's Zoo" for a reason: Why hide the fact that children are the reason parents go to the zoo? Children don't want to *look*; they want to *do*. Children use their sense of touch to examine boxes, such as one containing an ostrich egg; or use different stamps to create a new and imaginary animal; or listen to a World Wildlife Foundation six-minute tape, "Rain Forest Rap." Four plastic all-weather globes are located at different regional exhibits, and on a bulletin board are questions related to the exhibit and the globe. Americans young and old are not known for their sense of geography. These globes add a fun dimension of education to the zoo; I know of no other zoo that has such globes, but they all should.

One of my favorite exhibits is the bat exhibit. It is not large nor deep, but the lighting is such that the viewer can see some bats in motion, and some hanging, sleeping from the roof of the shallow cave. Harp wire, not glass, keeps the bats in the enclosure, which is most effective. You can hear, smell (maybe), and certainly see them better than through reflecting glass.

Adjacent to the bat exhibit is the outstanding aquarium; consisting of a single medium-sized tank, it is made marvelous by clear water and a mirrored ceiling and wall.

A one-acre aviary, built at a very reasonable cost of $50,000, is filled with birds on branches and in flight and sometimes perching on your head or shoulder.

Australia is 82 times larger than Indiana, and the Fort Wayne Children's Zoo is just 38 acres—yet into a corner of it is fitted Australia. How can this be done? Very well—so well, in fact, that a visiting Australian lady once told the director with emotion that the exhibit had so many Down Under touches, it made her homesick. What really did it was the red clay underfoot. The center of the Australian exhibit is a clean, tidy plaza surrounded by buildings modeled after actual buildings in Australia. From the plaza a clay walkway leads to a unique opportunity: a walk through the kangaroo exhibit. About 30 'roos hop past the visitor, ignoring human presence. They are a pleasure to watch and be with! Near the Australian exhibit, look for the Tasmanian devil, a really ugly creature. Perhaps not as ugly as the daubentonias (aye-ayes) of Madagascar, whom I actually rather like because they have character. Character can bring a form of beauty to the ugly. The Tasmanian devil and aye-aye are cases in point. So are naked mole rats.

The 22-acre African veldt is reached by a vine-covered boardwalk. One must look to find the animals, just as one would on a safari in Africa: zebras, ostriches, tommies (Thomson gazelles), greater kudus (a species of antelope), wildebeests, guinea fowl, and white storks. At the far end of the exhibit the visitor reaches a "village" where a safari car is available for the return trip through the veldt on a moving track. The only drawback is the noise made by the cars, which distracts from the "I'm in Africa" mood.

Wells believes that the Species Survival Plans (SSP) are not a sufficient basis for positive action to save species. He believes that zoos should take a more practical approach on the habitats of animals, identifying the species they can do something for. Fort Wayne Children's Zoo has targeted the endangered snub-nosed langur, which is found in the wild in the mountains of the Chinese provinces of Szechwan, Kansu, and Yunnan, for a captive propagation program. The zoo also developed a working relationship with Richard Tenaza on Mentawai Island, off the west coast of Sumatra, Indonesia, to work toward habitat preservation on the island. The zoo has provided uniforms for Indonesians which identifies them with the preservation project and gives them pride in their job. The project started in 1989, with $35,000 spent in the first two years. For one year all gift shop sales went into moving people from a village to establish a game reserve. Also $12,000 has been raised to save primates in Indonesia, the money providing geographic, zoological, conservation, and social anthropological training to the Indonesians.

➤ INDIANAPOLIS ZOO

1200 West Washington Street
Indianapolis, Indiana 46222
(317) 630-2001
Open: 9–4; weekends 9–5;
April–May 9–4
Best for: Dolphins; polar
bears; birds of prey

Year opened: 1988
Acres: 64
Animal population: 2,408;
371 species
Director: Roy Shea

Getting there: From the north: I-65 south to Exit 114, south on Martin Luther King Jr. Boulevard/West Street to Washington Street (Route 40), then west one mile. From the south: From I-70 take Exit 79A north on West Street and turn west on Washington Street. Horse-drawn trolley ride once you get there.

Conservation: Selective commitment to the SSP program.

Education: Teacher workshops, zoomobile, lectures, summer camp. For information, call 630-2040.

Special attractions: Show in Whale and Dolphin Pavilion.

Gift shop: Some unusual items.

Food: Fast food and snacks; ice cream parlor; pizza stand.

Roy Shea, the president and CEO of the Indianapolis Zoo, has strong ideas on conservation, the AAZPA, and education. Regarding Species Survival Programs, he believes that species are selected by popularity and for use in zoo exhibition, thus unattractive species are not selected. The SSP demands a lot of zoo staff time. It is time-consuming, distracts from regular zoo business, and each zoo must bear the cost. The Indianapolis Zoo is very selective in committing to the SSP program. Being a quality zoo for the public is its first priority.

Regarding reintroduction programs, Shea believes that some programs, such as that for the golden lion tamarin in Brazil, have been successful, but that they will not work for most species. A problem of reintroduction abroad could well be the introduction of disease by the animals reintroduced to their "native" habitat, but Shea thinks that local reintroduction programs may work.

Shea believes AAZPA has made some mistakes. One small but illustrative example of bad thinking on the AAZPA's part was a recommendation to the zoos that they all subscribe to the telephone service MCI. In some cases doing so would actually have cost zoos money, $2,000 a year in the case of the Indianapolis Zoo, while the AAZPA would make money from MCI by receiving a bonus. The AAZPA, by virtue of its accreditation program, is becoming a regulatory agency, which restricts or limits the opportunity of zoos in their efforts. Shea thinks that the AAZPA could perform a valuable task by bringing into focus areas for productive research. Neither the AAZPA nor anyone else has a research agenda, and research is undertaken at the whim of individuals, leading to zoos' commitments to research programs to the detriment—in terms of time, people and money—of the zoos' main operations. At the Indianapolis Zoo, Shea believes, research should be separate from the zoo operation and determine its own agenda.

When it comes to education, Shea believes that zoos must play a more all-encompassing role, "take a bigger part of the pie than just animals." Zoos must show people how they figure in global biological issues. Shea believes zoos are not doing enough in this regard.

Most zoos in the United States are handicapped in their effort to catch up with the move from cages and moats to natural habitats—but not the Indianapolis Zoo. The old zoo was opened in 1964 and closed in 1987. The $63 million New Indianapolis Zoo opened in 1988 and took two years to build. Current emphasis is on an endowment to provide funds for operating expenses, not further exhibit construction.

Giving the visitors what they want—a good time—the zoo offers carriage rides; camel, pony, and elephant rides; and an antique multicolored horse carousel. The $1.6 million Living Desert, under an 80-foot geodesic dome, is effective. A winding path made of decomposed granite draws the visitor through the desert past nearly 30 species of plants and animals, including tortoise, lizards, and mounds of cacti. A small pond is home to desert pupfish. Birds fly by and perch, just waiting for you to get a close look.

Aside from *Homo sapiens*, the primate best adapted to life in cold climates is the Japanese macaque, or snow monkey. The exhibit at the zoo includes a simulated hot spring, which the monkeys enjoy perhaps as much as people like saunas and whirlpool baths.

The Water Complex has on show 200 species, including sharks, sea lions, penguins, and polar bears, the latter having three separate panoramas. The Whale and Dolphin Pavilion is a stadium for 1,500 people to view seven bottle-nosed dolphins, two false killer whales that came from Osaka, Japan, and four beluga whales.

It has been stated that the most dangerous escaped animals are the polar bear, the Kodiak bear, and big cats. All zoos must be prepared for possible escapes, and at the Indianapolis Zoo, 14 personnel are assigned to the weapons team and are equipped with guns for such an unhoped-for event. They must be prepared to shoot to kill. On February 2, 1991, a Siberian tiger escaped by chewing through its steel bars, and was sighted on a service road. A member of the weapons team shot at the tiger, but missed. Fortunately, with patience and professionalism on the part of the team, the tiger was allowed to return to its enclosure.

🐾 POTAWATOMI ZOO

500 South Greenlawn Avenue
South Bend, Indiana 46615
(219) 235-9800

Open: 10–5

Best for: Monkeys; Siberian tigers

Year opened: 1917

Acres: 22

Animal population: 262; 97 species

Director: Johnny Martinez

Membership: Potawatomi Zoological Society
(219) 288-4639

Getting there: Located southeast of downtown, in Potawatomi Park. From I-80/90 (toll road), exit south at Route 23, turn left on Ironwood Drive, go south to Jefferson Boulevard, and turn right. At next stoplight, Greenlawn Avenue, turn left, and go over railroad tracks to zoo.

Conservation: Successful breeding program resulting in 16 wallabies; condor conservation program.

Education: Animal Resource Center (ARC) is focal point.

Special attractions: Australian walkabout.

Gift Shop: Run by the Potawatomi Zoological Society; modest.

Food: Snacks.

Potawatomi was the first zoo in Indiana, and was renovated in 1979 and again in 1988. Director Johnny Martinez arrived at the zoo as director in 1990 at a time when there was a complete turnover in staff. Previously the zoo director had been chosen "from within." My impression is that Martinez is a significant asset. At the time of my first visit in 1990 I looked at a sad little island in a dull five-foot-deep pond with unhappy-looking blue-bills, small-mouthed bass, and carp, along with a trumpeter swan and some waterfowl. Most unhappy of all were ring-tailed lemurs huddled in a pipe section on the desk-sized plot of an island.

Two years later Martinez told me that the lemurs had been taken off their miserable island. There are now two islands, with healthy vegetation. Flamingos are wading happily in the pond, and concerts have been given on the pond's shore in the summer. Things are changing at the zoo. One exhibit Martinez is particularly pleased about is an Australian Walkabout in process of being built that will be a feature exhibit.

Exhibits to be seen at Potawatomi Zoo include a nocturnal exhibit of fruit bats, Burmese python and boa constrictor; Eurasian brown bears with a waterfall; the Zoo Farm, opened in 1988, with potbellied pigs and a corral of goats; black-footed penguins from Namibia, who have a good swimming area; condors; and wallabies, which have proved to be a great breeding success (look for them where shade is provided by a wall). An outdoor winter complex is provided for Siberian tigers and a snow leopard. An Old World monkey exhibit contains colobus monkeys.

♈ EMPORIA ZOO

P.O. Box 928
Emporia, Kansas 66801
(316) 342-5105
Open: 10–4:30; call for summer hours
Best for: Waterfowl

Year opened: 1934
Acres: 8
Animal population: 382; 72 species
Director: David Traylor

Getting there: Located on Emporia's main street. You can't miss it.

Conservation: Participates in SSP.

Education: Classes, lectures, publications.

Gift shop: Minor.

Food: Small snack selection; the setting is the thing.

Emporia Zoo is without question a zoo, accredited by the AAZPA. But, thanks to the loving care of Director David Traylor, it is also a garden. David Traylor grew up locally. In 1973 he took over administration of the park in Emporia, and in 1980 he also assumed responsibility for the zoo, built in 1935 and in deplorable shape. The zoo now has taken on the appearance of a little Eden with trees, bushes, and flowering plants and is immaculately clean. The highlight of the zoo-garden is its waterfowl. The clear pond, bracketed with geraniums and other flowers, is alive with them nesting in small houses and lazing on duck-sized ramps from the water to the grass. Even the caged golden eagle appeared content when I saw him, devouring his morning breakfast of rat.

🐻 SUNSET ZOOLOGICAL PARK

2333 Oak Street (11th and Poyntz Streets)
Manhattan, Kansas 66502
(913) 587-2737

Open: 10–6; call for winter hours

Best for: Snow leopards; cheetahs

Year opened: 1933

Acres: 55

Animal population: 259; 94 species

Director: Donald Wixom

Getting there: Drive west on Poyntz Street, past Manhattan High School on right. Take next right on Oak Street, which leads to zoo.

Conservation: SSP participation. In 1992 produced red panda babies; breeding of Japanese and three other crane species; produced first U.S.-laid Andean condor egg, which was sent to the San Francisco Zoo for hatching and eventual release into Colombia's mountains.

Education: Major emphasis on education, including workshops, lectures, activities for children. Developing opportunities for teenagers as well as younger children and adults.

Special attractions: Primate exhibit and conservation center (construction started in 1993); children's zoo.

Gift shop: Some innovative items.

Food: Snacks.

Donald Wixom, director of the Sunset Zoological Park in Manhattan, Kansas, can trace his interest in animals back to one rainy day when he was five years old. The Kelly Big Train Circus came to town, and his family took him to the fanfare and fun under the Big Top. It continued raining during the performance. When the last animal left the ring and the last clown laughed, Don and his parents headed for the family car. The car started up. That was no problem. Mud was the problem. The tires spun around, with a whining sound, sinking the chassis deeper into the mud. Young Don peered out of the car window, and through the splash of mud and rain saw "a big gray thing," move up to, then push, their car. The shape was an elephant. From then on he was—and still is—nuts about elephants, although there is no elephant at Sunset Zoo.

With this push in the direction of wildlife he grew up with his nose pointed toward the television set every time *Wild Kingdom* came on the screen. As time moved on, he made three wishes: to go to Africa, to be in the zoo business, and to have his own television animal show. All three of his wishes came true. Since 1975 he has had a weekly local cable television show on animals, one of the longest running zoo-news shows in the country, he believes. Once when the station took him off the screen for six months, such a howl went up from viewers that they put him back on the air.

Sunset Zoo is alive with creativity, imagination, and energy. "Our zoo is small, but spunky," Wixom states. I was impressed by the children's zoo, which was well attended and offered barnyard animals and diverse educational activities. However, Wixom told me it was to be replaced by an aviary, then went on to tell me about plans for new children's activities. "The key is immersion. We're planning a multispecies primate conservation center to include tamarins, agoutis, lemurs, colobuses, olive baboons, chimps, with a rope tower for children to climb and view spider monkeys." Three grasslands exhibits are also planned: Australia (where Aborigines are explained, and kangaroos exhibited); Africa (Maasai are portrayed, zebra shown); North America (the story of the American Indian, with bison in the exhibit).

Wixom has already done much to improve the zoo. In the process of transforming a concrete chimp cage into a Himalayan monal pheasant exhibit, he gave both the chimp and the pheasant more space. Wixom's philosophy is that "the zoo is a show." The three priorities in building and maintaining an exhibit are (1) the animal, who is a captive guest; (2) the keeper, who must care for the animal; and (3) the "zoo guest," for whom the zoo exists and who will hopefully help the zoo to continue to exist. Wixom likes to give visitors an added treat when they visit his zoo. At the time of my visit an African fair had been set up for a week and the stalls were buzzing with treasure seekers. Wixom took me over to meet a Kenyan trader at his stall, where we exchanged a few words in Swahili.

The Sunset Zoo does what more zoos should do for point-of-exhibit education. For example, a sign suggests, "Meet the keeper at [time]." Since 1975 Sunset Zoo has had its WOLF program—Wildlife Outdoor Learning Facility—in which high school students study grassland ecology at the zoo and sleep overnight on the zoo grounds, listening to night sounds.

The day I visited the zoo was the day Jim Fowler, of *Wild Kingdom* television program fame, had promised to visit the zoo for his famous and educational birds and reptiles demonstration. Jim Fowler is a man who epitomizes the outdoor world, an adventurer with physical scars from his profession, a man whom some zoo directors call a showman, not an educator.

I believe Jim Fowler's showmanship *is* education. Whether on television or in person, he gives drama, spirit, and inspiration to everyone with whom he has contact. I watched Jim walk to the stage that had been set up for him. The audience—most of the children seated on the ground, parents scattered—quieted down. Jim introduced himself and asked for volunteers to come onstage. The first eight were selected. Then, to the oohs and ahs of parents and onlookers, a large boa was brought forward by handlers and placed in the children's hands. A tiny tot at the tail end looked scared and tried to retreat offstage. Jim persuaded her to return, and she bravely touched though didn't hold the reptile's tail. This was the *show* part of the presentation. Then Jim started to tell his snake bearers and the audience about the snake, about wildlife, about conservation. It was an afternoon not to be forgotten by those who may grow up to be savers of wildlife.

Fowler has very specific views regarding zoos. "The public must be educated on the destruction of habitat. Scientists must work with the public. Zoos have always focused on academic work. This is baloney. Universities and museums should do research. Zoos should be the advertising agency for wildlife, for nature. I have not heard one design person or company state why wildlife and wilderness is important to human beings. Zoos talk of research, endangered species, and conservation as their mission; they must talk about buildings for animals. Zoo designers create water and rock habitats which are costly. We need twenty- to thirty-thousand-acre captive wildlife areas. Zoo priorities should be changed from research and academics to involvement in the natural world. Zoos should focus on how the earth works. Zoos must affect the attitude of local people to nature; they must be told of how to enjoy nature locally by zoos, of where to go hiking or boating." He added, as a final shot, "Zoo directors like William Conway (President and general director, NYZS The Wildlife Conservation Society) should go on TV with an outreach program using the media to get a zoo mission message across."

🐎 SEDGEWICK COUNTY ZOO AND BOTANICAL GARDEN

5555 Zoo Boulevard
Wichita, Kansas 67212
(316) 942-2213

Open: 9–5; call for winter hours

Best for: Oryx; zebras

Year opened: 1971

Acres: 212

Animal population: 1,273; 279 species

Director: Mark Reed

Getting there: From Route 235, take Exit 10 (Zoo Boulevard) north to zoo.

Conservation: A breeding farm adjacent to the zoo will open soon. SSP participation: black rhino, golden lion tamarin, white-necked crane, Bali mynah, spectacled bear, Arabian oryx, Grevy's zebra, maned wolf, chimp, orangutan.

Education: Training teachers on use of zoo. Class for kindergarten children coordinated with school district. Class for seventh grade at the zoo. For information, call (316) 942-3602.

Special attractions: Children's farm—it *looks* like a farm. North American prairie opened May 1993 on 11 acres.

Gift shop: Environmental section.

Food: Snack food, salads, and barbecue.

The Sedgewick County Zoo's outstanding jungle building was the second to be constructed in the United States, the first being at the Toledo Zoo. It is damp and authentic: a dirt and tanbark path winds up and down four levels, past flowering trees, ferns and papaya, and you traverse a stream via a small rope bridge. Bats hang on trees and in a bat cave, and a golden lion tamarin, tricolored squirrel, and six red-ruffed lemurs watch you as you pass by them, unconcerned at your intrusion into their territory. Birds are to be found at every turn. You pass through a rock tunnel, viewing fish (pacu and jurupari) in a pond. Waterfalls abound, including a walk under one with a 20 foot drop. Future plans call for a swamp exhibit with rainstorms and a cloud forest.

Rainstorms for indoor rain forests are fine, but hailstorms outside can create considerable damage. In June 1992 hail fell on the zoo, ruining all of the roofs, which had to be replaced to the tune of $700,000. The roof on the jungle building, which needed to be replaced anyway, was given a new type of roof that allows light in and doesn't require much maintenance.

During 1992 the zoo completed a $1.7 million, 1½-year capital campaign. As a result, on May 30, 1993, the North American prairie exhibit opened with grizzly bears, pronghorn elks, bison, Mexican wolves, wild turkeys, cranes, native waterfowl and a walk-in prairie dog exhibit. If you take the zoo's boat canal trip you will be able to see the exhibit from the water.

The Wichita zoo has a hippoquarium with two hippos and, unfortunately, an inadequate water filtering system. As hippos are prone to do what comes naturally frequently, the water goes from cloudy to dense rapidly, but if you catch the hippos at the right moment, when their tank has just been filled and the murk has not yet set in, you'll enjoy the sight of these large, slow-moving creatures with pink faces in their big tub.

The herpetarium provides a close look at a Kansas riverbank with snapping, soft-shell, painted, and red-eared turtles and a nocturnal section that includes a boa constrictor, green iguanas, a rhino iguana, and a tegu hanging over the visitor on a large branch. Very effective!

There is considerable debate concerning the composition, design, and participatory activities of children at *their* zoo within a zoo, but professionals are nearly unanimous in holding that children's zoos are essential to the education of young minds at a susceptible age—the younger, the better. To have fun is paramount. Touching is an experience. To come into physical contact with another species is an act of communication, and, says Barbara Burgen, former curator of education, education "is the guiding force behind a zoo." To touch an elephant when she appears like a mountain before you is unforgettable. To touch a soft, furry thing, perhaps a rabbit or a ferret, is sensational. To look into the dark staring eyes of a knowing owl and to run the tip of your finger down its plumage is exciting. To feel the rough, leathery surface of a young alligator is an electric contact with danger. To submerge your hand in a tank of water and finger the slippery body of a sponge is eerie. Children can do all of these things at the Sedgewick County Zoo.

The Sedgewick County Zoo's farm has a feeling of authenticity, of being a real farm with an international population. The big red barn houses karakul (flat-tail) sheep, which date to 5000 B.C. in Persia, asses, ankole (Watusi) cattle, Barbados and Tunis sheep, Nigerian dwarf goats, zebus (more numerous than people on the island of Madagascar), domestic yaks, dromedaries, guinea hogs, and bantam miniature domestic fowl. It is the largest collection of rare and endangered breeds of domestic livestock—the so-called minor breeds, according to Director Mark Reed. Adjacent to the farm is an herb garden—sadly, usually bypassed by visitors. Not a part of the children's zoo, but to be counted as a children's exhibit, is a 10-acre prairie dog exhibit, the largest in any zoo, which ties into a one-mile nature trail.

✦ TOPEKA ZOOLOGICAL PARK

635 Southwest Gage Boulevard
Topeka, Kansas 66606
(913) 272-5821
Open: 9–4:30
Best for: Apes
Year opened: 1933

Acres: 30
Animal population: 377; 136 species
Director: Michael LaRue, acting

Getting there: Located one-quarter mile south of I-70 at the Gage Boulevard exit.

Conservation: SSP participation for orangutan, Asian wild horse (at a 180-acre facility out of town), gorilla, Bali mynah, golden eagle.

Education: Children's zoo opened 1992.

Special attractions: Tropical rain forest; Lion's Pride exhibit.

Gift Shop: Standard.

Food: Restaurant near entrance.

One zoo that has used its imagination to make a moderate budget go a long way is Topeka, a small zoo with just 136 species and an animal population of about 400. It provides some direct involvement between the two primates *Gorilla gorilla* and *Homo sapiens* at Discovering Apes, an outdoor walk-through. As I sauntered down a transparent acrylic tunnel a silverback gorilla casually walked up to me—a palm-print away—reached up and climbed slowly over my head and down the other side of the sturdy acrylic. If proximity has appeal—and it does—for humans seeking a relationship with a gorilla, this exhibit is a great success!

A tropical rain forest exhibit, opened in 1974, is home to birds, reptiles, and mammals and makes possible close encounters for the visitor. The exhibit Lion's Pride is commendable for the approach to the exhibit along a winding path through the brush, creating an element of suspense and pleasure when, rounding the corner, lions appear. Hill's Animal Kingdom contains a mata mata turtle from South America, and "spineless wonders" such as the Cuban cockroach and Haitian tarantula. A conservation window has a life-sized photograph of a man with several dead birds that are endangered species hanging from his hand. A sign says, "This man doesn't care." Adjacent to Hill's Animal Kingdom you will find an Aldabra tortoise, named for an island in the Seychelles in the Indian Ocean.

A 167-acre Asian wild horse breeding farm belonging to the zoo is half an hour away. Since 1986 the Topeka Zoo has released a total of 15 American golden eagles at the Wilson reservoir in western Kansas in cooperation with the Prairie Raptor Project. The zoo also has provided trumpeter swans—five in 1992—to the state of Minnesota for release in the wild. Sometimes the swans migrate back to Kansas.

The children's zoo, opened in 1992, has four separate areas. The Petting Area has miniature animals for small children to pet: miniature cows, donkeys, goats, and horses. There is also a fenced-off education section in the area where a keeper can give a presentation and children can put their hands through a flap and touch sheep, rabbits, and turtles. The second area, Play and Learn, has modified playground equipment allowing children to pretend that they are animals. A third area is for above-ground animals such as hamsters. The fourth is a gazebo and pond, where parents can relax and watch their children safely occupied.

✝ LOUISVILLE ZOOLOGICAL GARDEN

1100 Trevillian Way
P.O. Box 37250
Louisville, Kentucky 40233
(502) 459-2181

Open: 10–6; Sept.–April: 10–5, closed Mon.

Best for: Woolly monkeys; reptiles

Year opened: 1968

Acres: 133

Animal population: 2,156; 412 species

Director: Dr. William Foster

Getting there: Located 15 minutes south of downtown Louisville. Take I-264 (Henry Watterson Expressway) to the Poplar Level Road exit. Follow black-and-white zoo signs to 1100 Trevillian Way.

Conservation: Participates in program for black-footed ferret; Siberian tiger cubs born at the zoo in 1990.

Education: Program with schools to develop creativity; MetaZoo education center; outreach initiatives with various community groups.

Special attractions: Rain forest; the microscopic world; herpaquarium.

Gift shop: Modest.

Food: Lakeside café.

William R. Foster, director of the Louisville Zoo, has strong opinions on education at zoos. Zoo education must be creative. In Kentucky each school must teach creativity. Zoos can be a focus for that. "Excitement must be created for learning to occur," Foster says. At the Louisville Zoo the MetaZoo provides a wide range of participatory exhibits for an in-depth look at animals. A student may see insects under a microscope and then see the world as an insect sees it, or compare his voice pattern to that of an exotic animal. MetaZoo has been a prototype for zoos and parks in the United States and Canada as the first facility to serve as both a public exhibit and a living classroom. Over 50,000 Kentucky students from kindergarten through college benefit annually from the many programs designed to complement their school studies.

Under the umbrella of its education program the Louisville

Zoo has initiated a community outreach program to disadvantaged or hospitalized people and senior citizens. The zoo is interested in bringing people together through a common interest in the zoo. Louisville Zoo has worked with a halfway house. Outreach programs take the Louisville Zoo into hospitals and care centers whose residents might otherwise not have contact with the animal world.

Equuleus (known as E.Q.) is a zebra, born at the Louisville Zoo on May 17, 1984, (his present home is in Houston) whose biological father was a Grevy's zebra, but whose surrogate mother was a quarter horse. E.Q.'s birth was the result of the first successful embryo transfer from an exotic to a domestic equine. William Foster worked with equine specialist Scott D. Bennett to develop the techniques for the transfer, and Foster's joy at the success of the birth is that it gives hope to zoos that the same procedure may be applicable to endangered species such as Przewalski's horse.

On entering the zoo, if the visitor goes straight ahead he will find himself on a boardwalk where if he looks up he'll see Canadian lynx and puma (through piano wire), and if he looks down, bald eagles at very close range. Located in the center of the zoo, the modest $368,000 exhibit has an interesting perspective.

Woolly monkeys at the Louisville Zoological Garden are exhibited on two communicating treed islands, both with entry to inside shelter. They are given room to roam, and they need it: Woolly monkeys have a hypertension problem in captivity. In the wild, Director Foster explained, their blood pressure is 130/80, but when brought into captivity it rises to 260/230. Medical research has discovered that if the woolly monkeys can browse for themselves their blood pressure returns to normal. The reasons for this are not understood.

Nearly every zoo has its reptile house, and reptile exhibits still tend to be boxlike structures with a rock, perhaps some sand, and a light bulb. Nowadays, however, more and more zoos are creating miniature dioramas that challenge the viewer to find the reptile. Louisville's zoo has an outstanding small desert habitat exhibit, opened in 1989, where lizards lounge on rocks. The exhibit replicates as far as possible the biome, or ecological community, of the snakes and other interdependent organisms. This exhibit and other biomes exhibits for the zoo were created by herpaquarium curator John Walczak and design professionals Luckett and Farley. This team created a lighting system that is triggered to go on and off on different areas of the rock, causing the lizards to move to the warmer area. Modern technology also re-creates climates, sights, and sounds of the desert and rain forest. The snake collection includes the eyelash viper, cottonmouth, and anaconda. Each of the herpaquarium's biomes (desert, forest, and worlds of water) stresses the interrelationship of animals and plants.

Plans now on the drawing board include an orientation plaza with a Kentucky Café, several satellite classrooms (including one in the orangutan exhibit) that will be participatory learning environments, an Ohio exhibit showing among other things the state's prehistory, a five-acre Asian elephant exhibit demonstrating the species's interaction with humans throughout history, and a Plaza de las Américas leading into the Amazonia exhibit.

➤ AQUARIUM OF THE AMERICAS

P.O. Box 4327
111 Iberville Street
New Orleans, Louisiana 70178
(504) 861-2537

Open: Sun.–Wed. 9–5; Thurs. 9:30–8; Fri.–Sat. 9:30–6

Best for: Sand tiger sharks; Atlantic stingrays; white alligators

Year opened: 1990

Acres: 10

Animal population: 10,000; 500 species

Director: L. Ronald Forman

Membership: Audubon Institute, (504) 861-2537

Getting there: On the Mississippi River. Walk from downtown.

Conservation: Strong emphasis on turtles and coral reefs.

Education: Hands-on. Micro lab.

Special attractions: Gulf of Mexico (oil rig) and Mississippi River Delta exhibits.

Gift shop: Outstanding.

Food: Excellent; healthy food. River view.

The Aquarium of the Americas is a pretty grand-sounding name, and it is meant to be. The Audubon Institute, which oversees the aquarium, thinks big under the leadership of its president and CEO, Ron Forman. To begin with, the aquarium's location is dramatic, in downtown New Orleans, within a short walk of Bourbon Street's handsome iron balconies, jazz galore, oyster bars and antique shops. The first exhibit upon entering the aquarium is the Caribbean Reef, a rounded 40-foot acrylic tunnel "inside" a tank of bonnethead sharks, dazzling varieties of angel and butterfly fishes, and schooling pompano. Impressive.

Walking below a pier in the Mississippi River Delta exhibit, you encounter a multitude of species of parrots, and a super exhibit of adult white alligators. (For those who may have forgotten the differences between alligators and crocodiles: An alligator's head is wider than a crocodile's and only its upper teeth show when the mouth is closed.) From the pilings of a simulated pier the visitor can look up at an exhibit of crayfish.

A 500,000-gallon Gulf of Mexico tank is most impressive, with its simulated but most convincing oil rig platform visible through 16-foot-high acrylic panels. Oil rigs create an ideal microenvironment for many species. Inside the tank are sea catfish, spotted eagle ray, tarpon, red grouper, Atlantic black-tipper shark, Atlantic stingray, sand tiger shark, and more.

On the second floor are some of the most important exhibits of the aquarium—not only fun or dramatic, but highly educational as well. An exhibit titled "Living in Water" has specialized sections. In "Behavior" are found the mermaid purses that are the egg sacks of the chain dogfish. "Senses" has a "Taste and Touch" tank explaining, for example, that "barbels on a catfish's chin are more like tongues than whiskers," and that electric knife fish surround themselves with a sensory shield by emitting continuous waves of electricity. The micro lab has a monitor screen that shows brine shrimp squiggling about, and one can also see them under a microscope. Also at the micro lab are dissected marine life and bones encased in Lucite blocks for easy handling, and very informatively labeled. A nearby hands-on and hands-in touch tank is a major attraction.

The aquarium's exhibits all rate straight A's except for the Amazon Rain Forest, a disappointment because it's not genuinely tropical in atmosphere. Perhaps planting a vast amount of foliage over a long period of time will improve this solarium.

Most important is the aquarium's participation in conservation efforts. The aquarium coordinates the program of the vessel *Louisiana* for sea turtle rescues, responding rapidly to reports of sea turtles stranded or otherwise in trouble. If the turtle is dead, tests are performed to determine the cause. If alive but in need of medical care, it is cared for and, when well, returned to the sea. In 1992 the aquarium returned an endangered Hawksbill sea turtle to the Gulf of Mexico.

In the Gulf of Mexico, aquarium-owned SONAR devices are used to determine the effect of dredging on sealife. The aquarium monitors changes in the coral reef at the Flower Garden National Marine Sanctuary in the Gulf of Mexico; off the coast of Honduras, studies are taking place to determine the effect of tourism on the waters, and what action should be taken to save the coral.

☙ AUDUBON PARK AND ZOOLOGICAL GARDEN

P.O. Box 4327
6500 Magazine Street
New Orleans, Louisiana 70178
(504) 861-2537

Open: 9:30–4:30; call for summer weekend hours; closed for Mardi Gras and the first Friday in May

Best for: Cats; apes; birds

Year opened: 1914

Acres: 58

Animal population: 1,830; 438 species

Director: L. Ronald Forman

Getting there: Located on Mississippi River. By boat: From Aquarium. By streetcar: Out St. Charles Avenue. By bus: From hotels (586-8777); Grayline Tours (899-2027).

Conservation: Twenty-five percent of its collection, including plants, is on the endangered species list.

Education: Pathways to the Past, an interactive natural history museum; impressive Education Center. For information, call (504) 861-5103.

Special attractions: Louisiana Swamp; tropical bird house.

Gift shop: Five ZOOvenir shops, each with different items: posters, stuffed animals, and deluxe items.

Food: Cypress Knee Café for Cajun cooking at Louisiana Swamp. Pizzas at zoo entrance. Hamburger stand near children's zoo. Oasis Café near sea lions.

The Audubon Institute in New Orleans (not to be confused with the unrelated Audubon Society) has a $268 million grand plan called the 2000 Project. Part of the project is the Aquarium of the Americas (see previous profile), which opened in 1990 on New Orleans's downtown riverfront. The plan also includes a conservatory, a natural history museum, and the Louisiana Nature and Science Center in New Orleans's Joe W. Brown Memorial Park "to stress education, . . . to inspire in people a sense of stewardship for the natural world, . . ." and "to stimulate a sense of wonder . . . through creative exhibits and flexible programming, to provide recreational activities to visitors on and off site; to make learning fun." The Louisiana Nature and Science Center will include a 12,000-square-foot education complex, a teaching greenhouse, a library, and classrooms.

Audubon's Louisiana Swamp exhibit has a population of alligators and migratory birds, nutria, cougars, muskrats, and otters and incorporates both nature and cultural history. Director Ronald Forman notes that "people are confused, as to why a swamp was brought to New Orleans. Swamps are disappearing. It is an opportunity to educate future generations." "It is important," Forman added, "that we learn who the swamp dwellers were and how they lived." This emphasis on Louisiana's swamp couldn't be more timely with the howl that is being heard in the United States today about disappearing wetlands. (If you wish to visit a swamp in the area, one of the many tour companies that will take you for a two-hour boat ride is Cypress Swamp Tours; for information and reservations call [504] 581-4501.)

The South American pampas exhibit shows visitors a lonely world, an ancient orderly world where animal life has changed little for eons. See llamas, rheas, capybaras, and tapirs. Also, don't miss the Tropical Bird House, a very pleasant walk on a winding path, birdlife flying free about you, but also in cages at the side. The primate exhibit is good for the swing space of the siamang. Check on the time, but alligator feeding is usually at 3:00 P.M. on Sundays and Thursdays, spring and summer.

The Audubon Institute's education center "celebrates the zoo as a living classroom." A multipurpose wooden-beamed and -walled 95-seat auditorium is flanked by columns decorated with animal figures and has a projector room with the newest technology. Major stress is placed on presentations *at* the exhibits, using creative materials drawn from the lecturer's zoo-bag, such as a cloth-padded snake that unfolds to expose multicolored cloth internal organs. The education center is a magnificent facility, although the zoo may eventually need a larger auditorium and more classrooms. Not to be missed is Pathways to the Past, an interactive natural history museum at the zoo that focuses on the ancestral link between reptiles, dinosaurs, and birds. A dig site computer game is but one of many educational exhibits.

The Audubon Park's future plans also specify that eight miles from downtown New Orleans, on a 1,114-acre site on the west bank of the southernmost tip of land on the Mississippi River, will be located the Freeport-McMoRan Audubon Species Survival and Research Center and Wilderness Park. The park will operate under the Audubon Institute, with participation of the Alexandria Zoo, the Greater Baton Rouge Zoo, and the Louisiana Purchase Zoo in Monroe. The purpose of this conservation area is the "planned breeding of animals such as rhinos, red wolves, tapirs, gharials, tigers and tropical storks." The park will work closely with the Captive Breeding Specialist Group (CBSG) of the International Union for the Conservation of Nature (IUCN). Four hundred acres, to be "set aside for a wilderness park, stocked with native Louisiana animals," will be the first zoological regional species survival center in the South, and will also focus on embryo implantation research and study such concepts as "frozen zoos"—multispecies sperm banks (see CRES in the San Diego Zoo profile). The Survival and Research Center's conservation activities will be directed especially toward saving swamps, marshes, and hardwood forests. By focusing on these natural treasures Audubon hopes to create sympathy, understanding and resultant action on saving "all living things within the ecosystem."

GREATER BATON ROUGE ZOO

P.O. Box 60
Greenwood Park, Highway 19
Baker, Louisiana 70704
(504) 775-3877

Open: 10–5; weekends 10–6

Best for: Birds; ungulates; small primates

Year opened: 1970

Acres: 145

Animal population: 944; 210 species

Director: George Felton, Jr.

Membership: Friends of Baton Rouge, (504) 778-4009

Getting there: From Route 110 north of Baton Rouge, take Route 19 or Plank Road to Thomas Road (zoo entrance).

Conservation: Successful bird-breeding program.

Education: Outstanding. Zoomobile visits schools, hospitals, nursing homes, festivals, day camps in summer. High school students help build exhibits.

Special attractions: Only zoo in U.S. with purple-faced langurs.

Gift Shop: Fair.

Food: Poor; small choice.

This is a super homegrown zoo with a lot of heart. Its director, George Felton, worked for 18 years as a high school coach with the Louisiana Department of Parks and Recreation and has been with the zoo since 1959.

The reward of a drive north from New Orleans along the bridged highway over swampland is the Greater Baton Rouge Zoo. Zoos that exhibit their ungulates in such an imaginative way cannot help but attract more public attention to the animals. Sable antelope with their unusual horns and Nilguri Tahrs goats from India, silhouetted against the skyline as they wend their way to the top of a rock hill, are sights to be treasured. The hill of synthetic rock was built not by an architectural firm but by high school students, and antelope births have occurred on the peak. The suni (tiny dwarf East African antelope) exhibit is neat and grassy; swamp deer are coupled with saurus cranes. Kudus, dama gazelles, and ostriches live side by side.

Egyptian geese live in the exhibit with pygmy hippos, and don't miss the hammerhead stork. He's a small fellow, but a determined one who builds a nest large and strong enough for a man to stand on. There is a lake with two islands on which black-necked swans nest despite acrobatic performances by lemur. In another lake flamingo trot around an Aldabra tortoise, while a peacock displays. Greater Baton Rouge Zoo's breeding of the Abdim (white-bellied) stork has been a great success, I was told by the head keeper, Linda Sanders.

Some exhibits are cramped, but a five-year plan initiated in 1991 should give cats, monkeys, and other animals more space. The plan provides for a new veterinary hospital, a new cat exhibit with grassy knolls, and a children's exhibit. A natural swamp lies adjacent to the zoo. One innovative project under the Master Plan has already been implemented: A multipurpose man-made swamp with a boardwalk viewing area has been built over a $420,000 sewerage disposal system, to be paid for over a three-year period, through cost saving $150,000, currently paid to the city in sewer fees. The two-acre marsh has attracted wild waterfowl and 500 to 600 wading birds to the zoo, plus raccoons, nutrias, muskrats, bobcats, and foxes.

🐾 BALTIMORE ZOO

Druid Hill Park
Baltimore, Maryland 21217
(410) 396-7102
Open: 10–5:20; call for winter hours
Best for: Otters

Year opened: 1876
Acres: 158
Animal population: 1,522; 234 species
Director: Brian Rutledge

Getting there: From I-83 north of central Baltimore, turn onto Druid Hill Drive. Follow signs to zoo.

Conservation: Programs for the breeding and conservation of the lion-tailed macaque and black-footed penguin.

Education: Zoomobile, zoo lab, tours, classes, lectures, summer programs.

Special attractions: Children's zoo; African Watering Hole.

Gift shop: Inadequate.

Food: Fast-food snacks.

The children's zoo is the Baltimore Zoo's best feature. The aviary marsh is small but impressive under a big, walk-in mesh tent. Herons nest in trees on islets, and wooden walkways lead through an area that includes a large "nest" for children to play in and giant plastic lily pads on which children can leap like real frogs. Continuing the emphasis on water, a superb river otter exhibit can be viewed not only from above the water but also from inside a 10-foot tunnel under the pond. An acrylic section in the tunnel provides a view of the otters swimming underwater and skimming over the top of the acrylic. You are inside, and the otters are about and above you. Architecturally the concept is similar to the Topeka Zoo's gorilla tunnel.

A "wilderness cave" is appropriately dark and damp, and winds through the interior of a "hill," creating an effective, realistic sensation. Children can see stalagmites, stalactites, bats, bullfrogs, and fish.

The Kodiak bear exhibit has space, a good pool, and a waterfall, and the addition in 1992 of a six-acre African Watering Hole exhibit is a definite plus. Sadly, a number of exhibits are in need of renovation, and it is to be hoped that someday the entire zoo will be remodeled with the same imaginative effort as the children's zoo.

➤ NATIONAL AQUARIUM IN BALTIMORE

Pier 3, 501 East Pratt Street
Baltimore, Maryland 21202
(410) 576-3823
Open: Mon.–Thurs. 9–5, Fri.–Sun. 9–8; call for winter hours
Best for: Penguins; ocean mammals

Year opened: 1981
Acres: 3.25
Animal population: 8,561; 588 species
Director: Nicholas Brown
Sister Zoo: Simón Bolívar Zoo, San José, Costa Rica

Getting there: On the harbor waterfront.
Conservation: "A top priority," states Director Nicholas Brown.
Education: Tours, classes, teacher workshops, lectures. Hands-on: touch and hold horseshoe crabs, starfish, sea urchins.
Special attractions: Twelve major theme exhibits.
Gift shop: More than one, highlighting the penguin, aquarium mascot.
Food: Dozens of restaurants in all price ranges on the harbor.

The Baltimore aquarium gets my vote for the number one aquarium in the United States. It has 12 major theme exhibits emphasizing activities of sea life, for example the Atlantic Coral Reef exhibit. The reef exhibit is overwhelming, seen from an interior ramp that descends five stories, passing parrot fish, butterfly fish, angel and damsel fish—the inverse of Boston's New England Aquarium, where the visitor walks on a ramp that hugs the outside of the big circular tank. Other theme exhibits include Finland, an open ocean exhibit of a sand tiger, a sand bar, nurse sharks, and game fish; a tidal beach; and the South American rain forest, whose theme is "unity of life through water." The rain forest is located in a 65-foot-high glass enclosure atop the aquarium, sunlit from a skylight and doused in mist at frequent intervals. Among the more than 500 species of plants and animals, look for a two-toed sloth hugging a tree (her name is Rapunzel); blue-crowned mot-mots, tanagers, finches, and scarlet ibises flying freely in the forest; and five-foot iguanas crawling on the ground. The exhibit illustrates that whether on land or in the sea, water is essential to life.

Though smaller than some other super penguin displays (at the Sea Worlds in Ohio, Texas, Florida, and even Shedd Aquarium's in Chicago), Baltimore's exhibit (the penguinarium) is darn good. Then there is Baltimore Aquarium's oceanarium, focusing on marine mammals. The oceanarium provides a facility for continued study of whales and dolphin as well as a safe place for rescue and rehabilitation of marine mammals that have been stranded on West Coast beaches. The oceanarium's pools are the site of educational demonstrations. Baltimore's oceanarium has two giant video screens, on which a conservation pitch is made, but the audience's attention is on the action in the pool. The 20-minute presentation is followed by a 20-minute period when personnel are available for questions.

The Baltimore Aquarium gets top marks in education for its "Surviving Through Adaptation" series of exhibits that demonstrate feeding, hiding and displaying, fin power, activities of living together, and migration.

The aquarium's director, Nicholas Brown, captain, U.S. Navy (retired), did not grow up collecting squirmy or furry things. He believes that running an aquarium has very little to do with expertise in biology, and compares it to running a ship, where "everything is subordinate to the mission." In addition to managerial competence, however, Brown thinks an aquarium director should have an artistic eye, for the product is the exhibit, and the exhibit should be one that works. Furthermore, an aquarium director should be a leader able to instill a desire in those working at the aquarium to *want* to work there. Finally, a bit of knowledge of biology helps. Brown has all of them.

Brown believes that conservation is aquariums' and zoos' most urgent task—"Captive propagation is not worth the time." To those who have complained that the SSP has not paid enough attention to aquatic species, Brown responds that the methodology is not adaptable to fish and invertebrates, only to mammals. Brown also believes that a marriage between a zoo and an aquarium is a forced one; zoos that have tried to include an aquarium have not succeeded, Point Defiance, Washington, being an exception. Brown looks on himself as a conceptualist, and the aquarium as an urban development tool. The Baltimore Aquarium "peddles a mood of excitement; it is visual rather than cerebral. Aquariums address a different part of the human brain than megavertebrates at a zoo. An aquarium is an agent of change."

🐾 FRANKLIN PARK ZOO

Franklin Park Road
Boston, Massachusetts 02121
(617) 442-2002/2300

Open: 9–4, weekends 10–5; call for winter hours

Best for: Bongos; pygmy hippo; gorillas

Year opened: 1910

Acres: 80

Animal population: 1,576 (650 invertebrates, 386 birds); 257 species

Director: Charles Desmond

Getting there: Located in Dorchester, south of Boston. By car: From Route 93, take Exit 15 west to Columbia Road. Zoo is at end of Columbia Road. By subway (T): Orange Line to Forest Hills stop.

Conservation: Various programs related to species in the African Tropical Forest exhibit.

Education: Teacher workshops, lectures, classes, tours.

Special attractions: African Tropical Forest exhibit.

Gift shop: Fair.

Food: Substandard.

Both the Franklin Park Zoo, just south of Boston in Dorchester, and the Walter D. Stone Memorial Zoo in Stoneham, west of Boston, suffered when they were run by the Commonwealth of Massachusetts as the Metroparks Zoos. In 1990, however, an independent corporation took over responsibility for the zoos, and Stone reopened on June 13, 1992, with five exhibits and a master plan for the future.

In the 1980's $26 million was miraculously made available to the Franklin Park Zoo for the construction of a spectacular structure to house a three-acre tropical forest environmental exhibit. On September 9, 1989, the African Tropical Forest exhibit opened—North America's largest tropical forest zoo exhibit with no internal structural support. The drama of the architecture is worthy of the drama it contains: The structure's diameter is 250 feet and its highest point 75 feet. The roof is a Teflon-coated glass-yarn fabric supported by steel cables hung from three steel arches. It gives the illusion of being a massive, graceful aerial tent. (It was designed by Jerry M. Johnson, noted zoo architect/ designer.) Kept at a constant temperature of 72°F. and humidity of between 60 and 70 percent, it contains four waterfalls and has periodic rainstorms and a rainbow. The gorillas on their rock island made of fiberglass-reinforced concrete are seen immediately on entry and again from different angles as the spectator moves through the building, separated from the gorillas and other exhibits by only a moat. My reaction to the entire building and the dramatic setting it provides for the animals is one of astonishment. Other animals in the African Tropical Forest include a pygmy hippo, a very effective (you feel you are within arm's reach) exhibit of bongo antelopes, Nile monitors, African bullfrogs, forest buffalos, dwarf crocodiles, yellow-backed duikers, carpenter ants, and pottos.

In the Hooves and Horns Building are mouflons, aoudads (large North American wild sheep), addaxes, wildebeests, and Grevy's zebras. Like the Philadelphia, Toledo, and other older zoos, the Franklin Park Zoo has buildings of considerable architectural value, which should be enjoyed during a zoo visit.

→ **NEW ENGLAND AQUARIUM**

Central Wharf
Boston, Massachusetts 02110
(617) 973-5220
Open: 9–6; Wed.–Thurs. 9–8
Best for: Penguins; octopuses
Year opened: 1969

Acres: 3.2
Animal population: 9,760;
613 species
Director: John Prescott
Membership: New England
Aquarium

Getting there: By subway: Take the Blue Line to Aquarium stop. On foot: Walk from downtown Boston. By water taxi: From Logan Airport.

Conservation: The environment, from the Boston Harbor to the outer limits of the globe. Object: get people to conserve. Seventy exhibits make the point.

Education: "Education is the reason to be here." (Director John Prescott).

Special attractions: Cylindrical ocean tank with penguin area at base, seen immediately on entry. Dolphin and sea lion performances daily.

Gift shop: Outstanding. Wide choice.

Food: Choices abound nearby on Boston waterfront.

When you enter the New England Aquarium, the impression is dramatic. One is greeted by the superb 80-foot, 187,000-gallon Caribbean tank and, at its base, "ocean tray," a pond of effectively illuminated clear bluish-green water where jackass and rockhopper penguins swim about and hop onto small rock islands. The Caribbean coral reef tank contains more than 800 specimens of aquatic life, including a moray eel; a 32-year-old, 500-pound Green turtle; spine-covered balloon fish; small sharks—all swimming by your face as you ascend the external ramp to the open pool at the top. The aquarium has a strong educational orientation, providing detailed explanations for its 70 exhibits focusing on different aquatic habitats. The New England Aquarium also has a very good dolphin show on a barge adjacent to the aquarium, and many locals remember a seal named Andre, who swam from the aquarium to Rockport (north of Boston on Cape Ann) each summer, returning in the fall.

The New England Aquarium has had a rough recent past. Already one of the best, New England wanted to be better. Even though the plans didn't come to fruition, they deserve to be described, for their imagination and scope point up the potentials for the aquariums of the future. One proposal involved flooding an unused dry-dock; another proposal, for a point of land jutting into the harbor, would have had an underwater acrylic people passageway with sharks, sawfish, ocean rays, dolphins, and whales surrounding it. A sand dunes and marsh exhibit would have had birds flying free within the confines of the aquarium, and artificial waves breaking on a beach. More violent water would have been provided for seals, sea lions, and walrus at the rock shore exhibit. Other exhibits would have included a tank giving visitors a feeling of being suspended in the ocean; a coral reef; an Antarctic penguin exhibit with emperor penguins; a tidal pool; and hands-on teaching laboratories. Perhaps someday these promising plans will be brought forward again. In the meantime, plans have been made for the construction of an additional aquarium building adjacent to the present one, to be completed by 1997.

The story of the New England Aquarium's active involvement with conservation and other environmental programs gives an insight into problems of the times. In the 1980's conservation had begun to creep into the mission statement of aquariums, and the New England Aquarium worked with the government of Massachusetts on water issues. The aquarium was active in influencing the government, business, and the public. One environmental education specialist notes that Monterey, Shedd, Baltimore, and other aquariums are beginning pro-active conservation efforts in areas such as habitat restoration and in-house conservation. The New England Aquarium's Trustee Conservation Committee in 1989 adopted a resolution for a position of active participation on environmental protection of wetlands and regulation development, which was successful. The aquarium focused on off-shore drilling, showing its effect on the falling fishing catch on George's

Bank. The aquarium also had a major involvement in the Boston Harbor clean-up project, and was represented on two public works projects for clean water. A Marine debris program received their attention, and a sanctuary was designated. The New England Aquarium had a good program. Then came the nasty surprise: It was eliminated in October 1991 with many plans left unfulfilled. Elimination of the program was attributed to a lack of funds from the Massachusetts government and a decline in aquarium attendance, sales and contributions. Possibly the decision to eliminate the program was made by upper management of the aquarium without consultation with knowledgeable conservation staff. This was too bad, as only ½ of 1 percent of the aquarium's operating budget was being spent on the pro-active program, and some observers feel that had the staff been consulted the decision would have been different.

🐾 BINDER PARK ZOO

7400 Division Drive
Battle Creek, Michigan 49017
(616) 979-1351

Open: 9–5; call for summer hours

Best for: Bison; cheetahs

Year opened: 1977

Acres: 405

Animal population: 320; 72 species

Director: Gregory Geise

Getting there: Take Route 94 to Exit 100, 3 miles south to Beadle Lake Road. Good parking.

Conservation: Outstanding. Tied closely to education. SSP's: red panda, cheetah, gibbon, ruffed lemur. Mexican wolf and trumpeter swan breeding program. Works with National Zoo (Washington, D.C.) on breeding cheetahs.

Education: Excellent programs; outstanding education center. Workshops, lectures, summer camp. Three hundred volunteers. Zoomobile outreach to 33,000 schoolchildren is probably the largest outreach for zoo size in the country.

Special attractions: Waterfowl pond.

Gift shop: Outstanding. ·

Food: Excellent, attractive restaurant.

Binder Park Zoo in Battle Creek, Michigan, contains a surprise at the end of a thickly wooded boardwalk just inside the main entrance: a small meadow where one can encounter three bison at very close quarters. A large display board explains how the New York Zoological Society's persistent efforts under the direction of William Temple Hornaday saved the bison from extinction in North America. The bison population had gone from 60 million to fewer than 100 animals, but is now at 120,000. It is refreshing to see one zoo give another credit.

Binder Park Zoo has a good children's zoo, with about 22 goats to be touched and hugged. There is a waterfowl pond with a covered bridge and small waterfall at one end that is encircled by paths leading off to exhibits. Good observation platforms and other points exist where seats may be found to sit and enjoy the nature—including trumpeter swans being bred for eventual release into the wilds of Michigan. Cheetahs, located quite near to the pond, have a large enough area to run in, with high grass (seasonal, of course) to hide in, which sometimes makes them difficult to find. (They're becoming more difficult to find in the wild, too.) Binder Zoo has an off-site cheetah facility as well. In 1992 the zoo expanded to 405 acres, and over the next five to seven years the exhibit area of the present zoo will be doubled.

🐻 BELLE ISLE ZOO AND AQUARIUM

P.O. Box 39
Royal Oak, Michigan 48068
(313) 267-7160

Open: 10–5; Sun./hol. 10–6; closed Nov.–April

Best for (zoo): Spectacled bear; Western gray kangaroos

Best for (aquarium): Zebra mussels; albino glass fish

Year opened: 1904 (aquarium); 1980 (zoo)

Acres: 13

Animal population
(zoo): 1,541; 178 species
Director: Ron Kagan (also
director of Detroit Zoo)

Head zookeeper: Mike Reed
Membership: Detroit
Zoological Society
(313) 541-5717

Transportation: From East Jefferson, east at East Grand Boulevard, over the half-mile-long MacArthur Bridge onto 985-acre Belle Isle in Detroit River. Turn left on riverbank for 3-minute drive to zoo and aquarium.

Conservation: Zoo participates in SSP program.

Education: Zoomobile, lectures, tours.

Special attractions: Glass fish.

Gift shop: Modest.

Food: Snacks.

The highlight of the Belle Isle Zoo and Aquarium, located in a corner of the park on Belle Isle, is a three-quarter-mile elevated boardwalk, built in 1981, from which visitors look down on the animals. The zoo has an exhibit of siamangs, an endangered species of black gibbon from Sumatra and Malaya; their area has trees for them to climb and hang from. I was particularly struck by the dozen Western gray kangaroos who have a large tree-shaded area and a huge cement waterhole. One can also see a male spectacled bear, which has demonstrated unusual intelligence and ingenuity: Holding a stick, he has swung it at hot wires, disabling them. European white storks here are from five European zoos.

There is a master plan which, if realized, will take the visitor to ground-level viewing as well. In 1993 Ron Kagan, who had been acting director at the Dallas Zoo, took over as director of the Detroit Zoo and Belle Isle Zoo and Aquarium.

The Belle Isle Aquarium, which is the oldest continuously operating aquarium in the United States, and which specializes in freshwater fish, is a five-minute walk from the zoo. The building has a handsome façade, but inside is a bit dreary. Nevertheless, the tanks have clear water, and exhibits are simple but contain good plants and rocks. Dryers above exhibit windows defog the windows. The collection is divided into six color-coded areas: Africa, Asia, Australia, North America, Oceanic, and South/Central America. Signs are particularly good, with questions at the side of the exhibits and answers below the exhibit windows ("Do fish sleep?" "Yes, but they don't close their eyes; they have no eyelids.")

The aquarium has done a particularly good job on breeding threatened pupfish and checkerboard stingray. I especially liked the albino snapping turtle in the same exhibit with a Florida softshell turtle; and also a beautifully arranged exhibit of glass fish. There is also an exhibit devoted to the zebra mussel, an unwelcome invader from Europe that accidentally came to the Great Lakes in 1986; they eat algae, and attach themselves to intake pipes, which blocks water flow. The female lays 35,000 eggs per annum.

🐘 DETROIT ZOOLOGICAL PARK

P.O. Box 39
8450 West Ten Mile Road
Royal Oak, Michigan 48068
(313) 398-0903

Open: 10–5; Sun./hol. 10–6; call for winter hours

Best for: Elephants; chimps

Year opened: 1928

Acres: 125

Animal population: 1,654; 266 species

Director: Ron Kagan

Membership: Detroit Zoological Society (313) 541-5717

Getting there: A 20-minute drive north of central Detroit on Route 1 (Woodward Avenue).

Conservation: SSP participation.

Education: Small, informative insect exhibit.

Special attractions: Penguinarium; attractive plantings.

Gift shop: Modest.

Food: Snacks.

If you get to the zoo early in the morning, you may catch elephant Ruth walking through the zoo on her way to her exhibit. Ruth follows in the footsteps of Paulina, the zoo's famous and first elephant who lived at the zoo from 1928 until 1950 and came to Detroit from India by way of Hamburg. Paulina helped with construction and gave rides to an estimated 500,000 persons at the Detroit Zoo.

The Detroit Zoo is an exceptionally clean zoo. Water in the exhibits and ponds is clear. Of the three major ponds, one is an island of gibbons, hidden by weeping willow trees. Some of the zoo's architecture, such as the aviary, is old and worth saving; it will be turned into an education center. In the spring, summer, and fall there is a show of colors along borders, on the islands between walks and throughout the Michigan trail. The Garden Club of Detroit cares for the horticultural installations.

The penguinarium, located near the Woodward Avenue entrance, has four species of penguins: the blue, king, Marconi, and rockhopper, and features three distinctive penguin habitats. Penguins are fed twice daily (call and check for times). At the opposite end of the zoo, adjacent to two attractive lakes, may be found rhinos, kudus, zebras, giraffes, tapirs, hippos, bears, moose, otters, elks, prairie dogs, oryx, and hyenas. On the other side of the lake, near the chimpanzees, are elephants, lemurs, leopards, lions, tigers, sea lions, and reptiles.

The chimpanzees received a new exhibit in 1989: four acres of freedom. Chimpanzees like to examine the perimeters of their territory, and did. Using ingenuity and persistence, they found how they could escape, and did. This was before the electrified wire was installed. One chimp drowned, one nearly drowned, and a third escaped but was retrieved. The exhibit—now, one hopes, escape-proof—has an authentic-looking termite mound, filled with tantalizing food. The chimps extract the good stuff from the holes in the mound with a stick, lick it clean, and have another go.

Escapes were not new to the Detroit Zoo. In fact, one almost occurred on its opening day, August 1, 1928. The mayor, John C. Nagel, had difficulty in finding the zoo, and finally ended up at the rear entrance rather than the front where everyone was eagerly waiting for him. He decided to walk through the zoo. At that moment a keeper, looking around and seeing that nothing of particular interest was going on, assumed he was early. In his hand he had a bucket full of bread to be thrown into the splendid moated exhibit of Morris, a large male polar bear. The keeper placed the bucket down carefully on the ledge of the bear exhibit moat at the same moment that Mayor Nagel came around the corner of the building, passing the exhibit. Morris, who had been eyeing the bucket of bread for some minutes, could resist no longer and leaped over the moat to take possession of his rightful booty. The mayor found himself only a few feet away from the bear, to the horror of zoo officials. Seven keepers flew to the bear to entice him back across the moat, while the mayor proceeded calmly to the ceremony site, saying, "He wanted to shake hands. *He's* the reception committee." Those who knew were not laughing.

🐻 JOHN BALL ZOOLOGICAL GARDEN

1300 W. Fulton Street, N.W.
Grand Rapids, Michigan 49504
(616) 776-2591

Open: 10–6; call for winter hours

Best for: Cats

Year opened: 1949

Acres: 14

Animal population: 465; 167 species

Director: John Lewis

Getting there: Located in John Ball Park. From Route 131, turn onto Route 196 west to Exit 75.

Conservation: SSP's for snow leopard, Siberian tiger, maned wolf. Zoo maintains the clouded leopard stud book. Works with Michigan Department of Natural Resources and the Audubon Society on programs for native Michigan birds.

Education: Animal study units for elementary schools within 20-mile radius; zoo school run by Grand Rapids Board of Education for sixth-graders; self-guided class tours; preschool program. Animals presented by geographic regions, also "nocturnal" category. For further information, call (616) 776-2591.

Special attractions: Hands-on activities with boas; camel ride; aquarium with penguins; herpetarium; 60-foot waterfall.

Gift shop: T-shirts, etc.

Food: Several snack stops.

Like a number of zoos, John Ball started with rabbits. The number of rabbits grew and so did what is now the zoo; owls, hawks, and an eagle followed. This was in 1891, when, true to the times, the "zoo" was a "curiosity shop" of caged animals. By 1970 dramatic changes began taking place, and the zoo keeps changing. Today it is a compact, attractive, interesting place with a very strong emphasis on education.

The John Ball Zoo established the first-of-its-kind zoo education program in the country. The program is run by the Grand Rapids Board of Education, with zoo support. Highly motivated sixth-graders are selected from all schools in the city to attend a full year of education at the zoo. All regular subjects are taught, such as reading, math, and science, but with an environmental twist. A similar program exists for junior high school students at the Buffalo Zoo. John Ball Zoo's preschool program brings children to the zoo for a morning or afternoon session to hear basic information on animals. Teachers at elementary schools may borrow for classroom use "discovery boxes" containing items ranging from different types of body coverings for help in teaching animal classification to explanations of how birds fly. In the summer the zoo has discovery weeks from mid-June through August with a variety of classes ranging from Animal Art to Zoo Careers.

The emphasis in the Nocturnal/Herpetarium Building is on reptiles (alligators, boa constrictors, Argentine horned frogs) and nocturnal cats, which are housed in 8-by-15-foot enclosures. There are also sloths, owl monkeys, and marmosets. Big cats, the puma and snow leopard, have their own exhibits up a hill constructed in 1984, with ledges on the rock wall for them to climb to and lie down on. The high point of the zoo is a recirculating 60-foot waterfall.

Through its Fable Conservation Fund the John Ball Zoo offers $5,000 in grants (usually five $1,000 grants) for zoo conservation or basic research in the interest of helping animals in captivity and the wild.

⚡ POTTER ZOOLOGICAL GARDENS

1301 South Pennsylvania Avenue
Lansing, Michigan 48912
(517) 483-4221

Open: 9–7; call for winter hours

Best for: Penguins; rhinos; Rocky Mountain bighorn sheep

Year opened: 1917

Acres: 17

Animal population: 359; 131 species

Director: Douglas Finley

Membership: Potter Park Zoological Society
(517) 371-3926

Getting there: In Potter Park, on the Sycamore River where it runs into the Grand River. From Route 496 take Pennsylvania Avenue south to Potter Park.

Conservation: SSP for rhinos (smallest participating zoo in the U.S.).

Education: Classes, junior animal keepers program; summer programs; hands-on activities. For further information, call (517) 371-3926/4155.

Special attractions: Rocky Mountain bighorn sheep.

Gift Shop: Very small.

Food: Drink vending machine.

The Potter Park Zoo is located in a forest of beautiful oaks, and around the zoo buildings the planting—the accomplishment of the zoo and the School of Landscape Architecture at Michigan State University—is excellent and in the summer, colorful. A generous gift of $100,000 from an individual donor has spearheaded a fund-raising drive to renovate the zoo. The Lansing Parks and Recreation Department has also pledged support and financial commitment to the zoo since 1984. The Core Project will include exhibits from North America, Asia, and Africa. Plans also include planting along the forest path leading to the zoo, which should do much to make the zoo grounds look more attractive.

Potter Zoo has an active education program, with an emphasis on summer programs and hands-on activities. Classes for teenagers are offered on five summer Friday mornings, covering topics such as endangered species, reptile life, primate classification and behavior, careers in animal-related fields, and the importance of water. In addition to conservation messages regarding animals, the zoo makes the point that trash should be recycled, informing visitors that Michigan residents dispose of 32,000 tons of solid waste *a day*, 42 percent of which is paper, which should be recycled!

One of the zoo's main attractions is its Rocky Mountain sheep. In a centrally located, moated exhibit, the sheep may be viewed from all sides. Rocks have been cemented together to create a hill and dry moat. The sheep births have taken place in full view. The rhino is in the former elephant exhibit. (The zoo did not want to have an elephant, but one had been purchased in the 1970's with 5- and 10-cent contributions by children, so the zoo sent the elephant to the Indianapolis Zoo.) There is good rhino viewing for the public, because the exhibit is small and the rhino has nowhere to go.

A small penguinarium is outdoors in a pond provided with bubbling water and a sprinkler system. White umbrellas along the rocks give shelter to the penguins in summer and give the exhibits the appearance of a chic beach. Mandrills are in a renovated 1930 zoo building, along with gibbons, ring-tailed lemurs, lions, and snow leopards. Seven different temperature zones in the building replicate climatic conditions necessary for the various animals. An interesting nugget of background on Victoria, the tiger; she was nursed by a dog at the zoo where she was born.

♀ MINNESOTA ZOOLOGICAL GARDEN

13000 Zoo Boulevard
Apple Valley, Minnesota 55124
(612) 431-9200
Open: 10–6; call for winter
hours
Best for: Dolphins; beavers

Year opened: 1978
Acres: 485
Animal population: 2,060;
387 species
Director: Kathryn Roberts

Getting there: South of downtown Minneapolis. Take Route 35 or 77 south to Apple Valley.

Conservation: Strong emphasis on conservation through education. SSP for clouded leopard (view in tropics building). SSP's also for Bali mynah, white winged woodduck, and gibbon. Zoo has initiated an "Adopt a Park" program for the remaining 50 Java rhinos in Ujong Kulon in Java.

Education: Zoocamp: become a zookeeper for a day, discover how dolphins and bats communicate. Field trips (marine biology) grades 7–12 in Grand Teton and Yellowstone Parks.

Special attractions: Gibbon Island; Asia Tropics exhibit.

Gift shop: Very good, especially books.

Food: Fair. Snacks.

Zoos that are doing a good job on education get people involved, and the Minnesota Zoo has a whole slew of learning/experience opportunities for all ages. There are daily programs such as zoolab (an appreciation of "Living Earth"), animal demonstrations, the children's zoo, a bird show, and seven miles of trails for cross-country skiing. Guided tours include the timber wolf tour for grades 4–12: Students are taken to the wolf exhibit, where a guide using information provided in the Timber Wolf Species Packet tells them how the wolf lives in its rugged environment. The packet was cowritten with the Science Museum of Minnesota. There are also tours along the Asian Tropics Trail for an education on the rain forest, a meeting with a shark (in the exhibit) to discuss aquatic relationships and recognize the importance of saving the oceans, and a walk along the Minnesota Trail exhibit for a better understanding of the owl, the otter, and the construction of a beaver dam. A behind-the-scenes tour gives a choice of three topics: conservation, using examples of local and global wildlife; animal behavior, for example, how a wolf pack determines leadership; and animal management, where students see how applied science solves management issues in captive environments. Internships and classes are also available at the college level. The Minnesota Zoo offers career days for children to get an introduction to various animal-related careers.

The zoo fosters communication with the public by means of two bulletin boards, at the marine mammals exhibit and at the Coral Reefs exhibit. They provide information regarding exhibits at the zoo and current conservation issues. Also, the zoo has a telephone number posted on the wall in the exhibit areas for anyone to call on a 24-hour basis for information on conservation. First you hear a recording, but if you hold the line you can talk to a human.

The Southeast Asia Tropics building is the centerpiece of the zoo. Under a single glassed roof the visitor follows a winding cement path with "bamboo" rails made of epoxy past a gibbon island with rocks and trees made of concrete with fiberglass branches that flex, and a waterfall broken by rocks; demoiselle cranes; Malayan mouse deer; hornbills, with a feeder hidden in a high tree stump; larger Malay chevrotains; and sun bears with camouflaged service doors in their exhibit. There are also ducks and Oriental small-clawed otters. The coral reef contains no live coral, but the fish are colorful, and there are good signs (unfortunately poorly lit). The zoo has a pleasant presentation of nocturnal exhibits on the Minnesota Trail, which is a tunnel leading out of the Tropics building and is home to spotted skunks and bats.

The beavers are in a two-tiered exhibit with a waterfall. Daily, several trees are placed in the exhibit, which the beavers chew on with delight. The exhibit is somewhat controversial since Minnesota spends several hundreds of thousands of dollars annually to control the beavers in nature. At the zoo they're a great hit.

Four dolphins appear in an outdoor exhibit, open during the

summer and covered during the winter. Some underwater viewing areas allow one to see the dolphins from underneath. The entire exhibit is to be reconstructed with 1,200 seats.

The zoo's conservation activities include a program, since 1986, for the release of trumpeter swans in Minnesota—56 by the Minnesota Zoo and 50 by the state department of natural resources.

🐻 KANSAS CITY ZOOLOGICAL GARDENS

6700 Zoo Drive
Kansas City, Missouri 64132
(816) 871-5700

Open: 9–5; call for winter hours

Best for: Big cats; gorillas; orangutans

Year opened: 1909

Acres: 170

Animal population: 627; 168 species

Director: Mark Wourms

Membership: Friends of the Zoo, (816) 756-3560

Getting there: From Route 435 south of Kansas City take Exit 66A west onto 63rd Street Trafficway to Swope Park and the zoo.

Conservation: A number of SSP conservation programs: Bali mynah, white-naped crane, Indian lion, Siberian tiger, snow leopard, red panda, maned wolf, cheetah, lowland gorilla, Bornean orangutan, black rhino.

Education: Hands-on activities at Touch Town: Ostrich eggs, peafowl feathers, antelope horns.

Special attractions: Zoo train, to area where you want to walk around. Pony ride, for those under 100 pounds. Elephant ride for all ages.

Gift shop: Several. Average.

Food: Twenty snack locations.

The Kansas City Zoo asked the community what it wanted in a zoo and learned that the public wanted entertainment but also the most natural exhibits possible, ones that would make them feel they were in the wild. Sixty percent voted for a property tax that gave the zoo $50 million for zoo renovation and new exhibits; another $21 million is to be raised by Friends of the Zoo.

The $16 million (raised by the Friends of the Zoo) education pavilion will be the visitors' first stop, in which they will receive a multimedia sequence orientation to make them understand the problems conservationists face and let them know that they can be heroes in conservation if they participate. The pavilion will include a giant screen IMAX (the first of any zoo) which Wourms describes as a "powerful media, taking the visitor to locations they would never be able to go to."

A number of zoo directors I had asked about having IMAX at a zoo were against the idea, feeling it would detract from what the visitor would see at the zoo itself. Wourms's response was that the zoo wants to "try to orient visitors to expect something different," and that a film presentation *versus* live animals at the zoo is a balance "to be achieved." IMAX's natural history and nature films are top-rate. The film *Beaver* is absolutely outstanding. *Antarctica*, *The Great Barrier Reef*, *The Nomads of the Deep* (humpback whales), and *Ocean* (off Catalina Island) are all magnificent, as are *Tropical Rain Forest*, *Weaving Ants*, and *Darwin on the Galápagos*.

The first project was Australia, which was completed in 1993. The highlight of this $3.3 million, 8-acre site is a walk-through where 19 kangaroos and 8 wallabies romp alongside the visitor, and which also includes an aviary with black swans and geese, and a sheep station with angora goats and dromedary camels. Director Mark Wourms points out that the exhibit includes the culture of Australia and has the largest aboriginal mural in the United States.

By June 1994, two new exhibit areas will be opened: a domesticated animal area with a U.S.-style farm, plus a World Bazaar featuring interactive exhibits, including ferrets traveling through transparent overhead tubes and other tubes that allow children to ferret through a cylinder themselves. Another exhibit, also opening in June, is a naturalistic Elephant Walk that passes down a long, narrow path from which five or six elephants may be seen from several vantage points. As one stands at its edge, there appears to be only a handrail between the visitor and the elephants, who are mud-wallowing, scratching on a dead tree, or bathing.

In his concept of what the renovated Kansas City Zoo would look like in 1996 when the project is to be completed, Director Wourms wanted visitors to believe "they are somewhere they are not." An atmosphere of "suspended disbelief" should be created. Wourms told me of his hopes with vivid description. There would be a Garden of Life with large sweeps of color and old trees, overwhelming the visitor.

A number of zoos have various animal demonstrations, such as elephants standing on their hindlegs; sea lions barking, clapping their flippers in apparent joy, and diving off a high rock; monkeys and polar bears playing with a ball. Feeding time is often as much of an event for the public as for the recipient. Bird trainers at the Kansas City Zoo put on daily demonstrations with eagles and other birds of prey who are trained to fly without returning to the hand, but instead return directly to the cage. Seeing birds in flight and hearing from the bird trainer about their life and habits stimulates interest and, hopefully, concern. For the birds, it provides a moment of freedom. The zoo is open during the renovations and installation of new exhibits, and there is much to be seen. The elephants and zebras are together in a former rock quarry—the first "mixed" exhibit in the United States. Like most elephant exhibits, this one is bare, somewhat dusty, with a bit of rock, some concrete, and access to water. However, the quarry is being given a structural face-lift, and will only include elephants. Casey, born in 1951, is the oldest elephant living in any zoo. The zoo also has clouded leopards, Indian lions, and Siberian tigers. New naturalistic exhibits will display cats by geographic regions and ecologically. In the Tropical Habitat Building a visitor will see a Bali mynah, superb starling, tawny frogmouth, and Victoria crowned pigeon. Tropical Habitat is to become a centerpiece for an Asian theme exhibit.

A zoo guide book provides interesting and educational information on the species in the zoo's collections:

- Mountain lion—The cat family is divided into cats that purr and cats that roar. The mountain lion is one of the largest purring cats and doesn't roar at all.
- Snow leopard—Snow leopards can leap six feet straight into the air.
- Cheetahs—The cheetah has been clocked at speeds of up to 70 miles an hour, making it the fastest land animal.

Something to look forward to in 1995 is the opening of an 80-acre African plains exhibit that will include wildebeests, zebras, and antelopes. Trails will lead to areas where warthogs, lions, rock hyraxes, rhinos, hippos and crocodiles can be sighted, to an island of baboons and to a 3.5-acre hillside for chimpanzees. At the cheetah exhibit, the visitor may cross a swinging bridge to the African forest to observe colobus monkeys, duikers, and gazelles (gorillas have not been at the zoo since Big Mac died several years ago).

ST. LOUIS ZOO

Forest Park
St. Louis, Missouri 63110
(314) 781-0900
Open: 9–5
Best for: Gorillas; birds
Year opened: 1913
Acres: 83

Animal population: 4,364; 721 species
Director: Charles Hoessle
Membership: St. Louis Zoo Friends Association
(314) 647-8210

Getting there: From Route 64/40, take Forest Park exit. There are several parking lots and entrances, north entrance on Government Drive and south entrance on Wells Drive. At the zoo, take the Zooline Railroad.

Conservation: Numerous SSP's, for lemur, cheetah, gaur, Speke's gazelle, tuatara, hooded crane, banteng, tapir. The zoo works with the Captive Breeding Specialist Group (CBSG), the International Union for the Conservation of Nature (IUCN), and local universities, and is a member of a consortium to help establish wildlife reserves in Madagascar.

Education: The Living World education center; WildWatch teacher-training program; Conservation Academy; many classes and tours. Call (314) 781-0155 for further information.

Special attractions: Living World; Zooline railroad (with replica 1863 locomotive); Flight Cage.

Gift shop: Two excellent shops.

Food: Giraffe Café at Living World. Snacks elsewhere.

St. Louis Zoo Director Charles Hoessle's professional expeditions include collecting vampire bats and reptiles in Mexico, and photographic safaris in South Africa, Rhodesia, Botswana, Kenya, and Tanzania. More recently he's been to the Peruvian Amazon, on a panda study tour to China, and to Costa Rica, where he represented the AAZPA at the International Conference of the IUCN-SSC. Born and raised in St. Louis, Hoessle joined the St. Louis Zoo in 1963 as a reptile keeper. In 1964 he was asked by Director R. Marlin Perkins to establish an education department; in 1968 he was appointed curator of reptiles and education; and in January 1982, director. Hoessle was host of the *St. Louis Show,* a weekly nature television program, from 1968 through 1978 and is a director of numerous nature-related organizations.

As director of the zoo, Hoessle still considers education his top priority. Hoessle had an idea that would bring the future into the present and would establish a model for other zoos and learning institutions: the Living World, a $17.9 million, 55,000-square-foot education center. The pavilion in which it is housed has a 65-foot rotunda, under which is suspended a 28-foot-long, 1,000-pound fiberglass great white shark. On both sides of the rotunda are halls of education where high technology and live animals are combined in educational presentations on how life evolved. The effect is dramatic, even overpowering. There are 30 computer stations, 32 large and 20 smaller video systems, 10 interactive video systems (including an interactive laser disc to view footage about rain forests), 85 films, and 150 species of live animals. Some examples of exhibits in the Living World:

- A 60-foot-long eye-level "living model" of a Missouri Ozark stream, whose fast-flowing waters contain live fish, amphibians, and reptiles.
- A satellite weather station that can provide current reports on weather conditions anywhere in the Western Hemisphere.
- A Hypertext informational device to generate various types of ecological data. I gave my birth date, and Hypertext printed out text informing me that since my birth, 211 tons of soil had been lost to erosion in the United States, 18 species of insects had been declared threatened or endangered by the U.S. Fish and Wildlife Service, and 6.35 billion people had been born.

Another feature of the Living World is the IMRI, or Interactive Multimedia Resource Interface, developed by Arnowits Productions. IMRI is a multimedia computer-based station designed for educators that allows teachers to make their own two-hour videos, selecting material from a biology textbook (on disc), 500 color slides, and prepackaged multimedia curriculum sets, and classroom activities from a menu of zoology, ecology, and conservation topics. Teachers may even add a brief visual (their face) and audio (their voice) introduction, personalizing the production for use in their classes. Teachers from the St. Louis area need only call for an appointment and bring their own cassette. IMRI and instruction in its use is free. The system won an award from the Association of Visual Communications.

George Johnson, a former director of the Living World education center, has said that the Living World "is the price of entry into the future. You can't wait until children are six years old," he emphasized. "You must get them to think."

Another education program, pointedly called the Classroom of the Future, puts children in a classroom with 20 Apple CX computers with hard disks and a microscope. The teacher's computer is wired to the students', so the teacher can also direct material to the student's screen. "We bring six teachers together from city schools for three full days to teach [fifth-graders] a two-hour program," says Johnson. "The object of . . . this instruction is . . . for fifth-graders to learn that science is fun." The teacher resource center has more than 2,000 books on zoology and conservation, plus slide sets, videocassettes, posters, and classroom kits, all available on a loan basis.

Of course things don't always pan out perfectly the first time, but Hoessle says he is "committed to keeping technology and the exhibit at the 'cutting edge.' " The entire project has undergone considerable evaluation and fine-tuning.

Some criticism has been leveled at the Living World; for example, that it is a great exercise in the use of modern technology but that its electronic exhibits require too much maintenance. One might question the relative value of a large number of small exhibits vs. a few large ones. The Living World's plethora of high-tech exhibits may be overwhelming and therefore difficult to assimilate.

Proponents of the use of high technology in zoos say it is a learning tool. Many zoo directors have a negative reaction to the use of technology in zoos, because it distracts from the animals. They look on much of such technology as gimmickry—but gimmicks, properly used, may be useful to teaching.

The teacher-training program called WildWatch took three years to develop and consists of six weeks of multimedia classes for teachers in both city and county schools. It focuses on 208 threatened and endangered species and the role that zoos play toward their conservation. Working with an Apple Macintosh program, teachers of fifth- and sixth-grade students are then prepared to work with their classes, addressing general science objectives, but also delving into research, information handling, computer skills, critical thinking, geography, language, and arts.

The zoo has become the operator of a school, the converse of the Caldwell School in Tyler, Texas, which owns the Caldwell Zoo (see profile). The St. Louis Zoo's Conservation Academy is a two-year zoo personnel training program.

When you visit the zoo, a good place to start is the Flight Cage, with over 1,000 birds. The elliptical structure, built by the Smithsonian Institution for the World's Fair in 1904, is still one of the largest free-flight aviaries in the world. More birds will be found in the Aquatic House, the Bird House, and the Pheasantry. The St. Louis Zoo is one of only four zoos with a Congo peacock.

Reptile collections are always a draw, and St. Louis is no exception. Look particularly for the tuatara in the herpetarium: It resembles a lizard but has different skeletal and anatomical characteristics. The zoo tapes the tuataras' lovemaking in hopes of learning why there is never any result. Experts theorize that the female's reproductive cycle takes six years—but they can live to be 100.

Other species to be visited: king and Humboldt penguins, gorillas in the Jungle of the Apes; lemurs at the Primate House (the zoo is particularly proud of its black lemur breeding successes); and koalas. The zoo is working with eight other zoos and organizations in Australia to develop an alternate food product for the koala, either pellets or a supplement, which will make it possible for zoos that do not have a readily available source of eucalyptus (which doesn't grow in a cold climate) to put koalas on exhibit.

Note that in the immediate environs of the zoo are the Missouri Botanical Gardens, the Planetarium, the St. Louis Science Center, the Natural History Museum, and the Art Museum.

𐊜 JACKSON ZOOLOGICAL PARK

2918 West Capitol Street
Jackson, Mississippi 39209
(601) 352-2585

Open: June–Aug. 9–6;
Sept.–May 9–5

Best for: Wallabies

Year opened: 1921

Acres: 110

Animal population: 443;
140 species

Director: Barbara Barrett

Membership: Friends of the
Jackson Zoo, (601) 352-2582

Getting there: From Route 220, take West Capitol Street exit east. Zoo is on left, in Livingston Park.

Conservation: SSP for Siberian tiger, Asian lion, lion-tailed macaque, orangutan, red-ruffed lemur, snow leopard, white rhino, and cheetah. Reintroduction of king vultures to Belize. Also rehabilitation of hawks, owls in the U.S.

Education: Educational graphics at the zoo; school programs.

Special attractions: Elephant show on weekends; Children's Discovery Zoo, African Rain Forest exhibit.

Gift shop: T-shirts, etc.

Food: Snack concessions; picnic area.

Jackson Zoo is another zoo that started with rabbits. Housed in the Central Fire Station when it opened in 1919, by 1921 the zoo had grown and was moved to Livingston Park. In 1985 it expanded again when the African Rain Forest exhibit was constructed.

The one-acre Children's Discovery Zoo was opened in 1989. At the Bird Barn children learn facts of bird life by watching chicks hatch. Nearby are large shells children can climb into. In a night room full of the sound of crickets, clever children may catch sight of Max, the barn owl. There are a number of touch-and-pet opportunities: a miniature gelding horse named Cai, a Spanish goat, an earless Lamancha goat, and sheep. There are trees to climb and lectures to attend and guinea pig stalls, and there's a prairie dog exhibit with crawl-through tunnels, plus a playground with a spider's web and a chance to dig for fossils, and an opportunity to compare one's own jumping ability to that of other animals. And rabbits still inhabit the zoo.

The wallabies' exhibit area is adjacent to the hippo on the way to the African Rain Forest.

ᚦ OMAHA'S HENRY DOORLY ZOO

3701 South Tenth Street
Omaha, Nebraska 68107
(402) 733-8401

Open: 9:30–5

Best for: Polar bears; Siberian tigers; birds

Year opened: 1965

Acres: 130

Animal population: 9338 (2,889 fish, 4,768 invertebrates); 475 species

Director: Dr. Lee G. Simmons

Getting there: From Route 75 exit at Tenth Street (near I-80). Zoo is near Rosenblatt Stadium.

Conservation: Research focus is on ensuring genetic diversity.

Education: Speaker's bureau; classes and workshops; internships, and junior keepers. For further information, call (402) 733-8011.

Special attractions: Lied Jungle; aviary; 2½-mile scenic zoo train.

Gift shop: Some good items.

Food: Light food at several locations throughout the zoo.

The four-acre Lee Simmons Aviary (named after the zoo's director, Dr. Lee G. Simmons) at Omaha's zoo is exceptional in that it is outdoors and has more the appearance of an enclosed totally natural swamp area than an exhibit manufactured by humans. The aviary is the largest in the world, although Singapore is constructing a five-acre aviary. You walk through on a raised boardwalk that occasionally passes over water and angles through trees and a tangle of bushes and scrubs. The signs are good but faded and difficult to read.

Mutual of Omaha's Wild Kingdom Building houses administration offices, classrooms, a lab, and a very attractive theater. It also has an entire circular center for educational displays, with considerable emphasis on invertebrates, especially insects to be seen through microscopes, as well as other live and artifact exhibits. Some particularly strong exhibits are the pygmy hedgehog tenrec, saddleback tamarin, tawny frogmouth, kookaburra, flying gecko, African clawed frog, Burmese python, and a multispecies exhibit that includes the short-tailed leaf-nose bat, blue-crowned hanging parrot, and Chinese button quail. In the center of the room are a mangrove swamp biome tank and exhibits of the Amazon at both high and low water.

Across from Wild Kingdom, to the right of the zoo's entrance, is the sparkling new Lied Jungle, dedicated by Ernst F. Lied to the memory of his parents. This tropical rain forest exhibit seems larger than its 1.5 acres, and offers 60,000 square feet of viewing space of Asian, African, South American, and Australian rain forests. A jungle trail leads past tropical flowers, fruits, trees, medicinal plants, a giant tree, cliffs, and 12 waterfalls. Along the wall of the exhibit, looking treacherously high, are placed a swinging rope bridge, caves, and lookout points atop rocks. There are five underwater viewing areas with otters, crocodiles, pygmy hippos, tapirs, and fish. Lied Jungle isn't an exhibit you look at from the outside; you are *in* the jungle with 140 species of animals and 2,000 plant species. The education center, in the basement of the Lied Jungle building, which was not in operation when I visited the zoo, should provide interpretation of the rain forest and answers to questions regarding its importance to us.

The zoo's gorilla house is on the path from the Simmons Aviary to the Wild Kingdom. It was remodeled in 1985, but looks drab, with no vegetation or ropes for the gorillas to swing on. As with Lincoln Park in Chicago, proximity to the animals is often possible. A bored gorilla was backed up against the glass wall of his area, and if it appealed to you you could sit on a ledge on your side of the glass and be a thickness of glass away from the animal. Adjacent to the gorilla's area and also separated by glass stood an orangutan, so the gorilla had a choice of primates.

Omaha's Henry Doorly Zoo is involved in a number of significant conservation initiatives. The Conservation and Research Institute for Omaha has a veterinary program that focuses on artificial insemination, nutrition, DNA fingerprinting (on gaur, wild cattle, bears, and large cats), tissue labs, and a tissue bank. Dr. Simmons emphasizes that the zoo world must pay greater attention to genetics. Simmons is working with international colleagues on gaur herds in Malaysia, rhinos in Indonesia, bears in Saba, leaf-eating monkeys, and proboscis monkeys.

A good example of the zoo's research is that on the gaur, a large East Indian wild ox that was the first species in the Species Survival Plan (SSP). A look at research on the gaur is an education on the work of the SSP program. A wild cattle symposium was held at the Henry Doorly Zoo in June 1991 to advance thinking regarding the application of semen cryopreservation technology to endangered cattle species. In September 1991 the North American SSP gaur herd numbered 163 and comprised 52 males and 109 females in 12 SSP zoos (in Brownsville, Buffalo,

Los Angeles, Memphis, Miami, New York, Toronto, Yulee, Oklahoma City, Omaha, and at King's Island, and the San Diego Wild Animal Park). Omaha's Henry Doorly Zoo is conducting research on gaur captured in Malaysia and Nepal. Their semen is collected and frozen. The gaur are then radio-collared; in 30 days they are recaptured and disease-tested, and their semen is imported into Europe and the United States to expand the gene pool disease survey, which seeks to expand our understanding of the relationship between genetics and disease.

Barbara S. Durrant of the Center for Reproduction of Endangered Species (CRES) at the Zoological Society of San Diego has stated that interest in germ plasm storage "has increased dramatically with the realization that self-sustaining captive populations of exotic animals may hold the only hope for species conservation." (See San Diego Zoo profile.) The world's first test-tube gaur was born at Omaha's zoo on August 2, 1993.

In February 1993, Omaha's Henry Doorly Zoo was one of four zoos that received a citation for excellence from Mutual of Omaha's Wildlife Heritage Trust. (The other three were the Sunset Zoological Park, Manhattan, Kansas; North Carolina Zoological Park, Asheboro; and the Great Plains Zoo and Museum in Sioux Falls, South Dakota.)

🐾 BERGEN COUNTY ZOOLOGICAL PARK

216 Forest Avenue
Paramus, New Jersey 07652
(201) 262-3771
Open: 10–4:30
Best for: Capybara; Patagonian cavy

Year opened: 1960
Acres: 18
Animal population: 174; 67 species
Director: Timothy Gunther

Getting there: Located in Van Saun Park. By car: From Route 80, take exit to Route 17 north (Woodland Avenue), which leads into Fairview Avenue. After the intersection with Route 4, turn right on Century Road, then left on Spring Valley Road, which leads to Van Saun Park and the zoo.

Conservation: Andean condor, Patagonian cavy, and other species.

Education: Summer programs, include internships, camp. Zoomobile.

Special attractions: Covered bridge. Relaxing.

Gift shop: Poor; closed in winter.

Food: Fair; closed in winter.

The Bergen County Zoological Park is simple, tidy, compact. It has charm, and offers a small but interesting collection. One attraction is a replica of a typical Bergen County farmyard of the 1860's with a smokehouse, well, horse, chickens, huge domestic pig, Jersey and Hereford cows—and a Nubian goat and a privy. A small outdoor exhibit allows close-up viewing of Artic foxes. The foxes can take shelter under a roof, and they looked in excellent health, with thick, shiny fur.

The capybara, the world's largest rodent, resembling an enormous rat in a science fiction movie, has an area with large rocks and a cement pond. Most exhibits contain more than one animal, except in the case of some of the birds, including the Andean condor, and the mountain lion, who are in solitary residence. The lion has not only trees but a tiered waterfall tumbling down rocks. In individual elevated outdoor shelters can be seen the yellow-headed Amazon parrot, whom I saw enjoying broccoli, carrots, and oranges; three chinchillas, and two screech owls. In a wide, open area with two trees are an ocelot and a Patagonian cavy, looking like a hare because of its long ears and slender legs. The cavy is probably the pride of the zoo, but its presence is not highlighted. A guanaco (a South American mammal related to the camel) and rhea (a tall, flightless South American bird) occupy a small exhibit, with a rhea egg in a box at the exhibit site, an effective educational touch. Six black-handed spider monkeys prance and relax in a triangular cage with swinging "vines" and a waterfall.

The zoo has a great covered bridge in an attractive setting over water with ducks paddling. It's the kind of bridge that appeals to children of all ages.

ᚱ RIO GRANDE ZOOLOGICAL PARK

903 Tenth Street, S.W.
Albuquerque, New Mexico
87102
(505) 843-7413

Open: 9–6; call for winter
hours

Best for: Birds of prey; plants;
primates

Year opened: 1927

Acres: 65

Animal population: 1,137;
274 species

Director: Ray Darnell

Getting there: Located on the east bank of the Rio Grande, a 15-minute walk from downtown: Go west on Central Avenue, turn south on Tenth Street and walk seven blocks to the zoo. Trolley, buses available.

Conservation: Bald eagles released into wild in Kentucky.

Education: Zoomobile planned.

Special attractions: Nineteen species of primates; look for orangutan Sara.

Gift shop: La Ventana Gift Shop has film, gifts, souvenirs.

Food: Snack bars are average.

At the Rio Grande Zoo some birds live particularly well. The zoo has a spacious, high, semicircular enclosure, built in 1982, that is divided into four sections, each containing eagles who dine on quail. The Rio Grande Zoo places an emphasis on its reintroduction program of captive birds into the wild, and is one of five zoos that have had particularly successful programs (the others are Greater Baton Rouge, Columbus [Ohio], Lincoln Park [Chicago], and Topeka). Rio Grande has successfully released bald eagles into the wild in Kentucky.

Sometimes small owls squeeze through the harp wire for a nocturnal escapade into the countryside, to the detriment of local small birdlife, but the owls faithfully return to their wire retreat after a night of AWOL.

The Rio Grande Zoo's ungulates are displayed in a fenced-in area. The zoo's polar bear gets a special treat when the temperature rises above 100°F. about four or five times a year: The local radio station, KOOL-AM, sends ice.

Former zoo director John Moore hopes that the city of Albuquerque will approve the construction of an aquarium off Central Avenue on the Rio Grande. One proposed exhibit of great relevance would trace what happens to a drop of water in the course of its trip from the headwaters of the Colorado to the mouth of the Rio Grande. You may want to think about visiting the zoo during October, when the nine-day International Balloon Fiesta takes place in Albuquerque and 600 hot-air balloons of all shapes and colors lift off every morning into the New Mexico sky.

🐘 BRONX ZOO (INTERNATIONAL WILDLIFE CONSERVATION PARK*)

18th Street and Southern Boulevard
Bronx, New York 10440
(718) 220-5100

Open: 10–4:30

Best for: Tropical birds; gelada baboons; Sumatran rhino

Year opened: 1889

Acres: 265

Animal population: 3,959; 592 species

General director: William Conway (president, NYZS The Wildlife Conservation Society International)

Getting there: By subway: Number 2 or 5 train to East Tremont Avenue. By bus: BxM11 bus up Madison Avenue. For transportation information, call (212) 652-8400.

Conservation: Extensive programs through NYZS The Wildlife Conservation Society International (WCSI) and Wildlife Conservation Center—St. Catherine's in Georgia. See profile text for more information.

*As of December 1, 1992, the new name of the parent organization of the New York zoos and aquariums is NYZS The Wildlife Conservation Society. Under the new parent organization, in addition to the Bronx Zoo, are the Central Park Zoo (now Wildlife Conservation Center—Central Park), Queens Zoo (Wildlife Conservation Center—Queens), Prospect Park, Brooklyn (Wildlife Conservation Park—Prospect Park), New York Aquarium, Coney Island, Brooklyn (the Aquarium for Wildlife Conservation), and

Education: A wide variety of visitor- and school-oriented programs (see Appendix C). The Education Department is currently working on its new Habitat Ecology Learning program (HELP) in partnership with zoos in Dallas, Kansas City, Fresno, Grassmere Park (Tennessee), and Lowry Park (Florida).

Special attractions: Jungle World and adjacent Bengali Express monorail; children's zoo; remodeled Elephant and Reptile houses; African Plains, World of Darkness, World of Birds exhibits, and two aye-ayes on loan from Duke University's Primate Center. Plans are on the drawing board for a $16 million Congo Forest Exhibit, and for the $15 million Environmental Education Center.

Gift shop: Several gift shops throughout zoo.

Food: Good restaurant; snack bars throughout zoo.

I have had an association with the New York Zoological Society and the Bronx Zoo for nearly 100 years. In 1909, my grandfather, Colonel Anthony R. Kuser, asked William Beebe, curator of birds at the then New York Zoological Park, to venture into the valleys and mountains of the Himalayas, Borneo, China, Mongolia, and Japan to write a book on pheasants. Colonel Kuser agreed to pay for the expedition, plus fees for illustrators (in the end there were three painters, G. E. Lodge, A. Thornburn, C. R. Knight) and a draughtsman (H. Gronvold). Dr. Hornaday, director of the the zoo, was opposed to Beebe's undertaking the mission, feeling strongly that he should stay at his post and not wander off to suit the fancy of an "evil genius of the zoological park," as Hornaday called my grandfather. Nevertheless, Hornaday capitulated, and Beebe ventured forth. Ten years later, in 1919, a grand four-volume limited edition of 600 copies, *Monograph of the Pheasants,* was published "under the auspices of the New York Zoological Society." Beebe very nicely dedicated the monograph to my grandfather and grandmother and named a partridge after them. Dr. Hornaday publicly praised both Beebe

St. Catherine's (Island) Survival Center, Georgia (Wildlife Conservation Center—St. Catherine's). NYZS The Wildlife Conservation Society International was previously called Wildlife Conservation International.

for his work and Colonel Kuser for "having brought about the union of foresight and forces that produced the great result now laid before the bird-lovers of the world."

I joined the Board of Directors of the New York Zoological Society in 1965 and as of this writing am chairman of the Education Committee and serve on its Executive, Conservation, and Marketing and Communications committees. I'm prejudiced in thinking that the NYZS is tops. Fortunately, a number of others do, too.

The NYZS has recently gone through a difficult period of soul searching as to who it really is—or who the public thinks it is. One problem is that because the NYZS comprises several entities, the public and press often confuse parent and offspring. For example, the Wildlife Conservation Society International (WCSI) was the conservation arm of the NYZS, although this association was not clearly understood.

Another issue was aims: NYZS concluded that *conservation* was its key mission and that the names of the organization and the entities under its umbrella should be changed to reflect this (see note at beginning of profile). An objective that began to capture the imagination of most zoos only in the 1970's and '80's, conservation was already an interest of the New York Zoological Society in the 1930's and even earlier. (In 1930, Vincent Astor took his yacht, the *Nourmahal,* to the Galápagos on a New York Zoological Society expedition to look for and bring tortoises from Santa Cruz Island to the Bronx Zoo to be bred. Thirty years later the Charles Darwin Research Station was established on Santa Cruz with an on-site breeding program.) Talking to potential donors in the course of a $100 million capital campaign revealed that those who gave did so because of the NYZS's participation in conservation programs, not because of its exhibits. The word *park* replaced *zoo.*

In 1993, Wildlife Conservation Society International's conservation budget was $11.5 million and encompassed a $1,000 project in Panama and a $1 million project for the Brazilian rain forest. (Sixty percent of WCSI's 200 projects focus on the rain forest.)

St. Catherine's Island in Georgia, once the home of an Indian tribe, today is owned by the Noble Foundation, which has invited the NYZS to use it as a wildlife survival and reproduction center (not open to the public). It is a breeding site for 444 animals of 59 species of mammals, reptiles, and birds, including ring-tailed, black, and ruffed lemurs, and lion-tailed macaques. The lemurs, native to Madagascar, were the first animals to be set free on the island—no cages, no fences. They are free to swing from the trees, roam the forest floor, and explore the fields of the island looking for skinks, acorns, mescaline grapes, and Spanish moss, but are able to return to a known spot for human-provided yams, fruit, and monkey chow. Only a radio collar monitors their whereabouts. More recently the lion-tailed macaques, being prepared for reintroduction to the mountain range in India called the Western Ghats (where their numbers have diminished to about 4,000), have also been released into the wilds of St. Catherine's.

Besides the lemurs (there are now several troupes at liberty on the island) and the macaques, there have been a number of births of Jackson's hartebeest in the only viable group of this species outside its Kenyan homeland, as well as of sable antelope, slender-horned gazelle, Nile lechwe, Grevy's zebra, Arabian oryx, wattled crane, yellow-knobbed curassow, maleo, Leadbeater's cockatoo, and red-fronted macaw.

The NYZS/WCSI feels that conservation and education must go hand in hand. At Jungle World at the Bronx Zoo, the exhibits are also classrooms. Jungle World is regarded by many zoo directors as the best exhibit of its kind, and one of the outstanding zoo exhibits in the United States. It has set the standard for interior walk-through rain-forest exhibits that other zoos are now trying to match or exceed. The Jungle World building has an interior height of 55 feet and a total volume of one million cubic feet and contains 530 animals of 87 species, from millipedes to gibbons, hornbills, and gharials. A troupe of silver-leaf langurs gathers on the outreaches of a tree trunk, one clutching a bright-orange baby. Waterfalls small and large are most impressive, and a mist maker provides the humid atmosphere of the tropics. Jungle World is a vivid demonstration of biodiversity.

In a Jungle Lab classroom, participants work actively together, learning from nature without disturbing it; they can view Jungle World from within, with langurs on one side of the classroom and tapirs on the other. A class is in session. Tools at hand include binoculars, microscope, clinometer (a device that measures the height of an object), telethermometer (a sophisticated electronic thermometer used to measure the temperature of air, soil, and water), psychrometer (which measures the moisture content of air), stopwatch, compass, range finder, calculator, and field notebook. Today's lesson is on the forests of tropical Asia: lowland and montane rain forests; mangrove, scrub, and monsoon forests. The focus is on the tiger (world's largest cat), gaur (world's largest species of cattle), Komodo monitor (world's largest lizard), the Asian elephant, and the reticulated python. The class is told that tropical Asia's jungles support a great diversity of wildlife: 11 species of wildcats, nearly 50 species of primates, more than 100 species of fruit bats, and more than 1,000 species of birds. The students' jungle field notes contain artists' renderings on every page, with informative text. One page informs that a water monitor basks in the sun until its body heat reaches 95°F, at which point it is ready to hunt. Another describes how "the leaf monkey catapults across a 20-foot gap between branches, its arms, legs, and tail extended for in-flight balance. Do they ever fall?" Yes: Field scientists often record the discovery of langurs with broken bones. The setting, the surroundings, the inside-the-exhibit classroom, the material presented for study, all make Jungle World a model for environmental education.

Adjacent to Jungle World is Wild Asia, a 38-acre home to over 200 animals. The Bengali Express, a monorail, transports visitors across the river on a 25-minute trip to view eight large habitat exhibits. The first glimpses are of axis deer and Indian peafowl, then of Formosan sika deer, as the Bengali Express speeds on at six miles an hour. A gaur appears, then the train rounds a bend and beneath you are Siberian tigers—if you can spot them in the high grass. The Asiatic elephants are coming out of the shade, moving toward the waterhole. Other exhibits slide by—Nilgiri tahrs (wild goats)—and after a treetop view of a red panda, the train moves into the station.

The Bronx Zoo's Sumatran rhino, Rapunzel, is usually found at the Elephant House at the edge of Astor Plaza, but for 1994 is on loan to the Cincinnati Zoo. Sumatran rhinos point up the plight of endangered species. It is not known how many Sumatran rhinos survive in the wild, but it is known that between 14 and 21 were poached in Sumatra in 1991, including some in a "protected" national park. Four U.S. zoos (in the Bronx, San Diego, Los Angeles, and Cincinnati) made a collective effort to bring 10 Sumatran rhinos to their zoos, and an agreement was reached with Indonesia. A professional was employed to find and trail the rhinos, then trap them. There were setbacks, for the rhinos' home territory is being lumbered, legally and illegally. By 1993 the project had resulted in seven Sumatran rhinos in U.S. zoos, but two died in captivity. The world's captive population of Sumatran rhinos—in the U.S., U.K., Indonesia, Malaysia, and Saba—is 24. The cost of obtaining one captive animal is about $800,000, a high price to pay for one animal of a species that will most probably become extinct in the wild and has little chance of breeding in zoos.

People enjoy the songs of birds, and their presence provides companionship. It is therefore no great surprise that humans have built houses for birds at zoos. Thanks to the *Reader's Digest*'s Dewitt and Lila Wallace, the Bronx Zoo has a most effective World of Birds, offering visitors walk-through natural habitats with flowering foliage and waterfalls and the pleasure of searching for the birds hidden in the branches, using as guides placards on the railing with photographs or sketches of the birds. Some more conservation-oriented exhibits opened in 1993 at the World of Birds. One of them, of virgin New York State forest, contains a sign: FOR SALE: 256 SCENIC ADIRONDACK LOTS, DEEP WOOD DEVELOPMENT. Another shows cut and fallen trees with the sign NO ROOM TO HIDE. Birds are also found at several other locations at the zoo: at the Aviary near the Rainey Gate (main) entrance, at the wildfowl pond adjacent to the cafeteria, and in the Tropical Bird House.

The gorilla exhibit is unspectacular (although the collection is one of the most important in the country): It provides enough space for the gorillas and good viewing for the public, but lacks natural-habitat fanfare. Within the limitations of its present exhibit, the zoo educates the public on conservation by bringing gorilla babies before the public as soon as possible, so people get an early peek at young gorillas and their always enticing antics.

But the International Wildlife Conservation Park in the Bronx (the Bronx Zoo) has decided that what is needed is a *habitat* gorilla exhibit with an educational purpose. In the planned Congo Forest (still on the drawing board), the presentation of gorillas will provide information and analysis on the status of the gorilla, one of man's closest genetic relatives. The exhibit will be home to gorillas, other primates (including mandrills and guenons), and canopy-dwelling birds. In the center of the exhibit will be a 30,000-square-foot "invisible" (enveloped by rain-forest vegetation) Environmental Education Center, with training workshops, a multimedia resource library, and conference capability. A special emphasis will be placed on teaching teachers, using new tools such as videodiscs and CD-ROM programs. Teaching will integrate classroom settings and natural habitats. The Wildlife Conservation Society International will participate actively by setting up a program with the aim of educating policy-makers, professionals (scientists, parks managers), and the general public.

The World of Darkness exhibit, which opened on June 11, 1969, marked a big step forward in the techniques of displaying nocturnal animals by presenting them dramatically in an ecological context. The imaginatively fabricated walls and ceilings of the exhibits simulate caves, underground holes, and passageways. The Tropical Cave was modeled after an actual cave in Trinidad, which I visited when I was posted as ambassador to Trinidad and Tobago. The animals tenant the dimly lit spaces, with just enough illumination provided for humans to see. At night the lights are brightened, cueing the nocturnal creatures to sleep. The World of Darkness introduces the visitor to more than 200 bats, plus opossums, galagos, raccoons, kit foxes, herons, skunks, sloths, and sugar-gliders. This exhibit taught me that 50 to 60 percent of all creatures are nocturnal. The World of Darkness was created for educational purposes, but it has also been a breeding success.

An exhibit of the naked mole rat opened in 1993 as part of the World of Darkness. Neither mole nor rat, these animals are more closely related to guinea pigs. They live underground and create tunnels miles long, in which they search for sugar, starch, and water in the underground buds of certain plants. The naked mole rat has a social structure resembling that of some insects, such as ants or termites; until recently this social structure, called *eusociality*, was considered unique to insects. The Cincinnati Zoo's Insect World had the first naked mole rat exhibit in the United States. The International Wildlife Conservation Park's (Bronx Zoo's) naked mole rat exhibit contains two colonies living in separate tunnel systems, and is lit for public viewing by a fiberoptical system. Thirty-six of the more than eighty-five naked mole rats are named after members of the Board of Trustees.

The lesser, or red, panda looks very different from the giant panda: the former resembles an American raccoon, whereas the latter is usually classified with the bears. Like the giant panda, the red panda comes from China and Nepal. It is small, about 20 to 25 inches long and 6 to 10 pounds. Because of its sharp tree-climbing claws the red panda is a difficult animal to cuddle, but it is a pure joy to watch this white-faced and -bellied, rust-brown animal resting on the top branch of a tree. Exhibits such as the one at the Bronx Zoo that allow for viewing at eye level with the treetops are most effective.

The zoo has had an African Plains exhibit since 1941. The lions basking on a rock appear to be in the same unrestricted area with more than 40 other species, including animals normally their prey, but in fact they are separated by a moat. It's a very creditable attempt to provide a sense of what one can see in the wild, and reminds me of one morning in the Serengeti. It was shortly after six, and the Serengeti sky was clear. The sun had just risen, and the freshness of night still clung to the ground. The roar of the lion had been loud during the night and the message was clear: There had been a kill. Our guide, sitting next to the driver, gave instructions in Swahili. Go left—now straight. He knew where to find the lions. The vehicle slowed as we reached a rise, then cautiously moved forward to observe but not disturb. Directly before us, no more than 50 to 60 feet away, the carcass of a buffalo was stretched out. The adults had had their fill and had wandered off a short distance to collapse in sleep; two immature lions were playing, raising their paws against each other in mock battle; the cubs were dining, sniffing, climbing, and sliding over the dead buffalo. There were 19 lions in all.

The zoo's Himalayan exhibit contains snow leopards, frequently providing very close views through wire, with Asian timberline vegetation surrounding the exhibit. An alert ear or sensitive nose may get an additional sensory reaction to the cats from the proximity—without that barrier of glass—that is critical to an understanding of man's relationship with other wildlife. The NYZS has displayed snow leopards in the Bronx since 1903 and has bred 70 since 1976. The present zoo population is 18, and there are fewer than 1,000 individuals remaining in the wild.

Zoo people, whether doing research in the field or administering a zoo, are dedicated to their work. George Schaller, NYZS's director for science and holder of the Ella Millbank Foshay Chair in Wildlife Conservation, is a conservationist, environmentalist, zoologist, and anthropologist. He has been associated with NYZS The Wildlife Conservation Society since 1966. His concern and care have taken him to distant plains, rain forests, mountain peaks, and pockets of nature still relatively untouched by modern human society. He has researched and written about the mountain gorilla, the Serengeti lion, the Himalayan snow leopard, and giant pandas. Schaller has been honored by the World Wildlife Fund (gold medal) and decorated by the Order of the Golden Ark Netherlands and is an honorary member of the Explorers Club. Over the past 10 years he has zigzagged across Tibet and most of China, making a record of the status of wildlife, taking an inventory of species and their populations, analyzing what can be saved and how.

Schaller is adamant that natural habitats must be saved, which cannot be done if people build roads and invade fragile landscapes with economic ventures. "Conservationists love the term 'sustainable development,' " Schaller says, "which is utter nonsense. It cannot function in, say, a rain forest. When people move in, the system breaks down. Certain areas should be free of multiple use.

"Animals should not be 'used,' " Schaller says with a tone of bitterness, citing the Chinese approach to pandas: "The Chinese would be happy to put all pandas behind walls. They should not rent pandas to go abroad, including, inappropriately, appearances at the Olympics. Pandas should not be treated like tourists." (See profiles on the Columbus Zoo, San Diego Zoo, and National Zoo for more about pandas.)

Since 1984, Schaller has been working with WCSI on a project to designate the Chang Tang area and the contiguous Xinjiang and Qinghai as reserves totaling 154,000 square miles (three times the size of Greece). The Chang Tang area contains Tibetan wild asses, with herds of up to 200; wild golden yaks, which are becoming rarer as they are hunted for meat by locals, who shoot them from trucks; blue sheep, the diet of snow leopards; Tibetan brown bears, the rarest large animal; 60 species of birds; and a population of about 600 elusive snow leopards, who kill livestock and eat horses, to the displeasure of people.

It is the Tibetan antelope that earns Schaller's greatest attention. He notes that just as the wildebeest in the Serengeti define that ecosystem, the antelope populations define the Chang Tang ecosystem. Chang Tang is unique, and until now its remoteness has been a shield against destruction. However, even the most remote spots of our planet are being explored, invaded, and destroyed by humans. Tibetan antelope wool is being exported illegally to Nepal at $150 per pound (which equates to four animals killed), where it is woven into shawls that sell for as much as $8,000 in Europe and the States. Poaching must be stopped.

On our planet there are 6,931 protected and partially protected areas covering 651,290,000 hectares (1,608,686,300 acres, or

2,513,572 square miles), 4.8 percent of our land areas. In addition, there are 977 marine and coastal protected areas, 283 biosphere reserves (terrestrial and coastal environments), and 503 wetlands. But legal labels are not enough, and policing by rangers and guards may not suffice to ensure the survival of wildlife and habitat in these areas, to say nothing of areas not labeled as protected. We cannot save all wildlife any more than we can save all the people on our increasingly overpopulated planet. Zoos and aquariums can help to conserve species and even a few habitats, but the ultimate responsibility lies with governments and individuals. The work of people like Schaller shows us what has to be done.

Addressing himself to the subject of conservation in general, Schaller feels that all zoos should have a fund-raising arm for conservation and should work with other zoo conservation organizations under an umbrella organization to coordinate activities and set priorities. If anyone can accomplish the task of finding such an umbrella, George Schaller believes it is William Conway, president of NYZS The Wildlife Conservation Society. "One person like Conway is needed to pull it all together, even to bully other zoos. But first, zoos must decide on ethics, on principles, which they have not yet done."

William Conway has always loved animals. Bristol Grade School in Webster Grove, Missouri, was immensely pleased when graduate Bill Conway gave it his butterfly collection. Bill didn't collect only butterflies; scores of beetles, boxes of spiders—including black widows—and galaxies of grasshoppers, all collected locally, became permanent residents of the Conway home. Because of his interest in box turtles, Bill safaried down to the Reptile House at the St. Louis Zoo whenever he could to chat with the keepers, who quickly put him to work. The curator of reptiles, Moody Lentz, became a lasting friend, and when Bill was 14 Lentz took him on a collection trip, a milestone event from which Bill learned fieldcraft.

Bill's love of nature extended to birds. One day the curator of birds at the St. Louis Zoo left, and Bill was asked whether he would look after the collection on a temporary basis, in his "free" time before and after school and on weekends. Bill jumped at the opportunity. He learned how to care for the birds, and became enthralled by ornithology. Eventually, he himself became curator of birds. Bill's horizons widened and his eyes came to rest on the Bronx Zoo: To go there became his objective. One day he received word from New York to come to the Bronx for an interview. It turned out that John Tee-Van, general director of the New York Zoological Society, had trotted off to St. Louis to check up on Bill Conway.

On November 13, 1956, Conway joined the New York Zoological Society as associate curator of ornithology. In 1959 *The New Yorker* reported his capture for the Bronx Zoo of a mossy-throated bellbird in Trinidad, a species that had eluded capture for 142 years. Another important year for Conway was 1960: In that year he met the feathered love of his life, the flamingo. There are six species, of which three are found in South America: the Chilean, James's, and Andean. In 1960, Conway went to Chile with *National Geographic* magazine photographer Bates Little-hales and headed for Laguna Colorada, a lake high in the Andes at 14,800 feet, where they camped for a month. Because of the altitude, the sun was strong and the temperature near freezing. Using considerable ingenuity to overcome the obstacles, Conway returned with 20 James's and two Andean flamingos. Flamingos (particularly James's) became Conway's everlasting favorite species because of their curious and little understood society. Flamingos live as long as vultures—which means as long as elephants. Conway wants to get to know the other three flamingo species better and hopes to understand how they decide where to go and which other flamingos they wish to associate with.

In 1959, Conway became a NYZS associate director; in 1962, a director; and in 1966, general director. He counts three experiences as the most satisfying of his professional life. First, helping to save a piece of nature, as he has done with Punta Tombo,

Argentina, with its thousands of Megellanic penguins, pinnipeds, and other water and land life. Second, working with zoo and aquarium curators as they nurture and breed rare species such as the snow leopard, bird of paradise, and rare turtles. Conway stands out as a zoo director who continues to involve himself with animals, whereas many directors complain that the administrative overload keeps them from animals. (Edward Maruska, director of the St. Louis Zoo, calls Conway the "guru of the zoological world.") Third is Conway's association with people working in the field, particularly George Schaller and David "Jonah" Western, who, he says, have "contributed to my education." Western is a Kenyan ecologist and conservationist, past director of Wildlife Conservation International, and a prime mover in attempts to save the rhino and elephant in Africa.

Conway has clear convictions on the question of where zoos and aquariums go from here. The SSP (which was his brainchild) is not enough; as important as it is, we cannot stop with captive propagation. The next step is to save habitat, and Conway feels that a good start could be made if the AAZPA would provide a forum for a conservation program. Conway doesn't believe we must save all life forms. We pushed smallpox into extinction, he notes, and the Norwegian rat probably doesn't require human intervention to survive. What we must do, Conway states, is "choose those who will be our bedfellows from now on." Zoos should become "conservation parks" that take on the task of representing ecosystems, with a few species from each ecosystem. When I asked him about cost, Conway pointed out that what Omaha paid for its rain forest was worth every penny, because such an exhibit will excite people into action to save habitats. Pushing his point further, he added that while he applauds the work of the American Museum of Natural History, their $60 million Hall of Dinosaurs is not going to save dinosaurs.

🐂 BUFFALO ZOOLOGICAL GARDEN

Delaware Park
Buffalo, New York 14214
(716) 837-3900
Open: 10–5:30; call for winter hours
Best for: Indian rhino; spectacled bears; carnivorous plants

Year opened: 1875
Acres: 23.5
Animal population: 1,377; 212 species
Director: Minot Ortolani

Getting there: From Route 198 (Scajaquada Expressway) take Delaware Avenue exit. Follow signs to Delaware Park and zoo.

Conservation: SSP's include Indian rhino, Andean condor, lowland gorilla, Siberian tiger.

Education: Full-time school for eighth- and ninth-graders; interactive and educational exhibits; "clowning for conservation."

Special attractions: New (opened 1993) waterfowl exhibit; World of Wildlife and Diversity of Life exhibits.

Gift shop: Good variety, including educational items, games, books.

Food: Standard fast food; deli with salads, other healthy stuff.

Buffalo Zoo's master plan has been completed, and education features strongly in all the zoo's activities. The new (1993) World of Wildlife, an interpretative center with interactive exhibits, has four sections: (1) an exhibit of birds, bats, and bugs, with microscopes to look at the bugs; (2) the rain forest, which focuses on biodiversity and conservation, with the message: preserve. It has a walk-through tree for children and tells them what animals can be found in the forest canopy, from bugs to birds; (3) an orientation center to inform visitors about what they will find in the Buffalo Zoo's collections; and (4) a section highlighting plant and animal interconnections, such as how animals depend on certain plants for food and how animals carry seeds away from the plant so it can grow in a different area. The entire World of Wildlife exhibit is strong on graphics, taking as its model the Toledo Zoo.

Another educational innovation of the Buffalo Zoo is a full-time public school at the zoo for the eighth and ninth grade that provides all the regular courses *plus* a zoo science curriculum for up to 240 students. In the eighth grade the focus is on the mammal collection, and in the ninth, on birds and reptiles.

A further innovative teaching approach at the Buffalo Zoo is conservation through clowning, which has been a success since 1990. A docent who is also a clown had the idea that a professional teacher could also be a clown, and through skits get environmental and conservation messages into the minds of small tots. It has worked.

The Diversity of Life exhibit, which opened in 1993, is in a wing of the Lowland Gorilla African Tropical Rain Forest exhibit. It is also heavy on graphics and, featuring invertebrates, includes seven live exhibits of insects and spiders. Here you can also see carnivorous plants.

On the conservation front, the zoo has acquired a white tiger and also a one-horned Indian rhino, of which there are only 44 in the United States. The zoo also strongly supports the SSP program.

🐾 BURNET PARK ZOO

500 Burnet Park Drive
Syracuse, New York 13204
(315) 435-8511

Open: 10–4

Best for: Sloths; mountain goats; meerkats

Year opened: 1912

Acres: 60

Animal population: 997; 226 species

Director: Anne Baker

Membership: Friends of the Burnet Park Zoo
(315) 422-1223

Getting there: From Route 690 take exit 10, then follow signs to Burnet Park and zoo.

Conservation: SSP's: red wolf, Asian elephant, Asian lion, clouded leopard, white-handed gibbon, snow leopard.

Education: Tours for schoolchildren. Zoo is leaning toward public education of conservation.

Special attractions: Tracing 600 million years of evolution.

Gift shop: Small, with a good mix.

Food: Burger King.

The Burnet Park Zoo is well designed, clean and neat. The central entrance plaza has a fountain, some waterfowl, and a very attractive Japanese macaque exhibit that includes Japanese stone art (though jumping opportunities for the monkeys are restricted).

As you enter the zoo, on your left is a mock cave containing exhibits that trace evolution over the past 600 million years. The exhibit Vertebrates Leaving the Sea 375 Million Years Ago gets an A, and school tours are brought to this exhibit for briefings. In the summer a related five-week course, "Ancient Life in New York State," is offered; it features the geology and botany of the region as well as digging for fossils, teaching what existed hundreds of thousands, even millions, of years ago right "here."

An indoor exhibit on social animals includes meerkats, a type of small mongoose, on sand and pebble ground, with a debris scene of wheels, tree trunks, and a bamboo house for whoever lurks inside. Also on exhibit are ruffed lemurs, mandrills, hyacinth macaws, tamarins in a daylight exhibit, gibbons swinging on ropes, ringtail lemurs viewed from both in and out of doors, and vervet monkeys. (The latter are rascals. When I had breakfast at the Samburu Lodge Park, in northern Kenya, the vervets would perch high on branches of trees along the riverbank, waiting for an opportunity to swing down, jump, bounce, pounce and grab at the sugar bowl, upsetting it as they took a fistful— sometimes simply making off with the entire sugar bowl.)

While each exhibit in the social animal complex has merit, the tie-in among the exhibits could be stronger. There are plans to re-do the building using the theme of island biodiversity. A visit to the zoo will be pulled together thematically by graphics emphasizing conservation.

Top compliments to Syracuse for grouping exhibits of endangered or threatened species in spacious, attractive outdoor exhibits: the grizzly bear with a waterfall and "streams"; bald eagles in a high cage on high ground with sky as background; red wolf, extinct in the wild since the 1980's; and mountain lion and pronghorn antelope. (Once there were 40 million pronghorn antelopes in North America, but they were reduced to 30,000 in the 1920's; now the number is up to 500,000.) The zoo wants to make some changes. The puma has already been moved out of its exhibit, replaced by a snow leopard. The grizzly bear, grown arthritic, will be replaced by a spectacled bear; the bald eagle will move out to make room for an Andean condor and a sign will tell the story of saving the California condor. The whole area will be called Wild North America.

Burnet Park Zoo works closely with the Ralston Purina Company. (Indirectly, Ralston Purina provides funding for grants through an AAZPA conservation program). With the company Burnet has developed a program called, "Big Cat, Little Cat," which focuses on the similarities and differences between pet cats and "big" cats.

✦ CENTRAL PARK ZOO (WILDLIFE CONSERVATION CENTER—CENTRAL PARK*)

Fifth Avenue and 64th Street
New York, New York 10022
(212) 439-6500

Open: 10–5

Best for: Penguins; polar bears; tamarins; snow monkeys

Year opened: 1864

Acres: 5.5

Animal population: 662; 96 species

Director: Richard Lattis

Membership: NYZS The Wildlife Conservation Society (718) 220-5100

Getting there: On foot: A short walk from midtown up Fifth Avenue to entrance at 64th Street. By bus: Fifth Avenue or Madison Avenue bus.

*See note under Bronx Zoo profile.

Conservation: Wildlife Conservation Society International (WCSI) of NYZS The Wildlife Conservation Society has information on conservation programs and a changing exhibit at the Central Park Zoo.

Special attractions: Seal and penguin feeding (check schedule).

Gift shop: Small, with some good specialized items related to the Central Park Zoo; books, jewelry.

Food: Attractive outdoor setting, but poor food; stick to snacks.

The cacophony of city traffic is muffled and left behind when you turn off Fifth Avenue and enter the Central Park Zoo. From potholed, trash-littered streets you make a magic transition into the exciting world of exotic species. If you stand at the zoo's highest elevation, next to the otter exhibit, you see an incongruous background panorama of city buildings while you watch snow monkeys cavorting on their rock island.

I grew up in New York City, and that is where I first came into contact with wildlife. On special outings into Central Park I was taken to the zoo. We walked past cages of large animals hunched up in the shadow of their small space. The monkey house had a strong smell that made me swallow hard. It also left me with my deepest impression of the zoo. I still think of it when I visit some zoos. The memory comes back of those screeching little primates jumping from a straight bar perch onto the cement floor. It was an unhappy zoo, and became a much more unhappy zoo before the situation changed. But it was the only place in central New York where people could see "wild" animals.

Ultimately the Central Park Zoo has become a superb central-city zoo as a result of Mayor Koch's good judgment in asking the New York Zoological Society to take over its management from the city in 1980. It reopened in 1988.

The zoo has been redesigned as essentially an all-weather zoo, allowing visitors to move from one exhibit to another under cover. Large animals such as elephants are no longer to be seen at the zoo. Today it is divided into three contiguous zones, temperate, arctic, and tropic. The Tropic Zone Building takes you into a rain forest. You are in the home of the purple honey creeper, which flies past you along with dozens of other species of birds. You spot a newly born snow-white colobus monkey being tugged from an "aunt" by the mother atop a hollowed tree in an exhibit of 10 colobuses who romp or sit on rock ledges. Along the wall in a darkened area is a leaf-cutter ant exhibit, where you can see the workers tote a bigger-than-ant-size chunk of leaf uphill, then down into their tunnels. On the wall next to the exhibit are three color monitors that show in magnification what miniature cameras in the ant exhibit are photographing. Beyond the ants is the bat-cave exhibit, shaped to give the dramatic feeling that the observer is *in* a cave. Exiting from the bat cave, you climb wooden steps and catch a glimpse of the miniature forest's canopy, then enter a multiexhibit area of small jumping and wiggling things such as frogs and snakes.

The Arctic Zone is home to polar bears, penguins, a snowy owl, seals, and puffins. Polar bears are always popular at zoos. Though they don't smile like hippos, are not as big as elephants, and lack the prehistoric look of rhinos, they are graceful for their weight, playful, and at times resourceful.

At many zoos, the polar bear is one of the top attractions. The most effective polar bear exhibits have viewing opportunities from two levels: slightly higher than water level, and underwater. At many zoos, underwater viewing is from an underground passage below the tank, with a glass window, but frequently the tank is cloudy and the polar bear difficult to see. Generally, the outside area of the exhibit contains rocks for the bears to climb on and a flat terrace to lumber back and forth on, but not much more. Polar bears at the Central Park Zoo may be viewed from three levels in their domain of artificial rock, which breaks up the straight lines of the pool and allows the bears to find an edge for their paw as they turn in their swim. The polar bears frequently strike the underwater viewing windows with a thud, then rise to play together with a large plastic ball.

In the Central Park Zoo you will find the most outstanding central-city penguin exhibit in the United States, if not the world. The semicircular exhibit, which gives the illusion on entry that the scene of Gentoo and Chinstrap penguins continues forever, provides excellent viewing—particularly for children—of penguins as they dive, soar up through the water, and hop onto land, or move across the rocks gathering large stones in their beaks to make a nest. Breeding has been successful, with three hatchings in 1992, and three in 1993.

The Temperate Zone, between the Arctic and Tropic zone buildings, houses the exhibit of the snow monkey on an island, with swans gliding in the surrounding water. There is also an outdoor exhibit of two red pandas (whose habitat ranges from Nepal to the Chinese provinces of Yunnan and Szechwan); they might be seen climbing trees, but they spend most of their time maneuvering through the grass and around logs and a bit of water they share with ducks. (In 1992, 28 SSP institutions had red pandas on exhibit.)

The centerpiece of the zoo is the sea lions as they glide through the water around their rock island, very visible through glass. A sea lion exhibit was at the same spot before the zoo was renovated, but the new exhibit bears little resemblance to the smaller, less friendly old one.

Richard Lattis never thought of working at a zoo, but today he is running three as director of the city zoos of New York: the Wildlife Conservation Centers at Central Park, Prospect Park in Brooklyn, and in Queens, all of which are divisions of the New York Zoological Society. Lattis always loved frogs. As children, he and his friends would gather tadpoles, bring them home, and watch them turn into frogs. As a graduate student in biology, Lattis upgraded his passion from frogs to fish, but ultimately he switched to reptiles. Lattis's first zoo job was as assistant curator of education at the Bronx Zoo.

Lattis places great emphasis on Wildlife Conservation Society International's Wildlife Conservation Room at the zoo. In 1992, an exhibit was mounted on the crocodile skin trade. In 1991 2 million skins were imported into the United States, 1½ million of them illegally. As a result of the exhibit, CNN did a story on the issue and visited a New York City department store that was selling illegal skins. Lattis feels that this type of exposure of wildlife conservation issues involves the public and creates an awareness of the big picture, not simply the life of animals in captivity. Lattis is now looking at the possibility of an exhibit on the bird trade. (In 1991, 3½ to 5 million birds were sold in international commercial trade.)

Lattis believes signs can play an important role in getting the conservation message to the public. Overhead signs are less often read than those placed where the public can easily see them, and there should be an educational message in signs. Regarding exhibits, Lattis notes that the past emphasis on species is changing to one on habitat. Thus, through creative exhibit design, a small space becomes a large space. Videos are a strong zoo tool to entertain and educate the public on what a zoo does, and a video can provide messages and images that focus attention on issues.

The Wildlife Conservation Center–Central Park gave me an opportunity to do a video on what happens backstage at the zoo. My Central Park Zoo video is an audio-visual presentation on how food is prepared for all the animals in the zoo's kitchen. (Crickets are purchased from Fluker's in Louisiana by the zoo for their birds, golden lion tamarins, and lizards, and as snacks for monkeys.) The video also shows the construction, maintenance, repair, and improvement of exhibits; the professional TLC of horticulturist Nancy Tim; the back of the ant exhibit and how the exhibit works; the development of ideas in the graphics department; and feeding birds in the Tropic Zone exhibit before the zoo opens to the public each morning. The video is played periodically in the Wildlife Conservation Room at the zoo.

A number of zoos sell videotapes in their gift shops promoting their zoo, but while such a video may be a moderate money-maker as a souvenir, it is rarely designed to be educational. I would encourage all zoos to prepare educational videos for use in various facets of zoo education.

Teachers interested in incorporating zoo materials into their lessons should contact the zoo's education department (renamed the communications department) for education information available at the zoo in Central Park as well as educational material used by the zoo that it receives from the Bronx Zoo (International Wildlife Conservation Park).

Long before Mayor Koch asked the New York Zoological Society to take over the Central Park Zoo, my mother had an extraordinary experience. One mid-morning her cook, Ina, raced into her bedroom and announced that a big bird was on the railing outside the dining room window. My mother, doubtful but curious, followed Ina to the window. There, sixteen floors above the traffic of Park Avenue, was perched the largest hornbill the pigeons of New York had ever seen. Rushing to the telephone, my mother called the Bronx Zoo and reported her aviary sighting. The Bronx Zoo was well informed. The big bird had cleverly escaped from the Central Park Zoo. My mother commented that it was obviously a very unhappy bird and that it should not have to go back to the zoo in Central Park. The bird obviously knew how to get action. What the bird obviously needed was a transfer to the Bronx Zoo, and this is what it got.

➤ NEW YORK AQUARIUM (THE AQUARIUM FOR WILDLIFE CONSERVATION*)

Boardwalk and West Eighth Street
Brooklyn, New York 11224
(718) 265-3400

Open: 10–5:45; call for winter hours

Best for: Whales; walruses; penguins; sharks

Year opened: 1896

Acres: 14

Animal population: 8,331; 464 species

Director: Louis Garibaldi

Membership: New York Zoological Society
(718) 220-5100

Getting there: By subway: Take F or D train to West Eighth Street/ Aquarium stop in Brooklyn..

*See note under Bronx Zoo profile.

Conservation: Osborn Laboratory oversees conservation programs such as captive breeding for endangered fish of Mexico (dwarf pupfish, Monterey platy, golden sawfish) and breeding of cichlids from Lake Victoria in East Africa. The Pew and Packard foundations are leading an investigation regarding aquariums' efforts and programs on conservation education, which they have noted is "not that good." Seventeen aquariums were contacted in 1993, five of which were visited. They found only one—the New York Aquarium—that had a worthwhile conservation program.

Education: Keeper training. For programs for the public, call (718) 265-3448.

Special attractions: Sea Cliffs; Pharmaceuticals from the Sea; Discovery Cove; shark tank.

Gift shop: Good values.

Food: Good restaurant and snack bar.

The New York Aquarium has eye-catching, imaginative exhibits. In Discovery Cove, two waves, one long one and another breaking overhead, convey the movement and strength of the sea. Child-level glass viewing spaces protrude into exhibits, and there are waist-level tanks one can look down into, bubble tanks, and a video monitor below water level on the rear wall of the exhibit. The Bermuda Triangle exhibit contains creatures including the silvery tarpon, groupers, moray eels, and huge sea turtles.

The aquarium has focused on the marine environment of New York (as the New England Aquarium has emphasized the importance of the Charles River and the Boston Harbor), and in 1991 the Hudson River exhibit opened with five riverine habitats and a panoramic map devoted to the river.

Also in 1991 a Desert Spring exhibit opened with rare Mexican desert fish, a participant in a breeding program of endangered species. If you are fond of leeches (nostalgic memories of Hepburn, Bogart, and *The African Queen?*), then you should head for the Pharmaceuticals from the Sea exhibit (leeches are used in plastic surgery and limb reattachment). Also to be found at the exhibit are horseshoe crabs; it has been discovered that their blood can be used in testing and detecting whether there are any bacterial contaminants in food, cosmetics, and a number of other products.

When the 100-yard-long Sea Cliffs exhibit opened on April 22, 1993, it increased the number of exhibits at the aquarium by one third. The exhibit area is a complex of coastal habitats for walruses, northern fur seals (from the Seattle and Mystic aquariums), harbor seals, California sea otters (from the Monterey Aquarium), and black-footed penguins, with both above- and below-water viewing, accompanied by exhibits on ecology, conservation, and associated species. The California sea otter has not previously been on public display outside of California.

ROSS PARK ZOO

185 Park Avenue
(60 Morgan Road)
Binghamton, New York 13903
(607) 724-5461

Open: 10–5; call for winter hours

Best for: Red wolf; burrowing owl

Year opened: 1875

Acres: 90

Animal population: 151; 59 species

Director: Steven Contento

Getting there: From Route 17/81 take Exit 73 onto Route 363 south. Take Vestal Street west and turn left at first stoplight onto South Washington. Go past next light and turn left at stop sign to zoo entrance on Morgan Road.

Conservation: SSP participation for red wolf, golden lion tamarin, snow leopard, Siberian tiger, and spectacled bear.

Education: Zoomobile, summer camp.

Special attractions: SSP animals.

Gift shop: Small items, mostly in the rubber snake category.

Food: Light snacks.

The Ross Park Zoo is rightfully proud of its participation in the SSP program and of the five endangered species it has on exhibit at the zoo. The highlight of the zoo is the red wolf exhibit. On a hillside, viewable from above and below, the area is large, natural, and effective, with signs explaining such topics as REPRODUCTION AND FAMILY, STATUS IN THE WILD, COMMUNICATION—SIGNIFI-CANCE OF THE TAIL, HUNTING AND DIET—LOCATING PREY, ENCOUN-TER, ATTACK.

A burrowed owl exhibit deserves praise; the owl is easy to see. The cougar has a new, larger area than previously, but other exhibits are unexceptional, and indeed the zoo in general presents a rather sad aspect, still living in the thirties in its architecture and exhibition design.

Two non-zoo attractions that should be visited are the Carousel Museum, sharing the same 200-car parking lot with the zoo, and the Discovery Center of the Southern Tier, only a stone's throw from the zoo entrance, created for children but splendid for all ages. Especially entertaining are its Giant Market, Fire Station Truck, Airport/cockpit, and Greek Diner. Interesting and amusing.

🐘 SENECA PARK ZOO

2222 St. Paul Street
Rochester, New York 14621
(716) 266-6591

Open: 10–5; weekends/holidays 10–7; call for winter hours

Best for: Elephants; snow leopards; snakes

Year opened: 1894

Acres: 14

Animal population: 367; 133 species

Director: Daniel Michalowski

Membership: Seneca Zoological Society, (716) 342-2744

Getting there: About 20 minutes by car or taxi from downtown.

Education: Touch exhibits of animal bones, skulls, fangs, skeletons, feathers, skins, quills, shed fur, etc. Zoomobile.

Gift shop: New in 1992. Souvenirs.

Food: Food stand with snacks and cotton candy.

Zoo director Daniel Michalowski deserves a medal for his dedication, tenacity, and loyalty to the zoo for the past 30 years. During this period, five plans to upgrade the zoo were prepared and submitted to Monroe County, but none came to fruition. The zoo was so poor and attendance so low that it could not afford a cashier in the winter, so admission was free.

By 1992 the situation had changed. A six-phase plan for a new zoo was drawn up by zoo designer Jon Coe, and Phase I was completed in 1993. The primates already have an excellent new exhibit. Two orangutans from Borneo have space to climb, with cargo nets, ropes, and hemp and wire "walls" that give (as a tree branch would) when landed on. The white-handed gibbon, black-handed spider monkey, and ring-tailed lemur appear to be enjoying themselves. A Discovery Building will be built with interactive exhibits and an underwater river basin theme exhibit of the otter. A naturalistic exhibit will house four local species: bald eagle, porcupine, beaver, and some waterfowl. Michalowski would like to reintroduce into the outskirts of the local community endangered Eastern massasauga rattlesnakes, threatened timber rattlesnakes and Northern copperheads, but current New York State law forbids this. He asks the public not to harm those surviving in the wild, even if they turn up in the backyard.

The zoo is proud of an African elephant exhibit (for two females) built by zoo personnel without outside contractors. Unfortunately, though, the elephants will probably have to go, because by 1996 all zoos with elephants will be required to have a hydraulic system for handling them, and the system is very expensive—too expensive for Seneca, just rising from antiquated structures to become a smart little zoo.

Another notable achievement is the birth in the zoo of 23 baby snow leopards.

A word about Jon Coe, zoo designer who seems to be everywhere, undertaking relatively small zoo expansions such as

Seneca's and huge ones. His work has a characteristic style and imagination, stressing the "enrichment" of animals' zoo environments to improve their quality of life. "By putting animals in a zoo," Coe says, "we have taken choice away from [them]. We should give animals things to move. We think that we are better than the animals and therefore give them what we think they should have, not necessarily what they need. Giving the animals choice of light, temperature, and food reduces stress on them. We must determine how animals can exercise choice in a zoo environment."

Some examples of Coe's ideas on this theme of choice and enrichment: At the Toledo Zoo, a ball on lures at ceiling height gives giraffes something to play with. At Brookfield Zoo rhinos have suspended logs at which to charge. At Zoo Atlanta, the angle of the sun was taken into consideration prior to construction so that when the sun strikes selected spots on gunnite "rocks," they become a place for the lions to bask in the sun. At the San Diego Wild Animal Park cheetahs have a plastic lure that can be readjusted for different routings. The lure is modeled after ones used with greyhounds and gives the animals something to chase so they get exercise.

🐦 STATEN ISLAND ZOO

614 Broadway
Staten Island, New York 10310
(718) 442-3101
Open: 10–5; weekends/holidays
10–7; call for winter hours
Best for: Snakes

Year opened: 1936
Acres: 8
Animal population: 422;
1196 species
Director: Vincent Gattullo

Getting there: By car: From the Staten Island Expressway (Route 278), turn north onto Clove Road, which leads into Broadway. By subway/bus: Take the R train to 95th Street, Brooklyn, then take the S-53 bus from 95th Street and Fourth Avenue (near the subway) to the Clove Road entrance to zoo.

Conservation: SSP participation for Aruba rattlesnake.

Education: Billed as the first (1936) education zoo in the U.S. "Traveling zoo" goes to schools. For further information, call (718) 442-3174.

Special attractions: Rain Forest exhibit; children's center; African Savannah.

Gift shop: "Zoovenir" shop.

Food: Snacks.

The Staten Island Zoo is a ferry ride away from downtown Manhattan or a drive across the Verrazano Narrows, Bayonne, or Goethals bridges. The director of this small but educationally focused zoo is Vincent Gattullo, who teaches a course in cellular biology at the City University. According to Gattullo, the only consultants for the construction in 1960 of the children's center were children: 6,000 kids were asked what *they* would like if they could build their own zoo. Some of the answers were a covered bridge, chickens, cows, deer, and llamas. That's what they got. For the area available, the result is admirable—although the bridge is undistinguished.

The zoo has given attention to landscaping. Jim Rives is the zoo's horticulturalist, and he also helps members plan their own gardens. He has created a life-sized topiary version of Jalopy, a Galápagos tortoise, which rises from a flower bed. Jalopy was given to the Staten Island Zoo in 1933 by Vincent Astor on his return from a trip to the Galápagos aboard his yacht the *Nourmahal,* accompanied by zoologists from the New York Zoological Society. Jalopy died in 1983, but he is still at the zoo and can be found, stuffed, in the center of the serpentarium.

The South American Tropical Rainforest exhibit, designed by zoo architect Jon Coe, (see Seneca Park Zoo [New York] profile), opened in May 1991. It demonstrates that a rain forest exhibit need not be acres large to provide a sense of the rain forest: Staten Island's miniature rain forest does a superb job of portraying aspects of the rain forest. In one exhibit the visitor is put *under* a rain-forest canopy at the roots of a tree trunk that seems to rise to a canopy far above. Artificial vines and real greenery complete the scene. There are motmots, spider monkeys, a dramatically and effectively designed bat cave, an ant exhibit, and a tarantula. Other zoos that want to create a compact, effective rain-forest exhibit should trek to Staten Island for a serious look.

The zoo is putting the finishing touches on its new African Savannah exhibit, which replaces the old Mammal Wing. Leopards, baboons, hyraxes, and naked mole rats (now at zoos in Cincinnati, Philadelphia, San Francisco, and in the Bronx) will be in residence.

⟟ UTICA ZOO

Steele Hill Road
Utica, New York 13501
(315) 738-0472
Open: 10–5
Best for: Mouflons; fallow deer; yaks

Year opened: 1914
Acres: 80
Animal population: 223; 82 species
Director: Mark Rich

Getting there: From Route 790/5, exit at Faxton Children's Hospital onto Memorial Parkway. Pass through three traffic lights; the fourth is blinking yellow. You are there.

Conservation: SSP for ruffed lemur, golden lion tamarin, red panda.

Education: Attractions for children include a play area.

Special attractions: Boardwalk viewing platform with deer below.

Gift shop: Small; caters to young children.

Food: Snack bar (seasonal).

The best exhibit in this sad but strong-spirited zoo is the boardwalk viewing platform on a hill that overlooks fallow deer in a zoo exhibit below. Mouflons and domestic yaks roam on the hillside dotted with trees and interrupted by a ravine, and in the distance is a panorama of Utica.

A duck pond is well populated by animals and has good signs.

The zoo has a sole camel, a Grevy's zebra, two tigers, and a reptile house with five green iguanas in an exhibit along with peach-faced lovebirds. The 1920 primate house is very sad indeed. There are tiled floors and walls, some swings and ropes, but the space and facilities are very limited; there is barred space for the primates. Ruffed lemurs appear to long for their home in Madagascar.

The children's zoo is billed as a highlight. It has a small collection of goats, a guinea pig, a pygmy goat, two emus in a barn, roaming peacocks, two sea lions in a kidney-shaped tub of a pool, two swans, and a raccoon. The signs are good but corny.

¶ NORTH CAROLINA ZOOLOGICAL PARK

4401 Zoo Parkway
Asheboro, North Carolina
27203
(919) 879-7000

Open: 9–5; weekends/holidays 10–6; call for summer and winter hours

Best for: Birds; elephants; primates

Year opened: 1974

Acres: 1,448

Animal population: 814; 140 species

Director: David Jones

Membership: North Carolina Zoological Society
(919) 879-7250

Getting there: Located six miles southeast of Asheboro on Route 159.

Conservation: SSP participation (first coordinator for chimps). Reintroduced the Bali mynah to Indonesia. Breeding gerenuk and dik-dik.

Education: Excellent brochures on various animals in the zoo, especially gorillas, chimps, birds, rhinos, and plants; also on special services for the handicapped or elderly. Call before coming (919) 879-5606.

Special attractions: Ultimately, each continent will be presented on a grand scale.

Gift shop: Excellent.

Food: Lunch and refreshment stands.

North Carolina's zoo is big and can plan on a grand scale; ultimately, each continent will be represented in its own extensive area—a new continent every five to seven years. First was Africa, with a total of 300 acres, completed in 1991. (North America, 200 acres, is well under way with completion expected by the mid-nineties. Asia, Europe, South America, Australia, and the World of the Seas will follow.) As you exit the 53,500-square-foot, fiberglass-roofed African Pavilion (with 3,300 plants and 200 animals), a 40-acre plain opens before you, populated by 120 animals, including elephants, ostriches, bushbucks and impalas—with no man-made structures in sight. The elephants have 3.5 acres of space, which is grass, not concrete. Except for the fact that the vegetation isn't quite right, the plains could be Africa.

Gorillas are found in the Forest Glade, which was opened on August 24, 1989. The 16,200-square-foot exhibit (about the size of one floor of a large office building) includes a 1,850-square-foot holding facility and cost $375,000. An artificial rock boundary creates two visitor overlooks. A stream tumbles over artificial rock into a six-inch-deep collecting pool. The habitat's unique features include areas planted with vegetables to enable the gorillas to forage among cucumbers, watermelons, radishes, green beans, collards, and corn. Forest Glade's flora includes 2,200 plants representing 98 species, including lespedeza, Jerusalem artichoke, bamboo, and bulrush, and trees such as black willow, oak, and maple. The exhibit's males are Kwanza, Carlos, Ramar, and Joe Willy, and the female is Hope. The exhibit is simple and effective, though without the embroidery of West African habitat. It is quite obviously North Carolina. What has been done is to provide a relatively large, safe, landscaped area for the gorillas where they can easily be seen by people. A second gorilla exhibit is being built, and the first will be kept for breeding purposes. The zoo has produced a particularly informative, envelope-sized, fold-out brochure on gorillas called *The Gentle Giant*, with sketches and maps, which provides information and drawings on "their homelands, their faces, their place, their defenses, their nature, their families, and their future."

The R. J. Reynolds Forest Aviary is lush with tropical vegetation. The visitor walks along a winding path to sight, among the more than 50 tropical bird species, the regal paradise whydah, crested barbet, Brazilian cardinal, and lilac-breast roller, which I saw in great abundance along the shores of Lake Naivasha in Kenya.

The zoo is proud of its chimpanzee breeding program and one-half-acre exhibit, which former director Robert Fry claimed to be "one of the best in the world." An artificial termite mound has hidden fruits for a hunt-and-find game to relieve boredom and give the chimps exercise. The chimps are easy to see, though the best viewing that may present a face-to-face encounter is through glass. Although the zoo is against encouraging the creation of animal celebrities, North Carolina's Ham became a celebrity when he was the first chimpanzee in the space program. Ham may have dreamed of life in the wild from his zoo confinement, and must have been surprised when he went into orbit! Ham died on terra firma at the zoo in 1984 of a natural cause—old age.

The North Carolina Zoological Park works with the SSP captive propagation efforts to breed animals not normally bred in captivity, concentrating on the gerenuk (an unusual antelope that stands on its hind legs to reach juicy green leaves on a tree) and dik-dik (a miniature deerlike antelope). Here they take the view that every gerenuk (one of the 21 species of antelope found in Ethiopia, Somalia, and Kenya) born should be raised by its mother, a position opposite to that of former director Warren Thomas of the Los Angeles Zoo, who believes that the newborn must be hand raised by humans, isolated from the mother for five to six weeks, then returned to her. If left with the mother, they can never be moved; on the other hand, if they are hand-raised by humans, they are "lost"—will not reproduce. North Carolina's position is "hands off, keepers, except for elephants [who need to be scrubbed and exercised], and eventually elephants, too."

The zoo director also sees the need to "go back to the basics" on exhibits intended for children by featuring domestic species such as chickens and cows.

The North Carolina Zoological Park is a perfect example of a harmonious zoo-government relationship. The first animals to arrive at the zoo, in 1973, were two Galápagos tortoise; since then, there has been great progress in planning and supportive funding from the state. The zoo is a program of the North Carolina Department of Natural Resources and Community Development. Fifty percent of the zoo's budget comes from government; the other half is from revenues.

rʎ AFRICAN SAFARI WILDLIFE PARK

Port Clinton, Ohio 43452
(419) 732-3606
Open: First weekend in May through Sept.; call for confirmation of schedule

Note: Not an AAZPA-accredited zoo; owned and operated by International Wildlife Management, Inc.

Getting there: From I-80 take Exit 6 north on Route 53 to Port Clinton. Turn west on Route 2, watch for signs (Lightner Road).
Education: Nothing provided, aside from feeding animals, riding a camel or turtle (maybe).
Special attractions: Drive-through safari, feeding animals from the car.
Gift shop: Poor.
Food: None for you, just for the animals.

An increasing number of so-called safari parks are cropping up throughout the United States, representing a commercial approach to providing contact between humans and other animals. I've visited several safari parks. Some are better, some worse, but the experience is always two-edged. Yes, it's fun to feed animals and have them lick or slobber all over your hand. That's *real* contact with the beast. But when I look into the animals' eyes, they're sad. There's no real joy to be found. Not for the animals; probably not for you.

At African Safari Wildlife Park the entry fee of $17.50 for car, driver, and one passenger (subject to change) gets you a white plastic bucket of "food" pellets. An extra dollar will get you an additional one. Get two. The camels are already waiting for you. Open the windows halfway, and don't let the camels get the bucket—they have had more experience with this tom-foolery than you have. But, if you don't put the bucket out, the camels will put their long furry noses into the car, spilling food pellets that you will still be finding under the seat next Christmas.

Gazelles, uninterested zebras, and other hoofed animals are in three fenced-in areas through which your car—along with a likely line of other cars—passes. The animals look bored and dirty. At the park's entrance are two 12-foot-diameter cages, containing a Siberian tiger and a lion who have no room for a walk, and barely room to turn.

A visit to such a nonaccredited AAZPA "safari land" is convincing evidence that this is not the way wild animals should be treated. While the animals may well not be mistreated, neither their environment, nor their confinement, nor their routine can provide them comfort. No trace of an educational element is discernable. Such is the case at Port Clinton and at most (although not all) "safari parks." They are zoos of a kind but their sole purpose is commercial.

🐾 AKRON ZOOLOGICAL PARK

500 Edgewood Avenue
Akron, Ohio 44307
(216) 375-2550

Open: 10–5; closed Jan. to mid-April

Best for: Squirrel monkeys; river otters

Year opened: 1950

Acres: 24.7

Animal population: 238; 93 species

Director: L. Patricia Simmons

Getting there: From Route 59, exit at Wooster Avenue.

Conservation: Director stresses recycling: benches and park tables from recycled materials; containers for soda cans.

Special attractions: Aviary.

Gift shop: Very modest.

Food: Snacks.

The Akron Zoo is a small, private, not-for-profit zoo with dedicated leadership and staff, operating on an annual budget of $700,000 (about the same as Ross Park Zoo in Binghamton, New York). Director L. Patricia Simmons says the zoo exists because people want a zoo to exist. "They want a fun experience such as a symphony, ballet, or art museum provides." This does not mean that zoo visitors go to the Akron zoo expecting only to be entertained. The zoo also educates. The other two AAZPA objectives for all zoos (in addition to entertainment and education) are scientific research and conservation, which receive as much time as the small Akron Zoo can manage. Simmons, who gained her first interest in wildlife at her grandfather's trout hatchery, believes that the latter two aims may be accomplished as a result of the first two.

"Who is the customer of the zoo?" she asks. Most, she answers, are four-year-olds; when parents are asked what they liked about the zoo, they turn to their small child and ask the child. "Therefore," Simmons concludes, "a zoo must develop programs that appeal to four-year-olds." A live presentation is given to all school groups visiting the zoo. Simmons wants the zoo to be a "window to the world" for its visitors, who will see and be told of the history in the wild of animals such as ruffed lemurs and red pandas. The zoo has staff members placed as interpreters throughout the zoo; there are zoo talks throughout the day, which are announced over the loudspeaker.

The zoo's shaded aviary, through which one walks on a boardwalk promontory, is small but effective and includes a minuscule pond and an alert roadrunner. Simmons's favorite exhibit, river otters (she has always had a passion for the active, entertaining little creatures), is also the newest. Her zoo is associated with a program to reintroduce river otters into Ohio's rivers. The squirrel monkey exhibit at the entrance is a most effective hello or good-bye on entering or exiting the zoo. The cage is attractively constructed and offers a good opportunity to see the monkeys, who are usually quite active.

🐘 CINCINNATI ZOO AND BOTANICAL GARDEN

3400 Vine Street
Cincinnati, Ohio 45220
(513) 281-4700
Open: 9–6; call for winter hours

Best for: Sumatran rhinos; Komodo monitors; okapis

Year opened: 1875
Acres: 67
Animal population: 11,613 (including 9,100 invertebrates); 715 species

Director: Edward Maruska

Getting there: From I-71 take 562 (Exit 7) to I-75 south. From I-74 take I-75 north. From I-75 take exit 6 (Mitchell); travel east on Mitchell. Right on Vine to Forest (.9 miles). Left on Forest to Dury. Right on Dury and you are at the zoo's main gate.

Conservation: Participation in more than 30 SSP's including black rhino (for which the zoo holds the record in number of births), lowland gorilla, Asian elephant, Arabian oryx, Micronesian kingfisher, red panda, Puerto Rican crested toad (in 1991 a number were released into Puerto Rico), and Sumatran rhino.

Education: Pioneer in zoo education; emphasis on environmental literacy; 150,000 children visit the zoo annually.

Special attractions: Insect World; Butterfly Aviary; Gorilla World; World of Birds; Jungle Trails. Zoo's flora: 1,400 species of trees, shrubs, tropical bulbs, perennials, annuals.

Gift shop: Good selection.

Food: Quick and ready. Safari Restaurant. Picnic area.

Most people don't appreciate insects. If an ant's path crosses your path, the toe of your shoe stamps it out and you give it no thought. But did you know that about 10,000 ant species each have 10^{15} living individuals in any moment of time (according to ant expert E. O. Wilson, *Biodiversity*, National Academy Press, 1988)? Or that there are nearly one million species of insects, with

90,000 species in the United States alone? Today, insects are receiving increased attention by zoos and gaining the admiration of an amazed public. Zoos in Washington, D.C., Indianapolis, San Francisco, and New York City (Central Park Zoo) have good insect exhibits, but the Cincinnati Zoo's Insect World is by far the best presentation in the United States.

Presenting an understandable visual and narrative explanation of insects is a formidable task for entomologists (those who study insects and other arthropods). The Insect World exhibit succeeds, however, asking and answering questions in multicolored dramatic and effective graphics. What is an insect? Graphics trace the evolution of insects. The exhibit "Success of the Insect" details ecological specialization, locomotion, and reproduction. "What Insects Eat" provides the not-so-simple answer: roots, shoots of plants, fruit, flesh, flowers, feathers, fungi, buds, blood, hair, bark, sap, leaves, seeds, carrion, nectar, wood, dung, other insects. "How Insects Feed" illustrates chewing, piercing and sucking, sponging, siphoning. "Defense and Escape" shows insects' weaponry: camouflage and mimicry. "Insects in Motion" shows them jumping, crawling, flying, swinging. "Insect Lifestyles" singles out the solitary insect (e.g., Amazonian stinkbug), the gregarious (tropical walkingstick), and the social (termites, ants).

I was determined to find out more about Insect World, so I contacted Milan Busching, the curator in charge of this vast population of creepy-crawlies. Busching told me that he had been in love with insects since the age of seven, when he lived with his parents on a farm in Iowa. He would put insects in his pocket on his way home from school. Soon he also became interested in butterflies.

Busching is intense on the subject of insects. He notes with restrained ferocity that they are the foundation that the rest of life depends on, the building blocks of life. He refers to Edward Ross, the noted entomologist, who once said, "If all humans disappeared, the earth would return to the equilibrium it once had. If insects were to disappear, immediately all other forms of life would be disrupted."

Of Insect World's 70 exhibits, a magnifying glass that slides over an exhibit and a pull tray are favorites of children. Busching himself designed the leaf-cutter ant exhibit as well as the exhibit for the honeybee and naked mole rat. His fondness for butterflies has continued throughout his life; Insect World's live butterfly exhibit was the first in the United States. On expeditions to collect butterflies, they had to be placed in envelopes until they got "home," but they would die if contained in an envelope for more than five to seven days. Also, they had to be taken out daily and fed sugared water with an eyedropper. Busching told me of the process with the maternal enthusiasm of a Scottish nanny. "Then I would have to dip their feet in water and dry them," he whispered. "This all took time, besides care." Busching, who is an expert at butterfly feeding, clocks it at two minutes per butterfly. Mealtime usually takes 2½ hours.

In 1989, when New York City's Central Park Zoo's leaf-cutter queen ant died (and was given a decent burial), they called Milan Busching. "We need a new queen ant; in fact, we'd like three of them, two as backups," they said. "And we need them now." The ant exhibit at the Central Park Zoo is one of the big attention-getters, and without a queen ant action came to a standstill. Busching dropped other insect priorities and jumped onto a plane for Port of Spain, Trinidad, and then proceeded to a remote area on the northern part of the island by car. There he found a leaf-cutter queen's colony. He didn't go after *the* queen, but instead, the younger queens. Eventually he found 14 queens, three for Central Park and 11 for Cincinnati. "In one colony the queen was sitting there and the workers weren't working. They were crushing her." This was a tragedy that had to be righted. Down on his knees, Busching nursed the workers back to good health by providing moist soil to improve the fungus garden on which they feed, and by cutting twig leaves into squares for the worker ants until they were able to do it themselves.

Several months after my delightful evening with Milan Busching, I lunched in New York City with Professor E. O. Wilson of the Museum of Comparative Zoology at Harvard University, environmentalist (an authority on biodiversity) and entomologist

(coauthor, with Bert Holldobler, of the Pulitzer Prize–winning
The Ants). Professor Wilson stated his belief that "zoos must be
like great literature: They must open the minds of people to the
diversity of life." Furthermore, zoos should bring to the public
an understanding of the microwilderness. Technology can "mag-
nify a whole new world of miniature lions and tigers; . . . these
are the creatures that sustain our world." I couldn't resist asking
Professor Wilson about edible insects. He looked a little hurt.
"Insects need to defend themselves and don't have claws or teeth,
so their defenses must be different. Many are poisonous. However," he added, smiling again, "the queen leaf-cutting ant is
really quite good, as she has a lot of fat." A friend had sent him
a jar filled with queens as a present. "There is one problem," the
professor admitted, putting the tips of his fingers to his mouth
and pulling on an imaginary leg, "they get stuck between your
teeth."

If you accept that space is unimportant, that cats don't need to
exercise, then Cincinnati Zoo's cat house is good. It is designed
with dramatic exhibits of rock and wall-painted scenery, with
unusual angles for viewing. The cat house was opened in 1952 and
was renovated in 1985. It contains 16 different cat species, including rusty spotted, pallas, pampas, and serval cats, and the
clouded leopard. It is good but could be better. Currently the
exhibits provide entertainment, but little education. I stood for
10 minutes watching the crowd go by. A parent would say to a
child, "See him?" The child looked and was excited, but unin-
formed. The signs are neither dramatic nor easily visible in a
badly lit space to the side of the exhibits. In fact, I don't think
a single person glanced at the signage.

Cincinnati has a simple gorilla exhibit located outside in a good
hillside area. Still saddened by the loss of King Tut, who today
may be found, stuffed, at the Los Angeles County Museum, the
zoo plans a new $5.5 million primate exhibit focusing on the use
of the thumb.

Cincinnati Zoo's red panda has been given a beautifully land-
scaped natural habitat with unusual Chinese plant species. One of
the zoo's newest exhibits is Jungle Trails, which includes the first

public exhibit of an aye-aye, a highly endangered species of nocturnal lemur found wild only in Madagascar. By 1991 the zoo had bred 37 gorillas, 200 tigers, 27 species of cats, and 15 black rhinos.

♦ CLEVELAND METROPARKS ZOO

3900 Brookside Park Drive
Cleveland, Ohio 44109
(216) 661-6500

Open: 9–5; Sun./holidays 9–7

Best for: Lemurs; aquarium; white rhino and cheetah (together).

Year opened: 1882

Acres: 170

Animal population: 3,279; 506 species

Director: Steve Taylor

Sister zoo: Wuhan Zoo, Wuhan, China

Getting there: From Route 71 exit at Fulton Road and drive south to Brookside Park. Inside zoo, free tram service between exhibits (distances are considerable).

Conservation: "is the goal," says Director Steve Taylor. Taylor got orangutans for the Wuhan Zoo from a European zoo.

Education: Outstanding hands-on exhibits.

Special attractions: New Rain Forest Building; World of Birds; Waterfowl sanctuary.

Gift shop: Excellent.

Food: Excellent.

The Cleveland Zoo's $28 million Rain Forest Building is its newest and most important attraction. From the outside the building looks like the Crystal Palace. Inside are four multifloor-height zones that house major exhibits surrounded by smaller exhibits, some tucked into the walls. The newest technology has been used for all exhibits in placing vegetation in exhibits and on the walls. The two-acre Rain Forest contains 118 animal species and over 600 specimens, including 17 endangered species. Some

of the animals to be found in the Rain Forest are Bornean orangutans, small-clawed otters, scarlet macaws, tomato frogs, and
Madagascar hissing cockroaches. An artificial 30-foot tree that
looks real has an interior spiral staircase for visitors to reach the
Rain Forest canopy. The Rain Forest has become a major part of
the zoo's Ed"Zoo"cation Programs, for prekindergartners to
adults. Programs have also included an investigation into the
grasslands of the world (a discussion of animal interdependency);
bats, myth and reality; wildlife trade (the poacher, the law, and
the consumer); wonders of the reptile world; and college internships at the zoo in marketing, education, graphics, veterinary and
animal management.

Exhibits that give animals a measure of freedom in their captive environment are a pleasing sight. Cleveland Metroparks Zoo
has a waterfowl island sanctuary also populated by gibbons; adjacent are two islands, one for lemur catta (ring-tailed) and the
other for mongoose, which is also a breeding ground for waterfowl. All islands may be viewed from the shore of the lake. The
Birds of the World exhibit includes Marconi penguins, one of 17
species of penguins. It is somewhat modeled after the Bronx's
World of Birds with only wire or lighting being used to separate
visitors and birds—light for the birds and a dark area for visitors,
which the birds are not likely to enter as they prefer the light.

Still in need of attention are exhibits for the cats and primates
and the aquarium, all currently housed hodge-podge under one
roof, but to be separated in the near future. Plans are in the works
to renovate the building, with the large primates taking up resi-
dency in the Rain Forest Building.

Zoo director Steve Taylor came to the Cleveland Zoo in 1989
after having worked at the Los Angeles, San Francisco, and
Sacramento zoos. His first step at Cleveland was to develop a
mission statement with 12 goals, conservation being the main
one. Captive propagation, he feels, should be secondary to conservation. He agrees with National Zoo director Michael Robinson's characterization of captive propagation as being like an art
museum fire where only 10 or 20 works of art can be saved.
Taylor believes that zoos will succeed in saving a few charismatic

large vertebrates, with zoo experts managing small populations of endangered species—but it's not enough. To achieve conservation goals, zoos must educate the public about the interrelationship of animals.

It is up to zoos, Taylor feels, to bridge the gap between zoos and the public's understanding of their conservation activities. The story of the zoo's famous gorilla Tim illustrates some pitfalls other zoos should avoid. In 1991 the Rain Forest Building was being completed, and it was time for the gorillas to be moved. The gorilla Species Survival Plan (SSP) recommendation was for Tim, a 33-year-old male gorilla, to be transferred temporarily from the Cleveland to the Bronx Zoo to mate. The media picked up the story and loudly declared that "Timmy" was going to be torn from the loving and caring arms of "Katie" (known at the zoo as Kate), who had been brought to Cleveland from Kansas City to be with him. The fact that Kate was sterile was not publicized. Five hundred people signed a petition demanding that Timmy should not go. Tim had been at the zoo since 1966 and with Kate since 1990, but it had become apparent that Kate was not able to breed, hence the decision by the SSP that Tim should go to the Bronx. Kate was to be given a companion in Tim's absence, Oscar, from Topeka. This news did not quiet the disturbed press. In front-page headlines in September 1991 the *Plain Dealer* accused the zoo of ending a love affair between Timmy and Katie.

The Animal Protective League, the animal rightist group that was behind the whole effort to keep Tim in Cleveland from the start, hired a lawyer. The press reacted with gusto: a gorilla with a lawyer! The lawyer prepared to get an injunction. On October 27, 1991, a temporary restraining order was issued against the zoo, followed on October 31 by six hours of court proceedings. When told that the action was being undertaken on Timmy's behalf the judge asked, "What is his last name?" After the case had been presented in some detail in Perry Mason style, the lawyers were summoned into the judge's chambers. The judge ruled that there was no reason to prevent the transfer. Tim was ready to travel. He was taken by two veterinarians and two keepers in a truck on an 11-hour motor ride to the Bronx, where after a period of quarantine, Tim entered an outdoor exhibit on May 9, 1992. It was the first time in his life that he had ever been in an outdoor exhibit.

Tim quickly did what he was supposed to do. He mated with 18-year-old Pattycake. In public. The crowds were thrilled. The press rushed to the scene and cameras took X-rated footage (a baby was born in 1993). Though amusing, Tim's story was no laughing matter for the Cleveland Zoo. It learned, painfully, that one should not asume that a conservation issue is understood by the public. It learned the importance of being protective; establishing internal communications; issuing press releases; giving out information supported by scientific evidence; explaining the goals of the SSP (conservation) to the public; and taking advantage of the local media.

♟ COLUMBUS ZOOLOGICAL GARDENS

Box 400
9990 Riverside Drive
Powell, Ohio 43065
(614) 645-3400

Open: 9–5

Best for: Gorillas; cheetahs; moose; bald eagles

Year opened: 1927

Acres: 405

Animal population: 8,260; 680 species

Director: Jack Hanna (director emeritus); Gerald Borin, director

Getting there: By car: Six miles north of I-270 outer belt (take Exit 20). By bus: from Broad and High streets. For information, call (614) 645-3459).

Conservation: Breeding of endangered reptile species, cheetahs, marine life. Hanna: "We are saving animals to buy time" (against what appear to be overwhelming odds toward the loss of species). Work with ARCAS (Association for the Rescue and Conservation of Wild Animals), a nongovernmental agency formed by Guatemalans to protect and rehabilitate confiscated or injured animals, particularly from the illegal pet trade—mostly macaws, parrots, and cats.

Education: Complete range of programs, including excellent lectures. Photography club.

Special attractions: North American exhibit; the New Discovery Reef, a 100,000-gallon saltwater aquarium with 200 species of fish; film *Life on an Atoll.*

Gift shop: Excellent assortment of souvenirs.

Food: Wendy's Restaurant. Other restaurants near zoo.

The Columbus Zoo is at the top of the charisma league. Under Director Jack Hanna's upbeat, super-promotional touch, visiting the zoo is a treat in getting to know animals. Very much a showman, Hanna believes that "people must have fun when they come to the zoo." He must be doing something right, because Columbus Zoo has 1.3 million visitors annually. Proximity to a large animal has good psychological affects on people.

Hanna's aim is for the general public to become as familiar with the animals as possible. Those soft-furred, padded-pawed, floppy-eared bundles that seem to be asking for affection with a recognition look in their eyes are zoo favorites. Pandas and koalas are high on the list of animals loved by people visiting zoos, along with foxes, wolves, ferrets, lemurs, cats of many sorts, and—with some reservations—kangaroos, prairie dogs, otters, and mongooses—and almost any baby. Generally, it is not safe to touch them—for either you or the animal. The joy of the cuddly is generally in the viewing.

Columbus Zoo wanted to borrow a panda from China, and did so for three months in the summer of 1992. Only about 1,200, and perhaps as few as 700, giant pandas may still be found in their native habitat of southwestern China. About 80 pandas are in zoos in China, and 40 in zoos outside of China. In the United States, the only panda is Hsing-Hsing, in the National Zoo in Washington, D.C., a gift from the Chinese government in 1972. Beginning in 1984 arrangements were made for pandas to visit the United States on loan. They were shuttled from zoo to zoo, exhibited, then returned to China. In 1989 the AAZPA established a moratorium on pandas, taking the position that no more giant pandas should be brought into the United States unless they could be obtained on permanent exhibit. Jack Hanna had made his arrangements for a panda visit well before this decision. As a result both Hanna and the zoo were dropped from AAZPA membership for one year. (Both the zoo and Hanna were reinstated as members on January 1, 1993, after the pandas had been returned to China.) In 1993 the AAZPA announced the formation of the Giant Panda Action Group to reevaluate the moratorium on giant panda importations. Before the Group published its plan, and even prior to necessary approval by the Fish and Wildlife Service, the San Diego Zoo and Busch Gardens, Florida, were deeply involved in negotiations with the Chinese to "rent" pandas. The San Diego Zoo is willing to pay $1 million per year for three years (or perhaps 10) for two pandas, and Busch Gardens to pay $13 million for 10 years. The AAZPA, which receives considerable financial support from the San Diego Zoo and Anheuser-Busch, did not voice any public disapproval, but established two stipulations regarding panda rentals: that any funds from such rentals be used by China for the preservation of the giant pandas' habitats in China, and that the Chinese only rent pandas from their zoos and not pandas taken from the wild. Unfortunately, neither of these two conditions is effectively enforceable by American zoos or the AAZPA. (See San Diego Zoo profile).

Hanna is proud that while many zoos are spending millions on primate exhibits, Columbus's gorilla exhibit cost only $50,000. The outdoor exhibit is simple: a huge cage, with grass and shrubs, lots of ropes for the gorillas to swing from and perches for them to climb up onto. It is in no way a natural habitat—there are no exotic imported tropical plants—and there is little privacy.

Columbus's lowland gorilla population of 17 comprises four generations, including Mosuba and Mascombo, the first captive-born twins. Colo, whose parents were Baron Macombo and Millie Christina, was the world's first gorilla born in captivity, on December 22, 1956, and is still alive. More than half the male gorillas are on loan from other zoos for breeding purposes. The Columbus Zoo is careful when introducing a new gorilla to the group, as individuals come from different levels of socialization (translocated adult animals, nursery animals, nursery-reared infants, juveniles, and transfers from other groups at the same zoo). The gorilla being introduced is at first put in a cage next to the group to which it is to be transferred, and food and bedding material are placed into its cage near the connecting mesh. Then browse and pieces of cloth are put into the cage. If these articles are latter found in both cages, it may be assumed that a sharing activity has taken place. Next the newcomer is placed in a cage with a single gorilla, and seeds and browse are placed in the bedding to provide diversion. A newcomer is introduced to a silverback (older male) only after it has met all of the other gorillas.

Columbus's aquarium has 15 endangered species of fish, including the Australian lungfish. Western banded killi fish are endangered in their natural habitat but are breeding well at the zoo. The collection includes a number of fish from Lake Victoria, the bottom one-third of which is dead, according to the aquarium keeper, because there is no oxygen as a result of the introduction of perch. A program is currently underway whereby the Japanese are taking the perch out, but that means that the local population will be denied the perch as a food source. The best thing that could happen, the keeper ruminated, would be to kill everything in the lake and start all over again. Clearly, another way must be found; the study of the lake and its marine life may lead to a solution.

Director Hanna is also keen on moose (the largest member of the deer family), and without doubt Columbus has the best urban moose exhibit. The ground is level, leading to a 12-foot-deep pond in which the moose can swim. Individuals in the local community supply branches for the exhibit. It is easy to see the moose, often very close.

Jack Hanna was director of the Columbus Zoo from 1976 to 1992. As he tells it in his book *Monkeys on the Interstate* (Doubleday, 1989), he grew up on a farm in Tennessee. His idol was the Knoxville Zoo vet, Dr. Warren Roberts, with whom he started to work at age 11 for no pay until he went on salary at $10 every two weeks.

Eventually, Hanna became director of the Columbus Zoo. He feels that education, not conservation, is the primary purpose of zoos. While zoos must communicate with the public, the primary target of a zoo's educational message should be the eighth- and ninth-graders. People must be made to understand *why* we are saving the animals, otherwise it is no good saving them. The SSP is saving animals to buy time. We are saving the right ones because they bring out emotions in people, especially children. Children's zoos provide an intimate hands-on relationship that a child or adult will cherish. It makes people feel good: It's the maternal or paternal or sibling instinct, the perhaps arrogant but sincere thought that in holding or touching an animal *you* have conveyed a message of caring from human to animal.

➤ SEA WORLD OF OHIO

1100 Sea World Drive
Aurora, Ohio 44202
(216) 995-2121

Open: May–Sept.; call for times

Best for: Sharks; penguins

Year opened: 1970

Acres: 90

Animal population: 2,513; 374 species

General Curator: G. William Hughes

Getting there: About 15 miles southeast of Cleveland. From I-80, take Exit 13 to Route 306 north into Aurora.

Conservation: Cooperation with zoos, aquariums, and other institutions.

Education: Extensive educational presentations.

Special attractions: Killer whale and dolphin performances in Shamu Stadium. Pearl diving in Japanese setting. Ask about guided tours. Sky tower view.

Gift shop: Excellent; very wide choice.

Food: Fast and good.

Since 1989, Busch Entertainment Corporation, a division of the Anheuser-Busch companies, has owned and operated *four* Sea Worlds, in Orlando, Florida; San Diego, California; Aurora, Ohio; and San Antonio, Texas. In addition Busch Entertainment owns and operates Grant's Farm, St. Louis, Missouri; Busch Gardens, Williamsburg, Virginia, and Tampa, Florida; Adventure Island, Tampa, Florida; The Old Country, a European-themed entertainment attraction in Williamsburg, Virginia; Cypress Gardens, Winter Haven, Florida; and Sesame Place, a play park for children in Langhorne, Pennsylvania.

While there are major differences between the four Sea Worlds in size and composition, they work closely with each other and with other aquariums, zoos, and institutions such as the Woods Hole Oceanographic Institution in Woods Hole, Massachusetts.

This profile focuses on the Aurora, Ohio, Sea World; basic information on the other three Sea Worlds is given at the end of the profile.

At Sea World of Ohio, at 10:00 A.M. sharp the national anthem is played over the speaker system. All the employees in the park stop and stand at attention. One man driving a cart has not heard the music above the noise of his vehicle. He makes a sharp turn and a pole he had on the cart falls off. He stops to pick it up, hears the music, returns to the side of his cart and stands at military attention until the music stops. There is nothing like an injection of national spirit to start the day.

In addition to putting aquatic animals on view in spectacular surroundings, Sea World is performing important research in a number of areas. One of the most exciting is communication between humans and marine mammals (cetaceans—whales, dolphins, porpoises, etc.).

Ted Turner, the curator and animal trainer of dolphins and whales, told me about Sea World's Symbolic Tone Language System (STLS), which has the capability to duplicate vocalization frequencies of cetaceans, which have been studied in the wild by scientists for many years. Turner said that starting in about 1988 a transition from communication by means of hand signals (still very much in use) to a tone language system began. The maximum number of "words" produced by STLS from variations and modulation of tones is estimated to be about 1,100. Turner fiddled with his computer keys and produced a series of high-pitched tones for me, giving me a brief impression of the language.

The two Ohio whales are quick at learning "words," but humans don't yet fully understand what meaning the combinations may have to whales. Turner has worked with dolphins on the tone language, and he might work with a walrus at a future date; at the Florida Sea World he plans on using the tone language with eels. He is testing another system whereby whales can initiate a subject to "talk" (communicate) with people by touching with their snouts a huge underwater board containing lexigraphic symbols. Turner hopes that he will be able to teach the whales to use the board, or lexigram, to identify particular parts of their bodies. If whales are able to communicate the message "It hurts here," they will be providing direct information to humans toward monitoring their medical welfare.

After years of shark research, and other preparation, Sea World of Ohio opened Shark Encounter, the largest shark exhibit in the Midwest, on May 22, 1993. The 340,000-gallon tank, containing coastal sharks (including brown, sandtiger, lemon, bull, and nurse) as well as exotic reef fish, small-toothed sawfish, pilot fish, tangs, moray eels and coral, represents Sea World's expression of its commitment to education, research, and conservation. An educational video introduces the visitor to both the exhibit and sharks in general. The visitor learns that there are 350 species of sharks, of which only about 20 are dangerous to humans, and that sharks range in length from less than one foot to more than 40 feet. The tank is shaped like a "dumbell," rather than having the conventional oval or circular design, which enables the sharks to *glide* through the water. Visitors travel on an 85-foot moving walkway that takes them seven feet into the exhibit and six feet below the surface of the water. The sharks can be viewed through five-inch-thick, curved acrylic panels.

Penguins always make people feel good. We laugh at the waddling walk of these droll, sensitive, active creatures in their "for-

mal" attire. There are 17 species of penguins. The Sea World of
California in San Diego has a visually spectacular, authentically
simulated Antarctic exhibit of 300 penguins, representing six
species. Videos, plus clear, informative colored signs and an
audio presentation, are effective and dramatic. At Sea World of
Florida's $13 million Penguin Encounter, where 6,000 pounds of
snow is manufactured daily, the light changes according to the
Arctic seasons. A smaller population of 100 penguins occupies
the exhibit at Sea World of Ohio in Aurora, where the scene is
equally impressive. Again, the signs are outstanding, with videos,
shown on screens larger than those at the San Diego Sea World,
of the penguin species represented: Marconi, emperor, chinstrap,
Adelie and the blue-eyed shaf. It is believed that there are no
other blue-eyed shaf penguins in captivity in the United States.

At the San Diego Sea World there is a huge petting pool where
people may feed and touch the whales and dolphins, an experience children are unlikely to forget. Rocky Point Preserve
opened in May 1993 with two exhibits: Dolphin Bay (with bot-
tlenosed dolphins), and Otter Outlook (with five Alaskan otters).
The Forbidden Reef is a 100,000-gallon, 3,200-square-foot exhibit featuring unfamiliar friendly monsters. Visitors can watch
bat rays flapping their "wings" in what might be considered a
ballet as they glide through the water, and can also touch and feed
them. While a great many aquariums have some sort of hands-on
touch tank, nothing can beat this, except being in the water with
them. The number one attraction is a show by Orca (also known
as the killer whale), which brings crowds flocking to the water
stadium. Attendants warn those sitting in the first dozen rows
that they will be splashed, and the children are delighted when
Orca circles the pool and indeed gives the water a big whack with
his fin, sending a wall of spray into the people area.

At all four Sea Worlds, a ride up the revolving sky tower for
an aerial panoramic view of the marine life and people activity
below is a "must."

It must be admitted that Sea World is expensive; admission
fees range from $19.50 (Ohio) to $29.95 (Orlando) for adults and
from $15.50 (Ohio) to $25.95 (Orlando) for children. Parking,

sky tower trip, food, and a visit to the gift shop can add up to well over $150 for a family of four. These are prices that a not-for-profit zoo or aquarium would never dare charge. Before I visited Sea World my thoughts were negative. I felt they were out for big bucks and that was all. I was wrong. Sea World is very good, and worth the price. While they naturally want to make money, they have a strong interest in bringing the best to the public, *and* in conducting research, stressing education and promoting conservation. And people respond. The four Sea Worlds had 9,500,000 visitors in 1992.

SEA WORLD OF FLORIDA

7007 Sea World Drive
Orlando, Florida 32821
(407) 351-3600

Open: 9 A.M.–10 P.M.; call for winter hours

Year opened: 1973

Acres: 218

Animal population: 9,710; 406 species

General manager: William Davis

SEA WORLD OF TEXAS

10500 Sea World Drive
San Antonio, Texas 78251
(512) 523-3000

Open: Call (512) 523-3611 for hours; closed Dec.–Feb.

Year opened: 1988

Acres: 250

Animal population: 7,230; 180 species

General manager: Robin Carson

SEA WORLD OF CALIFORNIA

1720 South Shores Road
San Diego, California 92109
(619) 226-3901

Open: 9 A.M.–10 P.M.; call for winter hours

Year opened: 1964

Acres: 150

Animal population: 17,825; 541 species

General manager: Michael Cross

🐃 TOLEDO ZOOLOGICAL GARDENS

P.O. Box 4010
2700 Broadway
Toledo, Ohio 43609
(419) 385-5721
Open: 10–5; call for winter
hours
Best for: Birds; hippos; sea
lions

Year opened: 1899
Acres: 51
Animal population: 2,587;
463 species
Director: William Dennler

Getting there: Three miles south of Toledo.

Conservation: Strong SSP participation with island boas in the Caribbean, and the gorilla.

Education: The Roger Conant Research Fellowship, named for the zoo's first curator and established in 1990, provides for a two-month fellowship each summer, including housing and a $1,500 stipend.

Special attractions: Zoo building architecture; Diversity of Life exhibit.

Gift shop: Excellent.

Food: Recommended.

One of the primary sights at the Toledo Zoo is the lovely old zoo buildings themselves. Some zoos have had difficulty adapting their landmarked buildings to housing modern exhibits, since landmarked buildings may not be altered or restructured externally. Toledo and Philadelphia are two zoos that exemplify how zoos can update facilities for animals without destroying the architectural beauty of their older buildings.

The Toledo Zoo was built in the Spanish Colonial revival architectural style that was popular in late-nineteenth- and early-twentieth-century America. Eight brick or stone structures, with arched doorways, cornices, parapets, and even balconies, were built at the zoo by the WPA (Work Projects Administration) between 1923 and 1945 and have been classified as having historical architectural significance. They are the primate, elephant, carnivore, reptile and bird houses, the aquarium, the museum of science, and the amphitheater and are described in detail in a self-guided tour brochure.

The hippo is one of my favorite animals, languishing, nearly submerged, submerging, then rising like a new island amid his fellow beings. There is without doubt something appealing about this "river horse," as the Egyptians called the hippo. Hippos are massive and seem relatively docile, although a number of years ago Alan Root, the wildlife photographer, was badly bitten by a hippopotamus as he was exploring their water bed at Mzima Springs, Kenya. Early explorers reported tales of canoes tipped over by hippos and the occupants being savagely eaten by the beasts.

Thinking of hippo exhibits of the past conjures up a picture of a badly lit building with cement interior, thick bars or a wide moat separating the viewer from one or more hippos asleep in a corner, and a graded slope leading to a pool of unsightly, dark-colored water. Unfortunately, this is still the depressing picture at many zoos. The Toledo Zoo, however, has an outstanding hippoquarium in a four-acre natural outdoor setting in the African Savannah exhibit, within view of giraffes, rhinos, zebras, lions, leopards, and impalas. The hippoquarium's water is unusually clear as a result of four filters cleaning 8,000 gallons of the 360,000-gallon-capacity pool every 90 minutes.

The hippoquarium has provided a viewing of two births underwater, which had never been seen before. The behavior of baby and adults was observed, and a previously unknown fact was learned: that the male has a major role in the birth of a hippo. In zoos, males had previously been separated from the female when she gave birth. The hippoquarium provides a truly direct view of the hippo in their natural setting, far better and infinitely easier than in the wild. A video of a hippo birth that took place at the zoo, *in* the tank in front of the viewing public, has been placed on the visitor's side of the exhibit.

At most zoos, signs placed at an exhibit state the date of birth of a particular animal, but they rarely use the opportunity of the drama and appeal of birth to provide conservation data about the species. It is to be hoped that the more the public can learn of how wildlife lives in the wild, the more it will be motivated to conserve natural habitats. Toledo's video is a good example of what can be done.

The zoo's most popular attraction is the large sea lions exhibit, where the animals have their own island and the visitors another. Daily at 10:30 and 3:30 there are demonstrations of sea lions responding to commands from a trainer who educates the public on how sea lions swim, dive, and maneuver when ashore.

The penguins have been relegated to the old sea lion exhibit, which has underwater viewing but is otherwise rather dull.

The aquarium has two wings with excellent signage and good lighting. Exhibits are of mixed species, such as turtles and fish. Don't miss the huge colossoma, mata mata turtle, and red devil exhibits. Also interesting are the beautiful blue-and-yellow tang; the bright-orange Garibaldi; the gray Schwanenfeld barb with orange tail and fins; the lionfish; the bumble bee grouper; and the remora, fish with suction cups on some fins, allowing them to attach to other fish and ships.

The primate building has orangutans, chimpanzees and low-land gorillas; all except for the gorillas are free to move in and out of doors. However, gorillas may look forward to a brighter future: Under its 15-year master plan, Toledo has provided for a $1.5 million Ape House expansion, including a large outdoor exhibit for six gorillas. The zoo is proud of its gorillas and rightly so. In 1988 Malaika, one of the female lowland gorillas, gave birth to a baby, Johari, and then raised her, Executive Director William Dennler recounted with enormous enthusiasm. "I cannot emphasize enough the significance of this event. In the first place, we had been trying to breed our gorillas for years: we all know the story of Max, the German stud who wasn't, and Akbar, the southern gentleman who stole the ladies' hearts. Second, even though Shani had been born the year before, Malaika had failed to raise her, and she had been pulled for hand-raising. Third, our staff had put in a great deal of time and effort over the past two years into collecting daily urine specimens from all our female gorilla in order to learn as much as possible about their reproductive systems. Fourth, many long hours were spent by staff and volunteers nursing Shani in view of Malaika in hopes that she would 'get the message' about what a gorilla mother is supposed to do. It all paid off when Johari was born on February nineteenth. Then, on September twenty-third, Happy, Malaika's sister, gave birth to Togo, Jr., and to everyone's delight she, too, was a model mother."

Toledo's Diversity of Life exhibit offers a comparative examination of dead specimens, under a magnifying glass, and live specimens, such as tarantulas, scorpions, Madagascar hissing cockroaches, and leopard geckos. A list of causes of extinction is posted on the wall: (1) land and water destruction, (2) unrestricted killing, (3) introduction of foreign species, (4) unrestricted capture, (5) pollution and toxins.

Toledo's zoo has a relatively small outdoor African Plains exhibit with several viewing areas from which people on the other side of the exhibit cannot be seen. The multispecies exhibit contains three rhinos, plus kudus, giraffes, lions (with a heated rock), and meerkats. An automatic electric lift for hay has been installed in the giraffe's cage so that the keeper can fill it at floor level and then raise the hay to a suitable height for the giraffe.

The greenhouse, including the area surrounding it, is a treasure. It is delightful, usually not crowded, peaceful, and is ablaze with color. The entire grounds are delicately manicured and cared for.

Not to be forgotten: At any zoo that has a koala, the koala must be visited, and Toledo has two koalas on permanent exhibit.

Zoo Director William Dennler's mother loved animals, so she didn't mind his having hamsters, birds, fish or turtles as pets—but she hated snakes. Perhaps this is why his craving developed into a lifelong love for snakes; today Dennler still has snakes in his basement, though not poisonous ones (because of the children). His wife doesn't mind at all.

Growing up in the fifties and visiting the Bronx Zoo, he didn't like what he saw. When Dennler saw a Walt Disney television program starring Hal Holbrook, whose character ran a small zoo, he realized that being at a zoo could be an occupation. In 1972 he landed a job with the Cincinnati Zoo, preparing the animals' food and butchering horses that people donated when they were tired of them. Dennler remained at the Cincinnati Zoo for three years, during which time he decided he wanted to study herpetology. Just then, Ed Maruska, director of the Cincinnati Zoo, told him the Toledo Zoo was looking for a curator of reptiles. That was in 1975.

Dennler recounts as his most rewarding experience in his work with animals something that happened on a visit to Rwanda to observe the mountain gorillas in 1986. He was standing in the thick bush, peering through the branches at gorilla a short distance away, when a huge silverback silently stepped out of the bush and positioned himself between Dennler and another man. The gorilla seemed surprised and a bit off balance, so he reached out and gently but firmly grabbed Dennler by his arm to steady himself, then looked at him face-to-face. The gorilla leading, they walked together for a few steps. His first reaction to this encounter was not wanting to see *any* animals in zoos. Then he remembered how fragile the gorilla population is in the mountains of Rwanda, increasingly encroached on by "civilization," and that some must be saved in zoos. Dennler returned to Toledo wanting to improve the lives of the animals in captivity, On reflection, Dennler feels that the biggest mistake zoos and museums make is that they haven't worked enough with people, especially those who educate others. Dennler has found that many teachers cannot identify a single endangered species.

ᛞ WILD ANIMAL HABITAT

6300 Kings Island Drive
Kings Island Amusement Park
Kings Island, Ohio 45034
(513) 573-5742

Open: 10–8; closed mid-Oct. to mid-April

Best for: Giraffes; zebras; gazelles

Year opened: 1974

Acres: 100

Animal population: 304; 34 species

Director: Scott Shoemaker

Membership: None

Note: Admission to Kings Island Amusement Park,

$22.95, includes zoo. Kings Island was bought by Paramount Communications in August 1992. Changes are being made.

Getting there: About 24 miles north of Cincinnati. From Route 71 take Kings Island Exit about eight miles north of Belt Route 275.

Conservation: Participation in SSP programs.

Education: Each fall, 20,000 children are brought to the zoo for Discovery Day.

Special attractions: Monorail.

Gift shop: Books and stuffed animals.

Food: Amusement Park snacks.

Wild Animal Habitat is a delightful surprise, a tidy, quiet, distinguished little zoo beyond the crowds, noise, and fanfare of the entrance of the Kings Island Amusement Park. The monorail moves silently on its two-mile-long, 22-minute voyage. The first animal sighted is a giraffe (always a favorite of mine; for years my New York license plate was TWIGA, "giraffe" in Swahili). Next are close-up encounters with rhinos, zebras, gazelles, and an elephant. Moving from one regional habitat to another, the monorail passes ponds, then climbs to pass through treetops at 80 feet above the ground. My only negative comment on the Wild Animal Habitat is that some park support facilities have been placed too near the zoo, and an amusement ride intrudes on the space over the North American exhibit.

 **THE WILDS**

Zanesville, Ohio
(614) 228-0402

Open: 9–5

Best for: Hartmann's mountain zebra; oryx

Year opened: 1990

Acres: 9,400

Animal population: 53; 5 species

Director: Robert W. Reece

Getting there: Fifteen miles southeast of Zanesville, Ohio. Near the intersection of I-70 and I-77.

Conservation: The purpose of The Wilds is conservation, so animals can breed in the wide, open spaces.

Education: A cooperative effort of the zoos of Ohio for conservation and education. Exploration centers at The Wilds. A butterfly workshop has already met at The Wilds, conducted by the Captive Breeding Specialist Group (CBSG) of the Species Survival Commission.

Special attractions: Visitor's Center for a look into The Wilds' future.

Gift shop: A modest one.

Food: No.

At 9,400 acres, The Wilds, part of a trend toward megazoos, could represent one of the "solutions" being sought to save wildlife.

It has been estimated that a population of 500 animals is required (depending on the species) to conserve a species. (The SSP has programs for 72 species and targets plans to establish programs for 200 species by the year 2000.) It is recognized that only a limited number of animal species can be conserved in zoos. They may be exhibited, and captive bred, but not conserved in quantity. Consequently, megazoos that can support large populations of compatible species are being established, both in the United States and abroad. The Kruger National Park in South Africa is an early example of a fenced-in "natural" animal reserve. Of course, it is not natural; fencing an area in changes its ecology. In 1954, when I first visited Kenya's first park, the Nairobi National Park, a 10-minute drive from downtown Nairobi, it was eight years old and was fenced in on one side only. The park is now fenced in on three sides, including 15 miles of electric fencing. There is serious talk of adding to its 44 square miles and fencing in the whole area, which would result in the wildebeests, zebras, impalas, kongonis, and Thomson's and Grant's gazelles no longer being free to migrate into and out of the park. Nairobi National Park would simply become a mega-zoo—a real pity, but perhaps inevitable. This is the trend in the case of natural reserves or parks: the establishment of boundaries between people and animals.

Another park, in Nakuru, Kenya, has already been fenced in, creating a megazoo. While preservation has resulted, nature has been disturbed. Sadly, there may be no alternative to fencing in land in Africa inhabited by wild animals. Human population pressures and resultant political issues may be too great to reverse the trend. Only time will tell whether megazoos are a partial solution to habitat preservation.

The opposite is happening in the United States: Areas that have not previously been the natural habitat of certain animal species are being set aside, protected and populated by captive animals, a different kind of megazoo. The initiative in establishing these conservation areas comes most frequently from zoos, although individual ranchers in Texas, New Mexico and in some other states have privately undertaken the creation of zoo-parks. One problem with these zoo-parks is that they are generally managed—some very well—at the total discretion of one individual, the owner. No governmental or national organization has any control over the aims, ethics, or conduct of these private ranches, where the future of the animals and of the surrounding environment is dependent on one individual.

The Wilds is different. It is a megazoo that has been in the planning since 1978 and officially opened to the public in 1993. Though one man, Dr. Robert Teater, was the force behind The Wilds' becoming a reality, the zoo's base of support is so broad that it is not dependent on any single individual. As director of natural resources of Ohio, Dr. Teater realized that Ohio must save its zoos and must have state support. The governor brought Dr. Teater together with Ohio's directors of transportation and development. They huddled over the problem and recommended to the legislature "to participate in a land and water project which would provide a 'reservoir' for zoos." American Electric Power, which had been restoring land it had strip-mined near Zanesville since 1954, was interested in getting involved. They offered 9,400 acres to the state to create The Wilds. Dr. Teater established a task force in 1984 consisting of Ohio zoo directors and members of the planning firm of Jones & Jones to determine whether the site was right, and they concluded it was. The next three years of negotiation involved many legal problems, and some disagreements among zoos as to the value of the project. The Wilds' board of directors was established and includes the president of each zoo association and the director of each zoo: Cleveland, Columbus, Toledo, Cincinnati, Akron, and Wild Animal Habitat of the Kings Island commercial amusement park.

In October 1991 the first 21 inhabitants of The Wilds arrived: 13 Przewalski horses from the Bronx Zoo, two Hartmann mountain zebras from Madison, Wisconsin, five scimitar-horned oryx from the National Zoological Park Conservation and Research Center in Front Royal, Virginia, and one female North American red wolf (extinct in the wild until 1987, when wolves bred in captivity were released in North Carolina). Cuvier's gazelles were added in 1992, and 7 Jackson's hartebeests in 1993. David Jenkins, then associate director of the AAZPA and on hand for the occasion, commented, "The Wilds is a new kind of venture that reflects the tremendous changes that have taken place in zoos over the past twenty years." Senator John Glenn, a native of nearby New Concord, Ohio, was the keynote speaker for the occasion. "We'd better not louse this planet up," Glenn declared with the dual perspective of the astronaut-politician.

Some big questions lie ahead for the board and staff of The Wilds, especially concerning money. Teater believes $55 million is needed to develop the land and another $100 million or more to develop geographic "regions." Can—should—Ohio shoulder the responsibility for this conservation and education center? How much support from corporate, foundation, and individual contributions can be expected? Will out-of-state financing be attracted to the project? Will the project, despite its serious intentions, be pressured by costs to go Disney? There are already plans for a tram system to carry visitors throughout the 14-square-mile preserve and for education centers. But will animal shows in the The Wilds and commercial people entertainment facilities surrounding The Wilds also crop up? The temptation may be too great. Thinking optimistically, and thinking big, Dr. Teater observed American Electric Power's generosity to date and noted that "120,000 acres are still available should we want it." The result would doubtless be an international megazoo in the United States. Will the public support conservation on this scale (or greater, for even larger preserves are needed to conserve animals in this manner)? Where will the money come from?

Deep thought must be given to the ultimate purpose of The Wilds, and it is taking place. Bob Reece, formerly the director of Wild Animal Habitat at Kings Island, is now the director of The Wilds. Reece feels that zoos must determine their roles in conservation and education. While conservation emphasis should be on biodiversity, we must be selective. For example, there are two species of black rhino and two subspecies. Should all of them be saved? No. The aim should be to save genetic diversity.

Regarding reintroduction, if there is no habitat suitable for reintroduction, zoos should not try to reintroduce a species. Some zoos are latching on to the SSP program to give themselves a "conservation" profile. Yet many of the SSP species will be in a zoo anyway. What must be done is to concentrate on captive breeding, on programs such as developing germ plasm. The whole thrust, says Reece, is to support wild populations in captivity by captive breeding, research rather than reintroduction, and the training of management technicians. He cites Cincinnati Zoo and San Diego's Wild Animal Park, and even the Front Royal, Virginia, center (see profiles) as involved in research but not having a sufficient number of animals to breed efficiently and productively; this *can* be done in the extensive space of The Wilds.

While financial support is a continuing challenge, interest is growing. The state of Ohio has provided funds and has been helpful with a visitor's center. The federal government has provided funds through the Fish and Wildlife Service for work with the red wolf and wetlands programs. As many as 75 corporations have contributed funds. One particularly interesting and potentially productive idea is to establish a "participating institution" organization: Member zoos that don't have the room for their surplus populations could board them out at The Wilds for a fee. Ohio zoos would be first to participate, but other zoos could apply. This idea does have a potential flaw: Taxpayers provide financial support for *their* zoo, and may need considerable convincing to use *their* dollars for animals that can only be seen elsewhere. The Wilds is not yet a member of the AAZPA. The Wilds encourages interested supporters to become members of The Wilds and to follow its progress.

Education is a major priority of The Wilds. At zoos, organizations or activities are created with names that include "education," buildings are built with classrooms and demonstration or display centers, and literature is published saying how important it is to save wildlife. Most zoos, conservation centers, and similar-minded institutions pinpoint specific actions being taken to conserve and preserve. Species Survival Plans are master plans for individual animals. At The Wilds, the education emphasis is on the creation of a master plan for conservation education. Of course, The Wilds can't create such a master plan alone. It will be interesting to keep our eye on how the role of The Wilds develops in relation to zoos, conservation of species, and conservation planning.

🐎 OKLAHOMA CITY ZOOLOGICAL PARK

2101 Northeast 50th Street
Oklahoma City, Oklahoma
73111
(405) 424-3344

Open: 9–6; call for winter hours

Best for: deer (Indochinese sikas); Chinese dholes; gorals

Year opened: 1904

Acres: 189

Animal population: 1,999; 536 species

Director: Stephen Wylie

Membership: Oklahoma Zoological Society

(405) 427-2461

Getting there: In Lincoln Park. From Route 35, take Exit 132 west (Northeast 50th Street) to zoo. Near zoo are Forest Park, Remington Park Race Track, National Softball Hall of Fame.

Conservation: Special attention for ungulates, cats, apes. Quarterly publication *Zoosounds* is informative and conservation-oriented.

Education: In-house and outreach classes; close working relationship with schools. Something for all ages. Family zoo walkabout tour.

Special attractions: Great EscApe.

Gift shop: Very good.

Food: Moderate, improvements planned.

When the Oklahoma City Zoological Park was originally established in 1904 in Wheeler Park, it consisted of a small menagerie of native animals. In 1925, the zoo was reestablished under the city's Park and Recreation Department at its present location in Lincoln Park. In 1975 the Oklahoma City Zoological Trust was formed, separating the zoo from the government-administered parks department.

Today the zoo's purpose and goals are: recreation, education, conservation, and zoological research. It is the number one family recreation resource in the Oklahoma City area, and draws approximately 42 percent of its visitors from beyond a 50-mile radius. The zoo must meet the challenge of providing enough recreation. Continued government funding is not assured, and the zoo may have to reduce its educational and conservation-oriented activities, as well as its animal collection. This would be most unfortunate.

Director Stephen Wylie takes the view that zoos are local institutions and must have local appeal. The zoo has credibility and the public believes that its money is well spent. Meanwhile, the zoo continues to grow. Great EscApe is a 3.3-acre exhibit that opened in August 1993 where, as promised, visitors are "immersed in a lush, simulated tropical forest at a thicket edge leading to a series of forest meadows and clearings inhabited by Great Apes." The exhibit was designed by Jon Coe of Coe, Lee, Robinson, Roesch. Exterior exhibit areas of Great EscApe will be available for public viewing in the spring of 1994. There are two groups of gorillas, totaling 10, plus three orangutans and six chimpanzees.

Wylie places an emphasis at his zoo on wild dogs and ungulates, which have been given large fenced-in areas shaded by healthy elms. "Space is the secret to breeding," says General Curator Jack Grisham. Don't miss the Rocky Mountain goat—it likes to climb trees!

Recently the children's zoo, built in 1964, was demolished and 30,000 cubic feet of concrete was carted away, eliminating the last ugly exhibit at the zoo. Other projects are in the works: Bear Trek takes the visitor through a number of bear habitats, from the tundra to the boreal forest. Oklahoma Trail will be populated by white-tailed deer, pronghorn antelopes, bison, elks, black bears, wolves, cougars, and alligators. It will have a tram stop, a picnic area with parking, and a tepee village. The Galápagos exhibit built in 1975 will be rebuilt as an insular species exhibit.

Director Wylie wanted to be a vet when he was a child. Although he lived in town in Kansas City, he had pet ducks, rabbits, a dog, squirrel, and chickens in the backyard. Twenty-five years ago Wylie started as a keeper at the Kansas City Zoo, a position he held until 1970, when he became assistant curator of birds at the Philadelphia Zoo. In 1974 he moved to St. Louis, as deputy curator of birds, and in 1981 he was appointed general curator. In 1985, Wylie became director of the Oklahoma City Zoo (where the aviary is his favorite exhibit). He believes that a common characteristic of zoo directors is that they like working with animals more than with people—but when they get to where they are going they are put in charge of people and become immersed in administration. "It's frustrating not to have more time with the animals," he confides.

↲ TULSA ZOO AND LIVING MUSEUM

5701 East 36th Street North
Tulsa, Oklahoma
(918) 669-6202

Open: 10–6; call for winter hours

Best for: Siamangs; brown bears; mandrill baboons

Year opened: 1927

Acres: 70

Animal population: 1,224; 283 species

Director: Dave Zucconi

Membership: Tulsa Zoo Friends, (918) 834-9453

Getting there: In Mohawk Park, west of airport. From Route 11, take Exit 11 north on Sheridan Road to north zoo entrance off 36th Street North (parking).

Conservation: SSP participation for 10 species. First second-generation hatching of pancake tortoise in 1992.

Education: Mission: A better understanding of the natural world. Three full-time staff plus 150 docents for education alone.

Special attractions: Focus on culture throughout zoo. Eastern Forest; Southern Lowlands.

Gift shop: One in Zoo Building, and one in Southern Lowlands building.

Food: Snacks.

The zoo's logo has four elements symbolizing humans, animals, plants, earth. Each complex of exhibits carries out the natural history theme—the importance of every facet of nature.

The Southern Lowlands exhibit shows fishes of the coral reef, the Everglades, and a cypress swamp with alligator snapping turtles, who are attention getters with their claws, thorny heads, and pointed noses. This exhibit points up the importance of the Great Barrier Reef of Australia and the reefs off Belize in the Caribbean; the relationship between swamps and reefs; and the value of environmentalists' and zoos' stress on saving the swamps and wetlands of America and the world.

The Eastern Forest exhibit shows the life of water dwellers and a chart demonstrating the food chain in sequence: bottom organic matter on the pond bottom, insect larvae, mollusks, crayfish, sunfish, spotted turtles, painted turtles, bullfrogs, bullhead catfish, and watersnakes. There is a good nonlive exhibit of insects: bees and butterflies.

The Southern Desert exhibit is indoors, showing cultures of deserts as well as their wildlife. Artifacts and photographs are most effective. A wall exhibit provides a peek into private burrows, and with the push of a button the small nocturnal creatures are illuminated gently for a better look. There is a good cactus exhibit with a roadrunner actively making its way along the desert floor.

I have been to the desert area of Baja California, and much of the time my binoculars were riveted to my blurring eyes in search of birds perched on a cactus, or a perhaps a chuckwalla nestled under a warm rock. I have motored and walked through the northern parts of Kenya, visiting water wells where camel caravans gathered. I have seen the desert areas of now war-torn Somalia and visited areas outside of the cities of Kano and Kaduna in northern Nigeria, parched and flat. The wildlife that exists in these desolate lands is there, but difficult to see, for the struggle is to live, to survive. The role of zoos in bringing the desert before us so that we may understand it is an important one.

The zoo's walking path is well defined, offering the visitor a number of choices: past chimpanzee island to Southern Low lands, or through the Arctic Tundra, Southwest Desert, and Eastern Forest to Southern Lowlands. Each complex is separate and accessible by a raised walkway over land and water. After visiting Southern Lowlands, a long loop takes one past (or to, depending on one's age) the children's zoo, the southwest entrance to the zoo, elephants (who are getting a new building), the Zoo Building, the Sea Lion Pool (feeding daily at 2:00 P.M.), primates and cats, the African Savannah, hoofed animals, and rhinos; then back, past an attractive lake, to the ever central Southern Lowlands. For an easy overview of the zoo, visitors may board the train at either the southwest or northeast entrance to the zoo.

In the children's zoo are llamas, wallabies, river otters, prairie dogs, and golden lion tamarins—yet it is a generally poor exhibit. I applaud the fact that the zoo has a golden lion tamarin, but is this the place for it? Furthermore, he is hard to see. The river otters have little swimming space, and the llamas looks dreary. There is, however, attractive ground cover in the area of the children's zoo, a carpet of blue juniper.

On the other hand, the siamangs, on their island in 70-foot-high cypress trees, the ground cover thick with bush, are in my opinion a major attraction.

ᛜ METRO WASHINGTON PARK ZOO

4001 Southwest Canyon Road
Portland, Oregon 97221
(503) 226-1561

Open: 9:30–6; call for winter hours

Best for: Insects; elephants; chimpanzees

Year opened: 1959

Acres: 64

Animal population: 1,643; 192 species

Director: Y. Sherry Sheng

Getting there: By car: In Washington Park, on the Sunset Highway (Route 26) west of the Willamette. By bus: Tri-Met Bus 63 every hour. Call 231-3263 for times. At the zoo: Zoo train to rose and Japanese gardens.

Conservation: Elephants, rhinos, ungulates. Elephant Zoo-Do package sold to public (good present). Recycling initiatives.

Education: SAFE (Save the Animals from Extinction) program. *100 Ways to Conserve Resources* (brochure). For further information, call 220-2782.

Special attractions: Elephant Museum.

Gift shop: Both cute and serious items.

Food: Good snacks; restaurant overlooks glassed-in aviary.

Metro Washington Park Zoo specializes in breeding Asian elephants, both naturally and by artificial insemination, and works with Asian governments on improving captive propagation. The zoo has 1.5 acres of exhibit space for its Asian elephants, and research staff is undertaking behavioral research in order to determine the amount of space required by an individual. Y. Sherry Sheng, director of the zoo, told me that humans really don't know how much space an elephant needs in captivity—a question that should have been answered a long time ago. The elephants' quarters have hydraulically controlled doors leading to seven holding rooms and an 80,000-gallon swimming pool. Portland's zoo also has an unusual, effective, and informative Elephant Museum with fossil mastodont feet that were found near the city.

The weaver birds exhibit is superb. Often I have seen weavers on the plains of Africa make a flying dart to the bottom of their thickly woven nests secured to the branch of a thorn tree. They hang suspended for seconds, then disappear through the entrance to their nest. Portland's exhibit is large enough to allow some flight, and the strong natural light recalled these ever-working birds' natural habitat.

The zoo also has a good chimpanzee exhibit, where visitors can see the chimpanzees cavorting on their own island and darting in and out of man-made caves, and is involved in studying interactions among chimpanzees. When young are born, the question arises as to how long they should remain with the family before they are shipped off to another zoo. Usually they are packed and sent off in one or two years, but the zoo has determined that four to five years "at home" are needed for chimps to develop relationships and learn to reproduce.

Of all polar bear exhibits I have seen I was most impressed with the one at the Metro Washington Park Zoo. At the front of the exhibit is an angled pool. On the other side of the pool lies a flat cement space, in the center of which is a large tree trunk with a strong branch protruding out over the pool. Enter: a polar bear. She is playing with a white basketball-sized ball, pushing it with her paw, forward and under, trying to catch it as it bobs up out of the water. Then she heaves it out of the water and it lodges in the elbow of the tree trunk. The polar bear swims to the ball and pushes it, expecting it to bounce back into the pool. It doesn't move. She tries several times. The ball moves slightly but remains stuck. The bear swims away; has she given up? Not at all. She reaches the far side of the pool, lifts herself out, lumbers to the trunk, lies down behind it, stretches one arm out underneath the trunk and gives the ball a push. It splashes into the pool.

The Africa exhibit includes black rhinoceros, Hartmann's mountain zebra, giraffe, impala, ostrich, and hippo. There are excellent multiviewing opportunities. During the summer there is an insect stand near the front entrance to the zoo. Both the emphasis on invertebrates and the quality of the exhibit are laudable. Two well-informed staff members let youngsters (and others) touch tarantulas and other creepy-crawlies or let them climb up their arms.

In addition to members' cash donations and admission fees the zoo receives contributions in kind: an anonymous individual donates bamboo for the red panda, and cattle bones are received from a local meat packing company. This zoo, great already, will be even greater with the fruition of its 25-year, $100 million master plan, which calls for the creation of five new sections (Oregon, Africa, Asia, Waters, and Discovery Complex) providing interactive displays, video imagery, and computers. There will be eight climatic zones, support areas that will include education activities, plus a Rose Garden.

⬤ CLYDE PEELING'S REPTILAND LTD.

RD #1, Box 388
Allenwood, Pennsylvania 17818
(717) 538-1869

Open: 9–8
Best for: Reptiles
Year opened: 1964

Acres: 4
Animal population: 145; 58 species
Director: Clyde Peeling
Membership: None

Getting there: On Route 15, north of Route 80, south of Williamsport.
Conservation: Breeding and reintroduction of Siamese crocodiles.

Education: Excellent programs on reptile education. Call (518) 678-3557 for further information.

Special attractions: Highly informative presentations with live reptiles daily 10:30, 1:00; 3:00, 5:00.

Gift shop: Fun reptilian things.

Food: Simple, fresh, and good.

Clyde Peeling's Reptiland in Allenwood, Pennsylvania, specializes in—you guessed it—reptiles! (There is a second Reptiland near Catskill, New York.) Very instructive and entertaining hour-long presentations are made by Clyde's son, Chad, with the assistance of a live tortoise, turtle, rattlesnake, and lizard, which the public are allowed to touch. Peeling told me that his motivation in creating Reptiland and in giving the presentations is "to introduce the public to reptiles so that they will understand them better." Exhibits are simple but good. Reptiland also has a reintroduction program. (Peeling ran into a potential problem one dark night when he was on the verge of releasing some reptiles into the bush not far from Reptiland. Suddenly a police cruiser pulled up to him to investigate, and a quick explanation had to be given to the law man. "Look what I have just *found*," he improvised.)

The reptile house, with its vipers, cobras, giant pythons, and boas, is small but effective, with excellent window exhibits that are clean and well lit and have good viewing angles (carpeted steps for children) and educational signs. Two coin-operated machines encourage the visitor to feed a cricket to frogs or turtles—much fun.

Peeling notes that while others are building multi-million-dollar rain forests, he is fine-tuning the educational presentations at his Reptiland. There are four lecturers at Allenwood and three at the Catskills Reptiland. He is standardizing the presentations by adding six to nine projectors to make each lecture a "multi-image show." Peeling's aim is not to get bigger but to improve "each section a bit at a time." The Catskills Reptiland is all indoors and smaller than at Allenwood. It has tortoise and iguana. Reptiland is an instructive zoo, not just an entertainment center.

❡ PHILADELPHIA ZOOLOGICAL GARDEN

3400 West Girard Avenue
Philadelphia, Pennsylvania
(215) 243-1100

Open: 9:30–6; call for winter hours

Best for: Primates

Year opened: 1874

Acres: 42

Animal population: 1,739; 494 species

Director: Alexander "Pete" Hoskins (president and CEO)

Getting there: By car: From Route 76 take Exit 36 to Girard Avenue. By public transportation: Number 15 trolley, Number 38 bus. Call 574-7800 for travel information.

Conservation: Sumatran rhino; Micronesian kingfisher (world population is down to 54); Marianas birds.

Education: Strong emphasis on children's zoo education.

Special attractions: Zoo's architecture; children's zoo.

Gift shop: ZooShop is good.

Food: Food stands; picnic grove.

"Philadelphia is best at the unique," said Bill Donaldson, former director of the Philadelphia Zoo. "For example, like the London zoo, our zoo is involved in comparative pathology, but now Philadelphia is better and therefore has learned of problems in animals that may help people. For instance, woodchucks have problems with liver cancer and hepatitis, people problems." Other species can help humans understand their own health problems better.

The Philadelphia Zoo's $6 million, 1.1-acre World of Primates clusters gorillas, gibbons, and orangutans on four strategically divided but adjacent landscaped, naturalistic islands. The contiguous exhibits may be seen from several perspectives, from distant, panoramic views to face-to-face encounters. Tamarins, marmosets, and ring-tailed and ruffed lemurs may also be seen. The gorillas, gibbons, and orangutans are kept amused (and fed) with puffed wheat and other food that is hidden and scattered throughout the outdoor exhibit, not only relieving the primates' boredom but increasing their activity.

Thirty percent of the children visiting the Philadelphia zoo receive a lesson from their teacher prior to their visit on what they are going to see and experience. The zoo's objective is to increase the figure to 70 percent.

Philadelphia's Discovery House for children was previously the Antelope House. A landmarked building, its exterior could not be altered but its interior could be modernized. The philosophy behind the Discovery House is "To be, rather than to see." Children explore inside a tree like squirrels, climb inside a giant gallinule egg, peer through the eyes of a frog, and climb up a honeycomb. The idea is good, and has been implemented at the Bronx Zoo with enormous success. In my opinion, however, the atmosphere in Discovery House borders on the tacky; and while it provides a nice indoor play area on rainy days for entertainment of groups, it requires too much explanation and results in too little education.

Besides the animal exhibits, notice some of the architecture when you visit the zoo. The building Solitude, built between 1784 and 1785, was the manor house of John Penn, grandson of William Penn. It stands in a corner of the zoo grounds at the end of a walk, surrounded by beautiful trees, and looks today very much as it must have looked when it was built. Joseph H. Anderson may have been the architect of this plain but distinctive building in neoclassical style, although some believe it was designed by Penn. In the early days of the zoo Solitude's drawing room was used for reptiles. Today, it houses the president's office.

The 1916 neoclassical Bird House was renovated in 1950 and restored it in 1987. The Victorian gatehouses dating from 1876 remain intact as architectural treasures without being coveted by zoo designers on the lookout for new exhibit space.

☝ NATIONAL AVIARY IN PITTSBURGH

Allegheny Commons West
Pittsburgh, Pennsylvania 15212
(412) 323-7233

Open: 9–5

Best for: Parrots; cranes; toucans

Year opened: 1952

Acres: 1.5

Animal population: 550; 217 species

Director: Dayton Baker

Membership: None

Getting there: In West Park, north of Allegheny River. From I-279 exit at Arch street, go to West Ohio Street.

Conservation: Focus on endangered species: Rothschild's starling, Guam rail, Palawan peacock pheasant.

Education: For information on programs at the aviary and at schools, call (412) 323-7234.

Special attractions: Parrots in the halls.

Gift shop: No.

Food: No.

At the Pittsburgh Aviary, the only indoor bird facility independent of a zoo in North America, 550 birds of 217 species are mostly in natural habitat settings. The aviary places a special emphasis on parrots, Japanese and white-naped cranes, and toucans, and also has an alluring burrowing owl exhibit, small forest birds, and hummingbirds. The Marsh Room has waterfowl and wading birds: egrets, herons, ibises, and spoonbills. Endangered species are highlighted, among them Rothschild's starling, the Guam rail, and Palawan peacock pheasant. Two golden conure parrots hatched in September 1990, and a hyacinth macaw in February 1990; all had been artificially incubated and were handraised. Both the conures and macaws were the aviary's first breeding of these species. It is worth reflecting on the purpose of such birds' lives. From a conservation point of view, they may be among the few survivors of their species. From a P.R. point of view, exotic birds can attract attention. King Tut, a salmon-crested cockatoo at the San Diego Zoo, achieved and maintained celebrity status until his retirement. Saving a species and raising the recognition value of one parrot can make an educational point about the environment.

🐾 PITTSBURGH ZOO

P.O. Box 5250
Hill Road
Pittsburgh, Pennsylvania 15206
(412) 665-3639

Open: 10–6; call for winter hours

Best for: Tigers; red kangaroos; saddleback tamarin monkeys.

Year opened: 1898

Acres: 77

Animal population: 6,284 (1,483 fish, 4,406 invertebrates); 398 species

Director: Barbara Baker

Membership: Zoological Society of Pittsburgh (412) 441-9304

Getting there: In Highland Park, west of downtown Pittsburgh, on south bank of Allegheny River. On Hill Road off Allegheny River Boulevard. From Route 28 take Aspinwall exit.

Conservation: SSP participation for Siberian tiger, white rhinoceros, lowland gorilla, golden lion tamarin.

Education: In-school visits. For grades one to six, preparation for zoo visits, summer camp. For adults, programs with colleges on animal behavior, habitats, endangered species. For more information, call (412) 665-3762.

Special attractions: Tropical Forest exhibit; Aqua Zoo.

Gift shop: Shops at entrance and plaza, with good selections.

Food: Good fast food at visitors' plaza.

The Pittsburgh Zoo is in the process of implementing a master plan, due for completion in the year 2000, that will move it from this century into the next in more ways than one. In 1898, when the zoo opened, it was, like most zoos at the time, a collection of

cage exhibits. The children's zoo was opened in 1949 and unfortunately looks it. There are prairie dogs, which the children are told
bark but are not dogs—they are rodents; a Scottish Highland
cow; and goats. A new children's zoo is planned and will have
participatory learning experiences.

The Aqua Zoo filled its tanks and opened its doors in 1967.
Today the giant northern octopus, dramatic angelfish, and king
(South African) and Chilean rockhopper penguin may be seen
there.

The general situation at the zoo began to improve in the 1980's
when the outdoor Asian Forest exhibit was added, and an initial
renovation was undertaken of the Siberian tiger exhibit, which,
like most of the zoo, is situated on a slope. Now the resident tigers
have vertical as well as horizontal space in which to pace, which
they do with apparent pleasure. It is a very attractive exhibit.
Also to be seen in the Asian Forest, which doesn't really look like
a forest, are Asian waterfowl such as bar-headed geese and demoiselle cranes.

The African Savannah exhibit, added in the late 1980's, provides a good opportunity to see lions, flamingos, reticulated giraffes, African elephants, white rhinoceroses, Grevy's zebras, and
the common eland. Landscaping could have been used to hide
more of the background buildings and man-made objects than it
does.

Pittsburgh Zoo's $7.4 million Tropical Forest complex was
conceived in 1983 and completed in 1990. It houses eight species
of primates, including lowland gorillas, black- and white-ruffed
lemurs, spider monkeys, white-handed gibbons, and mandrills.
The message is strongly oriented toward conservation and saving
forest habitats.

🐾 ZOOAMERICA NORTH AMERICAN WILDLIFE PARK

100 West Hershey Park Drive   **Open:** 10–8; call for winter
Hershey, Pennsylvania 17033   hours
(800) HER-SHEY

Best for: Snowy owls; pumas; porcupines

Year opened: 1978

Acres: 11

Animal population: 213; 71 species

Director: Troy Stump

Getting there: Located east of Harrisburg. From I-81 take Exit 27 south.

Conservation: Participates in ISIS program.

Education: Volunteers used in lecture program.

Special attractions: North America as theme. Nearby Hershey Park, an entertainment complex.

Gift shop: Poor.

Food: Fair, minimal.

ZooAmerica North American Wildlife Park is an 11-acre commercial operation and part of Hershey Park, an "entertainment complex" adjacent to Chocolate World, all owned and managed by Hershey Foods Corp. The zoo is divided into five zones: Big Sky, Gentle Woodlands, Cactus Community, Grassy Waters, and North Woods. It seems to be more commerce- than conservation/education-oriented, although ZooAmerica is an accredited AAZPA zoo, with 213 animals and 71 species. The zoo brochure advertises the zoo as "frolicking," "fun" and "fantastic." My impression on visiting the zoo was that it was a commercial afterthought: "We have a valley that we aren't really using, so why not put a zoo there?" The zoo needs more attention than it is receiving. Even the monorail of the amusement park trespasses directly over the zoo. Corporate ownership of aquariums (for example, the four Sea Worlds owned by Busch Entertainment Corporation) has, in general, produced a far better life for fish than such ownership of zoos has produced for animals.

In the Grassy Waters exhibit can be seen roseate spoonbills, eastern diamond rattlesnakes, an armadillo, and an American alligator. The Florida Keys reef has good signs, one noting, "Coral formations are composed of skeletal remains of polyps, tiny animals that live in colonies." Cactus Community has a well-lit rotunda with sand, rocks, and cactus—although some are dying or already dead.

In the North Woods zone at Hershey Zoo there is good multi-level viewing of bison, white-tailed deer, eastern wild turkeys, ravens, bears, and a wolf, though the wolf has a large exhibit area and is difficult to see. Signs are generally good at the zoo, although the wolf is not identified. The snowy owl has a large wire-enclosed outdoor area near a stream with much vegetation, including trees, which is good for the owls but makes viewing hard for the visitor. Pumas are found on a large artificial rock area with a cave. They have little space for privacy or walking, but the exhibit provides good viewing for the public. The trees in the porcupines' area include two birches, although two other trees are dying. The public gets a good view when the porcupines are slouched on the branch of a tree.

⊰ ROGER WILLIAMS PARK ZOO

1000 Elmwood Avenue
Providence, Rhode Island
02907
(401) 785-3510

Open: 9–5; call for winter hours

Best for: Polar bears; Cattail Marsh; African Plains

Year opened: 1882

Acres: 35

Animal population: 492; 156 species

Director: Tony Vecchio

Membership: Rhode Island Zoological Society
(401) 941-3910

Sister zoo: Belize Zoo and Tropical Education Center, Belize City, Belize

Getting there: From I-95 south, take Exit 17; from I-95 north, take Exit 16.

Conservation: Exhibits nearly 20 endangered species, including gray wolves, Parma wallabies, cotton-top tamarins, and Puerto Rican crested toads (first SSP animal).

Education: Emphasis on conservation. Call 785-9450, ext. 80, for further information. ZOOPOWER is a program initiated in 1993 to train urban youth ages 14 to 20 as long-term environmental educators; the youths conduct natural history and science activities for school children ages 7 to 12.

Special attractions: African Plains; Cattail Marsh.

Gift shop: Super. Books upstairs.

Food: Hungry Bear Café very, very good.

The Cattail Marsh is a refreshing boardwalk engagement with a broadleaved cattail marsh. Look for redwinged blackbirds, carp, muskrat, American cot, green frogs, painted turtles (probably on a log), and bird nests in the spring. The New England Marsh is to the Roger Williams Zoo what the Louisiana Swamp is to the Audubon Zoo in New Orleans. Both exhibits exemplify a regional native habitat, and provide a few moments with captive nature.

The tahr is a furry, goatlike animal that lives on rocky mountain slopes and is difficult to approach in the wild. Their exhibit is in a partially shaded wood with some brush and rocks; in most other zoos, such as the Greater Baton Rouge, the tahr has no cover, only high man-made rock. In Baton Rouge the tahrs are active, climbing, while in Providence they are inactive, lying on the ground.

As a part of its $28 million Master Improvement Plan, and at a cost of $4 million, in 1991 the zoo created a mini African Plains exhibit where Maasai giraffes and elephants share the same waterhole but are separated by a "fallen" tree trunk and rocks and boulders. The exhibit is good, but the attempt to create the illusion of a natural habitat fails. While the public has a close-up look at the elephants and giraffes, there is no depth to the scene. In 1993 the zoo opened its Plains of Africa II exhibit with two male cheetahs, zebras, bongos, and oryx, which provided a considerable addition. However, medium-sized zoos such as Roger Williams and Sacramento would perhaps do better not to have large animals such as giraffes and elephants and to place more emphasis on other smaller species. Unless a zoo can really manage to create the ambience desired, it should not try—the days of the one-of-each-animal zoo are over.

The Tropical America building (formerly the elephant house), dating from 1930, has been put to effective and dramatic educational use. The restoration project, while modest ($125,000), does a superb job of bringing a bit of rain forest to Rhode Island. Because there are no signs in rain forests, a handsome brochure, called *Field Guide*, is provided for plant and wildlife identification. Don't just put it in your pocket; read it and enjoy looking for the animals pictured in the booklet. The New York Zoological Society's William Conway points to the Roger Williams Park Zoo as one that deserves commendation for its conservation efforts.

🐃 RIVERBANKS ZOOLOGICAL PARK

P.O. Box 1060
500 Wildlife Parkway
Columbia, South Carolina
29202
(803) 779-8717

Open: 9–6; call for winter hours

Best for: Reptiles; birds; tamarins

Year opened: 1974

Acres: 170

Animal population: 2,250 (700 invertebrates, 527 fish); 483 species

Director: Palmer Krantz

Getting there: From I-126 take Greystone Boulevard exit.

Conservation: Breeding of black howler monkeys, white-faced sakis, golden lion tamarins, toco toucans, milky eagle owls, blue-billed weavers, cinerous vultures, pied hornbills, eclectus parrots, Renauld's ground cuckoos, and crimson seedcrackers. Reintroduction of the Bali mynah to Indonesia. Rehabilitation of local birds of prey. Riverbanks has successfully bred 11 of its 17 endangered species.

Education: Programs to support the elementary science curriculum throughout South Carolina. Other child and adult classes on endangered species and animal behavior. The zoo's farm, with cattle, goats, sheep, swine, horses, and poultry, focuses on agriculture-related programs. For information on programs call (803) 256-4773.

Special attractions: Rainstorms in the Bird House; feeding of lions and penguins; two milking demos daily. At Christmas: "Lights Before

Christmas" (80,000 lights on 250 trees for a dramatic evening visit to the zoo).

Gift shop: Elephant's Trunk Gift Shop.

Food: A fast-food restaurant in a very attractive, relaxing setting overlooking the African Plains.

Many zoos are placing an emphasis on water as a theme. In 1989 Riverbanks Zoo opened a 22,000-square-foot, $45 million Aquarium Reptile Complex with 2,000 specimens of 350 species, emphasizing the diversity of life forms. The complex is particularly well designed, with excellent lighting. There are four galleries: South Carolina, the Desert, the Tropical Habitat, and the Ocean. My favorite exhibit is the 55,000-gallon Indo-Pacific coral reef. At the complex you will find endangered crocodilians, radiated tortoises, Madagascar ground boas, and Aruba island rattlesnakes.

The Bird House features exhibits on the habitats of the seashore, the desert, the swamp, and the rain forest. The birds are separated by barriers such as moats, water, and light. You can count on the weather in the rain forest: There's a rainstorm three times daily on weekdays and four times daily on weekends. Since 1974, the zoo has cared for injured birds of prey, including eagles, hawks, owls, ospreys, kestrels, kites, and vultures. More than 48 percent of the birds are returned to the wild after they have been treated.

Riverbanks has a semicircular primate building which has the appearance of a tunnel, flanked by exhibits in its compact, ultraneat zoo. There are also Saki and Titi monkeys, golden lion tamarins, and siamangs, and the largest captive group of black howlers in the world. Riverbanks's director, Palmer Krantz, is particularly proud of his zoo's successes in breeding endangered animals. As you visit different exhibits in this zoo keep an eye open for the endangered species. The zoo has received two awards from the AAZPA—one for outstanding achievement in breeding black howler monkeys, another, in 1981, for producing the first captive-bred white-faced sakis, which are native to Brazil. There are two breeding groups of golden lion tamarins at Riverbanks, which number only about 200 in the wild in Brazil. The zoo is fortunate in having a farmer's market only fifteen minutes from the zoo, which provides 10 to 15 varieties of exotic fruit daily.

The toco toucan, which had never been bred in captivity, was hatched and raised in 1977. A critically endangered Micronesian Kingfisher, once indigenous to Guam but now only found in zoos, was hatched at Riverbanks in early 1993. Total zoo captive propagation is now 60; when it reaches 160, it is hoped that a reintroduction program can be implemented.

𝒓 GREAT PLAINS ZOO AND MUSEUM

805 South Kiwanis Avenue
Sioux Falls, South Dakota
57104
(605) 339-7059

Hours: 9–7; call for winter hours

Best for: Deer; red-tailed hawk

Year opened: 1963

Acres: 40

Animal population: 271; 69 species

Director: Edward Asper

Getting there: From I-29 take Exit 79 east (12th Street) and turn south on Kiwanis Avenue.

Conservation: Accredited to AAZPA in 1991.

Education: Natural history museum with classrooms and theater. "How the Animals See" exhibit.

Special attractions: Delbridge Museum of Natural History.

Gift Shop: Poor.

Food: Minimal.

The bad news: The Great Plains Zoo contains one of the worst big cat exhibits I have ever seen, in a dreadfully run-down state. The snow leopard in his cramped cage prison had an off-the-floor board on which he could curl up and nightmare his life away. The cement was cracked, discolored. Snow leopard cubs in an adjacent cage were kept under similar conditions, as were two Siberian tigers and two lions. A tearful sight. A big sign on the spot and on the zoo map promised a "Future African Savannah."

The good news: The zoo knows it has problems. Director Edward Asper, former AAZPA board member, with experience as zoological director of Sea World Parks and 12 years with Marineworld Africa USA of the Pacific in Vallejo, California, has taken charge of the zoo and begun an initiative to improve it. On October 25, 1992, the zoo announced a $2 million campaign to tear down the 1963 pens and build a new exhibit, deigned by Jon Coe of Philadelphia, for the snow leopard and Siberian tigers. One tiger is a female and has a surprise in store for her: A Siberian tiger sent over *from Siberia* is waiting for her in Calgary, Canada, until the new quarters are ready. The zoo and the female Siberian tiger can thank the SSP for having selected her to mate. The other cats (puma and jaguar) will be placed at other zoos.

The primate building counts as its population a Diana monkey, white-handed gibbon, ruffed lemur, spider monkey, and boa. Their building receives a second priority assignment (after the cats), and is expected to be renovated into natural habitats. The various hoofed animals are displayed in similar enclosures, each with a wooden-log barn: zebra, camel, bison, llama (and an ostrich). A sign at the penguin exhibit carries a dramatic conservation message, that "sixteen cents in coins is all it took to kill one of our penguins" (owing to zinc poisoning). The children's zoo is contained in a compound within a fortlike wall, with a prairie dog exhibit in the center (although no "dogs" were visible at the time of my visit). Goats and llamas are pettable. The exhibit is in process of being upgraded. Smaller exhibits, such as lizards, are to be placed in a log cabin at the edge of the children's zoo compound, and more farm animals will be introduced. There is hope of obtaining a red panda (an SSP animal).

The zoo opened two new exhibits in 1992, Wild Dogs of America, featuring the timber wolf, red wolf, coyote, and red fox, and a rebuilding of nine pheasant pens into an exhibit of birds of prey, including the screech owl, snowy owl, kestrel, king vulture, barn owl, and Swenson's hawk.

The zoo owns a massive collection of stuffed animals, a gift of C. J. Delbridge, who bought the collection and gave it to the city of Sioux Falls. The animals had belonged to Henry J. Brockhouse, a resident of Sioux Falls, who hunted local animals during the 1930's and 1940's. In the 1950's he ventured to Canada and Alaska for hunting, and in the 1960's to Africa. His final killing sprees were in India, New Zealand, Australia, and Mongolia. When I saw them, the 138 dead animals, including eleven endangered or threatened species, were lined up in the zoo's museum like a company of Marine Corps recruits. Director Asper has tackled the problem of display by constructing a wall maze, creating a path for the visitor to follow. The animals have been properly grouped by geographic regions, with graphics to identify them and their native habitats. Also, the city has provided $300,000 for the construction of two dioramas, one of a panda in bamboo surroundings, and the other an Australian grassland. This collection has considerable potential value as an educational tool. Some of the animals will or may never be exhibited live, and their presence is a reminder of the dwindling list of live species.

🐾 MEMPHIS ZOOLOGICAL GARDEN AND AQUARIUM

2000 Galloway Avenue
Memphis, Tennessee 38112
(901) 726-4787

Open: 9–5; call for winter hours

Best for: African hoofed animals

Year opened: 1906

Acres: 70

Animal population: 2,342; 416 species

Director: Charles Wilson

Membership: Memphis Zoological Society
(901) 725-6999

Getting there: In Overton Park, off I-40 (Summer Avenue) between North Parkway and Poplar Avenue.

Conservation: SSP participation for snow leopard, clouded leopard, Sumatran tiger, cheetah, gorilla, golden lion tamarin. Also blesbok antelope.

Education: Activities take place in amphitheater and Discovery Center. For information call (901) 725-4768.

Special attractions: Cat Country; African Veldt; Primate Canyon in 1994, followed by Nocturnal Exhibit.

Gift shop: Quality merchandise, especially good on books; education corner with instructional materials.

Food: Carnivora Restaurant. In the future large glass windows will look out at ringtail and white-ruffed lemurs.

In 1901, Natch, a black bear cub, was the Memphis zoo's first guest. The only problem was, there was no zoo. Natch had been the mascot of the Memphis Baseball team, and no cages could be found, so Natch was simply tied to a tree in Overton Park, where any passerby could visit him. However, Natch began to grow. Something had to be done. When Natch was joined by a bobcat and a raccoon in 1906 the city of Memphis came up with money for buildings and a zookeeper.

In 1990, a $24 million capital campaign was launched to propel the zoo into the forefront of the development of the city of Memphis. Today zoo goers enter past a parade of concrete animal statues—rhinoceros, elephant, hippopotamus, gorilla, and crocodile—and find themselves on the bank of the . . . Nile. You see the seven cataracts of the Nile, and feel you are not in Memphis, Tennessee, but Memphis, Egypt, at the temple. You enter the temple court where you will find a replica of the Rosetta stone, which in fact was carved not in Rosetta, but in *Memphis* (Egypt) and then transported to Rosetta. The copy is the size of the original. The development of Egypt is portrayed over 2,000 years, with a live African lion overlooking the court.

The visitor moves through the zoo along two different routes: on a primary loop route through the zoo, and a second route which leads into special regional or species-oriented areas. One exhibit renovated in the capital improvement program is Cat Country, the zoo's newest pride. The Larson Company of Tucson has done the construction, making a point of enabling people to view the cats at eye level, across a watered moat. If the cat swims across the moat it cannot get out, because the wall on the visitor side has been so cantilevered that escape is impossible. Ethnographic elements have been introduced into the exhibit to remind one that people and animals live together. The ruins of Angkor Wat in Cambodia have been replicated, tumbling out into the visitor area, and one has the sensation of being *with* the Sumatran tiger. The path leading into Cat Country is thick with bamboo and wanders uphill to a rise (actually crossing a service road, which you never see) to an Asian pagoda. Along the way you can catch sight of clouded leopards, jaguars, cheetahs, and lions.

Education takes a leading role in the zoo's future. The Children's Village is to be renovated into a history of the American farm with grinding stone, miniature animals, etc. While there will be some touching opportunities, the public will not be allowed in the enclosures with the animals. A donation of 50 or 60 horseshoes of different types, from racing slipper up, will allow children to compare the shoe of a Shetland and a Clydesdale!

Another improvement should come about by 1995, when the African hoofed animal exhibit will become an African Fishing Village with museum-type displays demonstrating the interrelationship of the human and animal worlds. A Tropical Asian Forest with butterflies and small bird life and a Tropical American Forest are also to become realities. A passage from the latter will lead into a natural 200-year-old-plus forest in Memphis, making the point that there is great diversity in the world, but some of it can be found in one's own backyard.

Director Charles Wilson worked at the Oklahoma City and Little Rock zoos before becoming director of the Memphis Zoo in 1975. Wilson has been with the zoo since 1972. His master's thesis was on the golden lion tamarin. Wilson's studies and zoo work caused his philosophy to change: he no longer considers wildlife completely free. Very little wildlife is completely wild; it is all managed to some degree. But he is grateful for the opportunity to contribute to the knowledge of the golden lion tamarin and its reintroduction to the wild. If he had been told in 1972 that they could be reintroduced, he says he wouldn't have believed it. It is a shining example of what might be done for other species.

Wilson also observes that over the past 20 years the concept of conservation has changed dramatically, from a concern over natural evolution in the wild to the evolutionary impact of captivity on populations. "We are trying to freeze-frame species," he observes.

➤ TENNESSEE AQUARIUM

P.O. Box 11048
Chattanooga, Tennessee 37401
(615) 265-0695
Open: 10–6; Fri.–Sun./holidays 10–8
Best for: Otters; alligators; piranhas

Year opened: 1992
Acres: Under one acre
Animal population: 4,000; 350 species
Director: President Jim Hill

Getting there: In downtown Chattanooga on the Tennessee River. Public transportation: Downtown shuttle up Broad Street every 5 minutes (629-1473).

Conservation: Programs directed toward world's rivers, with particular emphasis on the Tennessee and Mississippi rivers.

Education: Teachers may request specific programs relating to topics being taught in their classes. For further information: (615) 266-9353.

Special attractions: World Rivers; Tennessee River; Mississippi River and Delta.

Gift shop: Attractive gifts: glass figurines, carved fish, Christmas ornaments.

Food: No food allowed. Go to 212 Market Street, a splash away.

The $45 million, 12-storied Tennessee Aquarium, which opened May 1, 1992, prides itself on being the first major freshwater life center in the world. The aquarium, which was designed by Cambridge Seven Associates, focuses specifically on the Tennessee River and other great river systems. The exhibit designers were

Lyons/Zaremba of Boston, and the exhibit fabricators, the Larson Company of Tucson, Arizona. The aquarium's Nickajack Lake tank contains 139,000 gallons of water and is the largest freshwater tank in the United States. The Tennessee Aquarium was privately financed by contributions from individuals, corporations, foundations, and other organizations.

A publication of the Tennessee Aquarium notes that, "even though 70 percent of the Earth is covered in water, 97 percent of that is saltwater. Of the remaining three percent, which is freshwater, two-thirds is locked up in polar ice caps and glaciers. Most of the rest is underground. Therefore, of all the water on Earth, only 1/100 of one percent is freshwater found in our rivers, lakes, and streams. We are polluting that water at an alarming rate, killing turtles and darters—the main indicators of healthy water systems—in the process. All creatures are here for a reason, and we may not know how important those creatures are until we destroy their populations and are faced with the consequences."

The goal of the aquarium is *education in a natural setting.* There are no sea lion, dolphin, or other trained animal shows at the aquarium. The aquarium has hands-on and interactive exhibits, a 200-seat auditorium, two classrooms, and a wet lab. Children in Kentucky enthusiastically anticipate visits to the aquarium and have an exuberant reaction to the experience. For example, one school group hopped onto a bus, still half asleep, at 2:30 A.M. in order to arrive at the Aquarium for a 9:00 performance of interactive skits that focused on conservation of the Tennessee River, accompanied by graphic slides and loud music. They loved it.

The exhibits take the visitor on a trip beginning in the Appalachian high country from which water runs into the Tennessee river. One also visits the Mississippi Delta and the rivers of Africa, South America, Siberia, and Asia. The aquarium highlights waterlife but is all-encompassing in its approach, and exhibits also include birds, amphibians, reptiles, mammals, and insects that rely on rivers for their existence. Exhibit areas include:

- Appalachian Cove Forest
- Tennessee River Gallery
- Mississippi Delta
- Discovery Falls
- Rivers of the World (Amazon, Zaire, St. Lawrence, Shimanto, and cold and warm Eurasian rivers)

Endangered plants are included in exhibits: a pink ladyslipper from a logging site, an American chestnut tree in the Appalachian Cove Forest exhibit, ginseng and trillium. At the Discovery Falls exhibit videos show the life cycles of several aquatic insects and the importance of bogs and swamps in our lives. Another exhibit shows the life cycle of mayfly nymphs, who live for only one day and have no mouth parts. Twenty species of birds (Carolina chickadee, winter wren, downy woodpecker, migratory kingfisher, eastern bluebird, cedar waxwing) fly free among the hardwood trees of the Appalachian Cove Forest, where river otters may be found, along with minnows, perch, and sculpins. Over 30 species of fish, including fingerlings, bass, and catfish, are to be seen in the underwater terrain of the aquarium's Nickajack Lake, the original created by the Tennessee Valley Authority in the 1930's. After passing through the exhibits, the visitor enters a canyon for a view through large acrylic windows into the dimly lit exhibit tanks.

ᛤ CALDWELL ZOO

2203 Martin Luther King
Boulevard
Tyler, Texas 75710
(903) 593-0121

Open: 9:30–6; call for winter hours

Best for: Anteaters; reptiles

Year opened: 1952

Acres: 35

Animal population: 1,445; 276 species

Director: Hayes Caldwell

Getting there: From I-20 east of Dallas exit to Tyler Loop. Caldwell Zoo is off Loop and King Boulevard, five minutes from I-20 turnoff.

Conservation: Endangered-species exhibit with skins, bones, ivory at zoo entrance. SSP-oriented.

Education: Zoo owned by the Caldwell School. Discovery Center.

Special attractions: Aquarium and African Plains.

Gift shop: Outstanding.

Food: Good cafeteria; two other food stops.

By far the best small African plains zoo exhibit is to be found at the Caldwell Zoo in Tyler, Texas. There are many varied viewing opportunities, including one perspective of the plains from an attractive restaurant and gift shop housed in a pseudo–East African lodge. Both close-up as well as distant views are obtainable of giraffes, elephants, zebras, and other plains animals. A male black rhino and a female on loan from the Cincinnati Zoo produced a female weighing 80 pounds on May 30, 1993.

The Terrestrial Exhibit, containing an aquarium, birds, and reptiles, has been built on a corner of the plains and is absolutely outstanding. At water level in the aquarium, which is at just the right height for children to look at and over, there are rocks and vegetation, behind which are glass panels providing a sweeping view of the African Plains. There are 582 fish representing 48 species, including African peacock cichlids, Malawian eye-bilers, lemon cichlids, and regal peacocks. Reptiles to be seen include Madagascar pleated lizards, African giant pleated lizards, Sudan rough-scale lizards, and African spur-eyed tortoises. Birds at the Terrestrial Exhibit include lapwinged plovers, Cape teals, and white-faced whistling ducks. To the right side of the exhibit, through another wall with a naturally sculptured hole in the gunnite "rock," can be seen three lions relaxing, yawning, and stretching. Viewed from a different point the lions in the foreground (separated by a moat) appear to be in the same area as gazelle, which in the wild would be their natural prey.

At the zoo's Flight Cage exhibit, South American anteaters may be found along with king vultures, egrets, and 20 species of ducks. They relish a soupy concoction of commercial horse meat, milk, and egg. They love it! And I enjoy watching the anteaters.

Billy, a blue and gold macaw, is a zoo celebrity used in education talks.

Don't miss the colobus, leopard, and bongo exhibits (not a part of any specific geographic exhibit), which are a walk down (or up) the hill. These exhibits may be viewed through one cage into another, which creates a feeling of cohesion. There is an attractive waterfall. The Texas exhibit includes a hands-on farm area.

If I had to choose two smaller zoos as "the best" they would be Fort Wayne (Indiana) Children's Zoo and the Caldwell Zoo.

♛ CAMERON PARK ZOO

1701 North Fourth St.
Waco, Texas 76708
(817) 750-8400

Open: 9–6; call for winter hours

Best for: Gibbon island

Year opened: 1993

Acres: 50

Animal population: 125; 40 species

Director: Tim Jones

Membership: Central Texas Zoological Society
(817) 776-9036

Getting there: Near downtown Waco on the Brazos River.

Conservation: SSP participation: Sumatran tiger, white rhino, Grevy's zebra, white-handed gibbon.

Education: An education building like an old Texas farmhouse with "as many programs as we can get."

Special attractions: A brand-new zoo. African Treetops Village overlooks giraffe, zebra, kudu, rhino, and elephant.

The new Cameron Park Zoo (formerly the Central Texas Zoo) occupies 50 acres on the Brazos River, seven acres of which are to be devoted to telling the story of the Brazos River and exhibiting 125 specimens of local marine life. The new location places the zoo closer to Baylor University, with which it has a close working relationship on education programs. Furthermore, the zoo has joined an association of eight area museums, formed in

Waco in 1992, to develop education programs. The zoo's emphasis will be on anthropology, with a tie-in to the 15 mammoth
fossils that may be seen at their original site halfway between
Waco and the airport.

In addition to the SSP species mentioned above, the new zoo
has a giraffe (from the Audubon Zoo in New Orleans), a white
rhino (from Fossil Rim, Texas), and an African elephant (from
the San Diego Zoo). There is an African treetop viewing platform
and a 100-foot-long pond with many plants and secluded spots for
flamingo. Designs have been completed for a reptile house containing 100 species to be opened in late 1994. Johnny Binder, the
zoo's general curator, is a herpetologist, and a large number of
reptiles are native to the area in Texas, so people are interested.

➤ DALLAS AQUARIUM

P.O. Box 150113
Juanita Craft Station
Dallas, Texas 75315
(214) 670-8453
Open: 10–5
Best for: Queenland grouper
Year opened: 1936

Acres: 1
Animal population: 2,875;
375 species
Director: Richard Buickerood
Membership: Dallas Zoological
Society, (214) 943-2771

Getting there: Three miles south of downtown Dallas. From I-35 take
the Ewing Avenue exit and follow the signs.

Conservation: Interaquarium research.

Education: Classes, speakers' bureau.

Special attractions: "Different Strokes" exhibit.

Gift shop: Simple.

Food: No.

The Dallas Aquarium, which is one large rectangular room,
is predominantly a showcase of geographic areas. African Rift

Lakes are especially good. When I was there, poster graphics in English and Spanish appeared to be temporary and hastily put up, but were in fact very readable, to the point, and informative. A shell collection in the center of the aquarium building is a display I have not seen at other aquariums. Good idea. No hands-on or touch tank. Some small tanks are rather too high on the wall, separated from the viewer by railings, which children climb up on. At the end of the one-room hall is a nurse shark, horse eye jack, and lemon shark; and a good piranha and small, blue neon tetra are definitely worth seeing. Don't miss the Queenland grouper, which can grow to 10 feet and weigh up to 850 pounds. The exhibit "Best Camouflage" is a tasseled wobbegong shark from the Great Barrier Reef that blends into its surroundings. Signs on the seahorse exhibit inform visitors that the female deposits her eggs in the male's pouch for hatching. The "Different Strokes" exhibit shows that not all fish swim the same way: angelfish swim by propulsion, rays use flat pectoral fins, triggerfish rhythmically wave dorsal and anal fins forward and backward, moray eels use snakelike movements, wrasses use sculling motions, and puffers flutter and use their tail to guide them like a rudder.

All in all, the aquarium has merit, but needs an interior architectural face-lift. (It is no longer accredited by the AAZPA.)

🦌 DALLAS ZOO

621 East Clarendon Drive
Dallas, Texas 75203
(214) 670-6825

Open: 9–6; winter
(Oct.–March) 9–5

Best for: Large mammals;
birds; reptiles

Year opened: 1888

Acres: 105

Animal population: 1,487;
332 species

Director: Richard Buickerood

Membership: Dallas Zoological
Society, (214) 943-2771

Getting there: Three miles south of downtown Dallas. From I 35 take Ewing Avenue exit and follow signs.

Conservation: Dallas Zoo mission statement: "Strengthening respect and understanding for animals."

Education: "Imagine Africa" children's program. Children's zoo (summer only).

Special attractions: Wilds of Africa; monorail; nature trail (with guide brochure) to view the okapi, white-headed buffalo weaver, hammerkop, hyrax, bongo, duiker, more . . .

Gift shop: One at main entrance, another in Africa Plaza.

Food: Snacks.

A Dallas sixth-grader spends a day at the zoo. Freddy has signed up for a program called "Imagine Africa," and Africa is where he is going. He will need equipment for the trip and is given an airline guide to find out how to get there. He must know what it is going to cost, and receives a pad for his budget preparation. Alas, he is informed that the country he is going to in Africa does not use U.S. dollars; he must convert his dollars into a foreign currency. Binoculars slung over his shoulder, Freddy receives a Polaroid camera and is shown how to use it. He is then ready to join the group for their safari. A guide greets them, speaking Yoruba. Freddy climbs into a zebra-striped van (like the ones in East Africa), all his newly lent possessions secured in a knapsack. The group is divided into teams and given a task, a question to answer: The minister of tourism wants to establish a second lodge in the game park. What will this do to the park? Freddy's group visits animals at the zoo that are identified as being in the game park. Freddy takes photographs and is given research materials. He is glad when it is time to eat; he and his fellow adventurers sit down to an African meal and talk about what they have seen and the problems of the park. When Freddy leaves the Dallas Zoo he takes home with him his own field journal, a smart-looking, solid-cover record of his day on safari. In 15 pages he reports his impressions of Forest Habitat, Mountain Habitat, Woodland Habitat, River Habitat, Desert Habitat, Bush Habitat, and Savannah Habitat, with room for one picture on each page. A map of Africa follows, and the last page is for his conclusions. The conclusion of grown-up observers: The "Imagine Africa" program is an outstanding educational opportunity for children.

In constructing its Natural Habitat Gorilla exhibit the Dallas Zoo seems to have lost sight of its objectives. The exhibit, which opened in April 1990, is located within a 25-acre plot called The Wilds of Africa, featuring six native African habitats: desert, bush, river, mountain, woodland, and forest. The five gorillas' $4 million subplot is two acres, sporting more than 5,000 plants, including blackberry bushes and grapevines, heated rocks for dozing, waterways for "splashing and drinking," and "fog nozzles [to] help simulate the humid, misty atmosphere of a rain forest." There is lots of bush, brush, grass, leaves, and upright and fallen trees, and I was told the gorillas were there—but I failed to see even one during my visit. If one purpose for gorillas' incarceration is for humankind to see them and as a consequence care for the welfare of their relatives in Africa, then the purpose is not being served if they cannot be seen. If this exhibit is supposed to provide an educational message, it fails. If the exhibit is for the benefit of gorillas, then wouldn't the gorillas be happier on the slopes of Virunga? (In West Africa a gorilla's range is 1.5 to 11.5 square miles. The Dallas Zoo has five gorillas on two acres, which means that one gorilla has the space of one-half an acre. That's more than most captive gorillas get, but still cruel if the incarceration is pointless.)

A window allows visitors to observe gorillas when the animals show themselves. The acting director of the Dallas Zoo, Ron Kagan (now director of the Detroit Zoo), told me the story of the zoo's silverback. He was sexually attracted to all human females who passed by, and would start masturbating the moment he saw one, in evident frustration. This caused some embarrassment and amusement, and definitely captured the attention of zoo visitors, but was not the kind of education program intended for small tots. Something had to be done. A special glass coating was installed allowing visitors to look in but making it impossible for the sexually hungry silverback to see out. As a consequence the big gorilla stopped masturbating. One day, however, through primate perseverance if not instinct, the silverback managed to find a loose edge and peeled off the coating, and what to his wondering eyes did reappear but tantalizing human females. Overjoyed, he was immediately stirred to repeat his sexual act. What conclusions may be drawn from this tale? Ron Kagan's comment was that "gorillas find us fascinating, therefore we must impact—not alter—their actions in our relationship with them."

The Dallas Zoo's gorilla exhibit raises questions as to what constitutes a good gorilla exhibit, and which zoos have the "best." How are the exhibits constructed? What purpose do they serve? In the wild, gorillas are vegetarians and eat leaves, shoots, and stems, and small amounts of wood, roots, flowers, and fruits. What is their menu at a zoo? In nature gorillas live in bands (also referred to as groups, and sometimes troops) of two to 20. The leader of the band is a silverback. Do zoos accommodate the need of gorillas for companionship? How do zoos use their gorilla exhibits for the purpose of education, to trace the history of gorillas, their status in Africa, work being done to understand them, initiatives to save their relatives in Africa as a species?

Other exhibits at the zoo include the Bird and Reptile Building with its collection of 130 reptile and amphibian species; the Neotropical Aviary, where 300 species of birds are free to fly around you; and a children's zoo with a prairie dog town and pettable animals.

🐻 FORT WORTH ZOOLOGICAL PARK

1989 Colonial Parkway
Fort Worth, Texas 76110
(817) 871-7051

Open: Weekdays 10–5; weekends March–Oct. 10–6; June–Aug. 10–8; hol. 12–5

Best for: Texas town; primates; Asian rhinos; birds

Year opened: 1909

Acres: 59

Animal population: 4,200 (2,400 are fish); 725 species

Director and CEO: Position open

Membership: Fort Worth Zoological Association (817) 871-7000

Getting there: From Route 30 (East-West Freeway) take Exit 12A south onto University Drive, leading directly to the zoo.

Conservation: Exhibits of 44 endangered species, including harpy eagle (one of three zoos in U.S.); red-vented cockatoo (one of two zoos in the U.S.); eastern saurus crane (one of two zoos in the U.S.).

Education: A leader in zoo education. Works with schools' curriculum. First-grader visits to zoo. Outdoor experiences at zoo. For further information, call (817) 871-7055.

Special attractions: African Forest, herpetarium, aquarium (150 exhibits), 11-acre Texas pioneer town. Newest exhibit: Raptor Canyon, a three-acre walk-through aviary.

Gift shop: Zootique has super assortment.

Food: Yellow Rose Café, with its pressed tin ceiling and proscenium stage, for Texas food; Zoo Creek Café for fast food.

Fort Worth Zoo opened in 1909 with one lion, two bear cubs, an alligator, a coyote, a peacock, and a basketful of rabbits from a traveling carnival. The elephant, Queen Tut, was purchased in 1923, and the first animal shelter was built, a stone house costing $1,774 that is now a llama barn. Two American bison and the zoo's first zebra were acquisitions resulting from small visitor contributions.

Asian Falls (opened 1992) is chiseled out of the rocky hillside, and viewed from a boardwalk that appears suspended above the exhibits. Exhibited are Siberian and Sumatran tigers, and Neela, the white tiger, as well as sun bears. In Raptor Canyon can be seen harpy, bald, and Japanese hawk eagles; king vultures; and Andean condors.

The Fort Worth Zoo has re-created an 11-acre, $2.3 million turn-of-the-century Texas pioneer town for animals now found in Texas. A 12-stall barn is a dominant feature of the town with cows, pigs, and Dominique chickens. A central area with Texas longhorns, bison, javalenas, Jersey cows, and black-tailed prairie dogs (children may go through a tunnel on their knees to poke their heads up face to face with a prairie dog) is surrounded by a one-room schoolhouse, operating blacksmith shop, saloon, and a ranch house facing onto a town square. Look up and you will see a working windmill. The Texas town is reached by moseying down a tree-lined lane. Relax on the square by sitting underneath a mesquite tree with a cool drink in your hand while you ponder the 40 years of diary writings, displayed on 4-×-6-foot panels, of frontier woman Ella Algar Bird Dumont, the wife of a buffalo hunter. Afterward take a walk along the banks of Trinity River.

The impressive World of Primates exhibit, which opened in 1992 and houses all the families of the greater apes, is claimed to be the only such exhibit in the United States. The Sid Richardson Foundation in Fort Worth provided $7 million for the 2.5-acre exhibit, which includes an indoor, climate-controlled tropical rain forest housing endangered lowland gorillas, a gorilla nursery, colobus monkeys, and free-flying tropical birds. Trees and vines grow throughout the exhibit, and two 768-square-foot "living walls" within the enclosed rain forest, covered in live moss and tropical plants, are the largest of their kind in the nation. Indoor waterfalls flow into a moat that separates the gorillas from the zoo guests. Six separate areas house the lowland gorillas. Dr. Douglas Pernikoff, Fort Worth Zoo veterinarian, observes that "during the first few years of development, baby gorillas and baby humans are quite similar. Baby gorillas play and establish their place in the group just like human toddlers. They have their toys and favorite blankets." A huge artificial rain-forest tree with a 12-foot diameter rises from the center of the exhibit area and serves as a natural backdrop for the apes. The primates, housed in areas surrounding the tree, can be seen through unevenly shaped windows facing inward as well as one with a view of natural trees outside the exhibit building. A connecting outdoor exhibit features various other primates, including chimpanzees, orangutans, gibbons, bonobos, and mandrills, on lush islands. On my visit to the primate building, chimpanzees Cleo and Cleopatra were still in confinement in the basement of the building. Their daily schedule was simple, mostly eat and play, but they did have time to paint. One of their originals is framed and hangs on the wall of my kitchen. The Fort Worth exhibit puts people in the center, surrounded by primates. Gorilla Samantha likes to be photographed. She will give you a coy wave with the tips of her fingers. Samantha came from Cincinnati, where she threw snowballs at visitors.

Rhino Ridge is the name of Fort Worth's Asian rhino exhibit. Thirteen zoos in the United States are trying to save the Asian rhinoceros, also known as the greater one-horned Asian rhino, an effort spearheaded by the Fort Worth Zoo with the support of Edward P. Bass in association with the World Wildlife Fund (WWF). In the early seventies Nepalese farmers' clear-cutting for agriculture had divided rain-forest areas lived in by the rhinos into isolated islands. Poachers added to the problem, killing the rhinos for their horns, to which is attributed medicinal value. By the mid-1970's the rhino population in Nepal had been reduced to well under 100, with the world's total Asian rhino population at about 1,200. Three conservation goals were set up: to preserve the rhino's native habitat, to expand native habitats, and to encourage reproduction of the species. The Bass Foundation financed a relocation program for about 30 rhinos from one park to another in Nepal, where the rhinos now number 450. Maintaining rhino populations in more than one area is advantageous so that in case disease, weather, or unknown factors reduce one population, others will be saved. In 1990, a male, Arun (meaning "rising sun"), and a female, Arati (meaning "prayer"), arrived at Rhino Ridge, at the center of the Fort Worth Zoo; it is hoped that they will mate in 1994.

According to the 1985 master plan, future plans include the construction of an African Savannah, an entry fountain, water gardens and a sidewalk café, an Australia exhibit, World of Darkness (nocturnal animals), and an infant care center. There are plans to renovate the herpetarium (opened in 1960), the James R. Record Aquarium (opened in 1954), and the porpoise wing (added in 1962).

⚡ FOSSIL RIM WILDLIFE CENTER

P.O. Box 2189
2008 County Road
Glen Rose, Texas 78043
(817) 897-2960

Open: 9–two hours before
sunset; closed Thanksgiving
and Christmas

Best for: Cheetahs; white
rhinos; addaxes

Year opened: 1984

Acres: 2,900

Animal population: 946;
48 species

Director: Jim Jackson (owner)

**Vice president,
conservation:** Bruce Williams

Getting there: South of Fort Worth, from Route 35W go west on Route 67 to Glen Rose. Three miles southwest of Glen Rose turn south at the sign to Fossil Rim.

Conservation: SSP participation, including Grevy's zebra, addax, scimitar-horned oryx, dama gazelle, cheetah.

Education: Tours of center.

Special attractions: Overnight stays of three to five days at Foothills Safari Camp in the park, open year-round. Reservations required, (817) 897-7691 or (800) 245-0771 or fax (817) 897-3785. Six private double-occupancy tents with attached bath and heat and air conditioning. Attractive in- and outdoor dining area.

Gift shop: Outstanding, with unexpectedly large selection costing from pennies to big bucks.

Food: Simple, delicious, mostly homemade. Informal atmosphere. Striking view from a high vantage point of the ranch with an opportunity to spot wildlife.

There are nearly 500 ranches in Texas, and more in other states, with populations of exotic and superexotic animals. At most of these ranches animals are protected, though some exist to provide expensive sport for hunters.

The size, animal populations, and management of ranches varies widely. One example of a well-run private wildlife ranch is the Fossil Rim Wildlife Center, which is accredited by the AAZPA.

A different type of wildlife experience may be found at the Fossil Rim, a 3,000-acre chunk of Texas, about 80 miles south of Dallas, well off the beaten track, where animals have plenty of space. Here you can look forward to a 9½-mile drive over hillsides scattered with juniper, live oaks, and scrub brush that can take as long as four hours at the 16 mph speed limit, with stops for animal viewing. Fossil Rim seems and is remote. The main difference between Fossil Rim and other zoos, explained Director Bruce Williams, at Fossil Rim since 1981, is that Fossil Rim is "round the clock; zoos are not": The animals are not put away for the night as are most zoo animals, who are on show in their "native habitat" for public enjoyment for only eight hours of the 24. Fossil Rim offers an educational experience. It has some very good collections that are well displayed.

Fossil Rim is associated with the Species Survival Program, and has had great success breeding cheetahs, which are difficult to breed in captivity. Most of its population of 55 cheetahs are on loan elsewhere. Five acres are given to two cheetahs, who need space to exercise. I remember seeing a cheetah make a kill on the Serengeti plains in Tanzania: The cheetah searched for prey, a Tommie gazelle, across the plain, then moved stealthily through the grass, body pulled low, head pushed forward, eyes on the target, hindlegs raised by tight muscles readying for the spring forward; finally, the 70-mile-an-hour dash. It is good to see cheetahs have space, as they do at Fossil Rim. I cringe when I think of cheetahs on cement floors behind bars. Fossil Rim has more than 30 species of endangered, threatened, and exotic animals, including the red wolf, extinct in the wild (though a release program is contemplated for North Carolina); the Mexican wolf, whose DNA identifies it clearly as a distinct species; Mac and Ollie, the resident African white rhinos; and 90 addaxes—the largest captive collection in the world. Fossil Rim is a for-profit organization, though it is heavily endowed by Jim Jackson, its president and executive director, whose business is building yachts. Fossil Rim is what "safari parks" *should be* but, sadly, aren't.

The Role of Exotic-Animal Ranches

Ranches can play a very important role in conservation. According to Louis R. DiSabato, director of the San Antonio Zoological Gardens, wildlife conservationists and many zoo managers underrate the actual and potential value of Texas wildlife ranches, which started up in the early 1930's. Ranches that do not allow hunting could well be an asset to overcrowded zoos. At his zoo DiSabato has an antelope-breeding facility of 50 pens. A number of years ago DiSabato realized he had an antelope population of 500. He was interested in a number of particular species (he had 32 species at the time), but not in an accumulation of such a huge population. Ranchers helped him absorb his surplus, while he retained breedable numbers.

Some ranches also breed animals that are supplied to zoos. Zoos prize the small populations of topi, dama gazelles, and addaxes in their collections, while the total population of addaxes resident in Texas ranches is probably an astonishing 1,000. The kongoni (Coke's hartebeest), DiSabato points out, was once visible in great numbers in Africa, but no longer. Texas zoos had them, but didn't give enough attention to them. DiSabato believes that if they had been on ranches they would have been saved. "The blackbuck in zoos probably all come from Texas ranches," DiSabato said. Elvie Turner, former director of the Dallas Zoo, pointed out that there are probably 30,000 blackbuck in Texas, more than in India, where they originally come from.

The role of exotic-animal ranches in conservation is intertwined with the complex and emotional question of zoos selling animals to ranches to be hunted. The problem stems from zoos having surplus animals as a result of their breeding programs, which emphasize endangered species. The space and money available for surplus animals in zoos is limited. A tiger costs about $20 per day in upkeep. For the most part these animals cannot be returned to the wild. For example, there are 1,000 Siberian tigers in zoos and 300 in the wild, but surplus Siberian tigers cannot be reintroduced into the wild because their habitat will not sustain a larger population. Euthanasia is humane, but why should a zoo kill an animal if it can sell it and thus raise money for conservation efforts?

The AAZPA is studying this problem, and will release a report in 1994. Previously, the AAZPA expelled any member institution that sold animals to ranches to be shot. Now, the AAZPA accepts the position that an animal may be sold to a ranch where hunters shoot animals as long as the specific animal sold is not killed, but only its offspring. What wild kind of logic is that?

In mid-1993 the AAZPA focused on the issue by appointing an Exotic Game Ranch Committee to communicate with ranchers and "encourage them to participate in the Association's conservation programs." It stated the aim that research on contraception should be given a high priority for AAZPA's Conservation Endowment Fund's (CEF) awards and grants. It also stated its strong opposition to the "sale, trade, or transfer of animals from zoos and aquariums to organizations and individuals which allow hunting of animals directly from or bred at zoos and aquariums." The threat not to provide CEF grants or awards is a bit hollow, since the AAZPA decided not to provide *any* grants or awards in 1993. A number of zoo directors question the AAZPA's being in the conservation business at all. Nevertheless, AAZPA started a campaign on January 1, 1994, to raise $5 million for their CEF program by 1998.

𝕿 HOUSTON ZOOLOGICAL GARDENS

1513 North MacGregor
Houston, Texas 77030
(713) 525-3300

Open: 10–6

Best for: Primates; tropical birds

Year opened: 1921

Acres: 50

Animal population: 2,762; 661 species

Director: Don Olson

Membership: Zoo Friends of Houston, Zoological Society of Houston, and Assistance League of Houston
(713) 529-2632

Getting there: In Hermann Park. Within walking distance of Rice University. By bus: Eastern Metro Transit.

Conservation: SSP participation for cheetah, snow leopard, clouded leopard, golden lion tamarin, Galápagos tortoise, St. Vincent parrot, lowland gorilla, Siberian tiger, margay.

Education: Brown Education Center, including the Young Discovery Room. Art After School project and ecology lectures. Call for information, (713) 525-3362.

Special attractions: Kipp Aquarium; McGovern Mammal Marina; Discovery Zoo (barnyard animals). Alligators fed at 2:00, Thursday and Sunday, April–September; bats at 2:30 in nocturnal section of Small Mammal Building; sea lions at 11:00 and 3:00 in the Marina.

Gift shop: Usual zoo stuff; expansion planned.

Food: Concessions at both ends and center of zoo.

The $6.5 million, barless, cageless Wortham World of Primates, opened March 1993 on a three-acre site, is the pride of the Houston Zoological Gardens. It is home to about 150 primates of 13 species of prosimians, monkeys, and apes in 11 natural-habitat exhibits: boreal orangutans, siamangs, mandrills, Kikuyu colobus monkeys, Patas monkeys, spectacled langurs, black- and white-ruffed lemurs, ring-tailed lemurs, red-crowned mangebeys (found at only three U.S. zoos), howler monkeys, golden lion tamarins, emperor tamarins, and Bolivian gray titi monkeys.

With a climate that favors plant life, the Houston Zoo has made good use of flora in a renovated small mammal house (opened in March 1993) that includes a rain forest exhibit. Horticultural expertise is also demonstrated in the fish and bird garden. Birds to look for are the Bali mynah, Mauritius pink pigeon, turaco, and breeding Hawaiian forest birds. Natasha Schischakin, conservation curator, is leading a crusade to save the pale-blue Spix's macaw, native to Brazil, of which only 29 survive. Most of these endangered birds are in captivity and have a purchase price of $80,000 to $125,000. Schischakin feels strongly that zoos in the United States should focus on working together on regional programs; they should not work in isolation.

In 1988 the George R. Brown Education Center opened, with the Young Discovery Room for children aged two to six and an auditorium with multipurpose space where various types of exhibits can be mounted. For example, a snakes of Texas exhibit and a touch tank with sea anemones was on display in 1992. Lisa Ottman, education curator, is enthusiastic about the zoo's two Bioscanners (a type of magnifier). One is in the Reptile House and the other in the Brown Education Center.

The zoo's emphasis on education includes a series of Discovery Classes, specially designed for children from 3 to 12 years old, with names like "Night Critters," "Armored Animals," "Meerkats Make You Smile," and "Hidden Animals." A four-part course for junior curators examines the challenges of designing a zoo for the twenty-first century.

The Houston Zoo works with the school system on a program called "Say Yes to a Youngster's Future," designed by the National Urban Coalition and Shell Oil. The program encourages students to think of careers in math or science. During a morning at the zoo, teachers receive materials for classroom activity as well as training on how to use the zoo. Some students who participated in the program were so enthusiastic that they composed a rap song with lyrics that included the refrain "good to go to a zoo," and they returned to the zoo to sing it.

Usually the zoo is a nice quiet place to stroll in, look at animals, and think about nature. In 1986, however, there was a moment of wildness when an escaped psychiatric patient tore through the zoo fence with a bulldozer he had borrowed from a construction site and plowed into an antelope enclosure, then through another fence and into a zebra enclosure. He continued his trip into a third enclosure, where there were two rhinos. None of the other animals were injured, but the rhinos went into shock, from which it took them some time to recover; the patient was placed in captive custody by the police. In recounting the incident, curator

David Ruhter commented that "people are one of the most dangerous things in a zoo."

The Houston Zoo receives its support from the Houston Parks and Recreations Department, which wants the zoo to be the crown jewel of the park system. The zoo is currently implementing a 20-year master plan that began in 1989. Until more of the master plan is realized, the Houston Zoo will remain a hodgepodge of the old and the new. Meanwhile, it achieves excellence in its programs and staff enthusiasm.

⚘ SAN ANTONIO ZOOLOGICAL GARDENS AND AQUARIUM

3903 North St. Mary's Street
San Antonio, Texas 78212
(512) 734-7184

Open: 9:30–6:30; call for winter hours

Best for: Koalas; antelopes

Year opened: 1914

Acres: 50

Animal population: 3,325; 811 species

Director: Louis DiSabato

Sister zoos: Kumamoto, Japan, and Guadalajara, Mexico

Getting there: In Olmos Basin Park, ten minutes from downtown or airport. From Route 281 take Hilderbrand Avenue exit east.

Conservation: Particular interest in antelopes.

Education: Speaker's bureau, zoomobile, internships, films, workshops. For information, call ext. 113.

Special attractions: Forest Trail; Australian Walkabout; children's zoo.

Gift shop: Excellent, including books.

Food: Riverview Restaurant; various snack stops.

Ten minutes from downtown San Antonio, at the headwaters of the San Antonio River, are limestone cliffs shaded by oak, pecan, and cypress trees. This is the site of the San Antonio Zoo and shows how a natural landscape may be effectively adapted to the needs of a modern zoological park as well as demonstrating most effectively how old iron-barred cages can be transformed into modern exhibit areas. Visitors can move from the central part of the zoo onto trails with multiple viewing opportunities and close encounters with animals. The Australian Walkabout, opened in 1989, features dingoes, giant red kangaroos (capable of leaping 26 feet), Goodfellow tree kangaroos, wallabies, wallaroos, wombats, and two Queensland koalas.

San Antonio is one of the six U.S. zoos exhibiting koalas; the others are Chicago, Los Angeles, Miami, San Diego, and San Francisco. San Antonio's African antelope collection is one of the largest in the world. The zoo once had a gorilla, but not at present; a new primate exhibit area is to be built. Birds on exhibit include lories, rosellas, and emus (the second largest bird in the world).

The children's zoo has a tropical tour with a boat ride that passes flamingoes on "Galápagos Island" and visits miniature exhibits; it also has a playground, desert building, Everglades exhibit, rain-forest exhibit, and animal nursery.

The zoo's magic is due to the imagination and ingenuity of zoo director Louis R. DiSabato. DiSabato started his zoo career at the Columbus (Ohio) Zoo, where he was a keeper for 15 years; then he went to the Seneca Zoo in Rochester, New York, before becoming director of the San Antonio Zoo in 1968.

🐎 NATIONAL ZOOLOGICAL PARK CONSERVATION AND RESEARCH CENTER (NOT OPEN TO THE PUBLIC)

1500 Remount Road
Front Royal, Virginia 33630
(703) 635-6500

Best for: Arabian oryx; Pere David's deer; Przewalski's horses

Year opened: 1975

Acres: 3,150

Animal population: 1,014 (410 mammals, 604 birds); 37 species

Director: Chris Wemmer

Owned by the Smithsonian Institution and managed by Board of Regents. Under the direction of the National Zoological Park, Washington, D.C.

Getting there: From Route 66, turn south at junction with Route 522/340.

Conservation: The main purpose of the center.

Education: Teacher training and training of foreign nationals.

Special attractions: Research.

Front Royal, Virginia, lies 80 miles west of Washington, D.C.'s, National Zoological Park (see profile). Southwest of Front Royal, in magnificent scenery on the slope of the Appalachian Mountains near the northern entrance to the Skyline Drive, is situated the zoo's 3,150-acre, double-fenced Conservation and Research Center (CRC). The space and rolling hills patched with forest make it an ideal refuge from the plight of our planet for any animal, humans included. It is a place where people are inspired to think about conservation. The CRC, on grounds formerly used as a government livestock research station and—during World War I—a German POW camp, was established in 1973. The center, which is dedicated to captive propagation of endangered species and education, is not open to the public. The center protects 37 species with an animal population that exceeds 400 mammals and 600 birds; there are no reptiles and no primates. A population of 96 Pere David's deer pause to look over a sturdy but unthreatening fence at 24 Przewalski's horses in one direction and 53 sable antelopes in another. Only 800 Przewalski's horses remain in the world, all in captivity. Across the valley, walking in a long line silhouetted against the sky, is a herd of 28 scimitar-horned oryx.

CRC places special emphasis on its birds, which include 117

Redhead ducks, 140 Bahama pintail ducks, and 115 northern pintail ducks. CRC is particularly pleased with its Guam rail breeding successes and also has six Japanese cranes, which are also called mandarin cranes; the politically neutral name "red-crowned crane" is most often used. The mandarin crane is believed by the Chinese to be the bird you will meet on your way to heaven.

CRC is supported by the U.S. government through the Smithsonian Institution. CRC is a member of the AAZPA and cooperates with other zoos; in fact, it considers itself *a* if not *the* leader in conservation thinking. However, its conservation coverage has limitations, and its contact with institutions abroad is no more and may be less than that of some zoo conservation efforts.

American conservationists with international associations have realized the great value of training foreign nationals so that they may take an educated, active, and productive role in conservation efforts in their own country. CRC's Wildlife Conservation and Management Training Program provides such training on an international level. Courses are conducted at Front Royal (CRC), and at locations in Venezuela, Malaysia, and China. A CRC staff instructor has organized a special environmental awareness program in Malaysia, working with the Malaysian Department of Wildlife. The program's long-term objectives include conservation education, training of instructors, collaboration in scientific research, establishment of overseas centers, career development assistance to trainees, and international networking.

In 1991 CRC celebrated its International Wildlife Conservation Training Program's tenth year with a residential course for 30 students from 20 countries who arrived at Front Royal with their luggage to stay for 10 weeks. The instruction they receive is comprehensive, even including a religious perspective on animals presented by Faisal Dean, who was conservation advisor to the prime minister of the State of Bahrain and now lectures at CRC on subjects which include ethical considerations regarding wildlife. Another program, Zoo Biology and Animal Management, began in 1988 with the purpose of teaching education, research, and conservation aspects of zoo management in developing countries. CRC collaborates on international conservation and educational programs with a number of U.S. zoos, including the Lincoln Park Zoo (a program in China); the Dallas Zoo, Miami Metro Zoo, and Milwaukee County Zoo (on zoo biology training); the New York Zoological Society; the Philadelphia Zoo; and the Columbus (Ohio) Zoo, as well as, of course, the National Zoo in Washington. CRC has also established a valuable communications learning tool: the Conslink computer bulletin board, which provides an electronic medium for discussion of all aspects of biological conservation. The bulletin board, which may be reached on BITNET, includes files such as: meetings (conferences, symposia, and workshops on conservation), field stations (list of field stations in tropical countries), reference (conservation-related material), and a newsletter of IUCN's (the International Union for the Conservation of Nature) Captive Breeding Specialist Group.

CRC has bred more than 100 golden lion tamarins at Front Royal. The golden lion tamarin, a South American marmoset, is highly endangered, with only about 400 living in their native habitat in the coastal mountains southwest of Rio de Janeiro, Brazil. The golden lion tamarin is a beauty to look at, with a thick lionlike mane covering its ears, and an alert, hairless face. Its coat is golden fur. A number of zoos participate with Brazil in a reintroduction program, placing the tamarins back into their home-country mountains. This animal truly deserves more publicity than it has received for its beauty, its endangered status, and for the fact that there is a working, successful program to reintroduce it into the wild. Of course, some cynics will rightly say: And how long will they be able to live in the wild? Meanwhile, the CRC and zoos with breeding programs are doing the right thing.

🦌 NORTHWEST TREK WILDLIFE PARK

11610 Trek Drive East
Eatonville, Washington 98328
(206) 832-6117
Open: 9:30–6:30; call for
winter hours; closed
Mon.–Thurs. Nov.–Feb.
Best for: Ungulates

Year opened: 1975
Acres: 680
Animal population: 515;
56 species
Director: Gary Gebbes

Getting there: South of Tacoma, off Route 161 north of Eatonville.
Conservation: Conservation of nature and habitat, thus of animals.
Education: Discovery Center.
Special attractions: Tram ride; trails; lake. Grizzly and black bear exhibit.
Gift shop: Interesting.
Food: No.

Northwest Trek Wildlife Park, in Eatonville, Washington, is a drive-through park, but in sharp contrast to many other drive-throughs, feeding of animals and private cars are not allowed. (There is adequate space for parking in the shade of trees outside the entrance to the park.) The pasture grass is green, and the hilly landscape is thick with trees offering refreshing shade. Enticing Horseshoe Lake attracts many species of waterfowl, and there are five miles of nature trails to explore at a leisurely pace on foot. If you want to see more of the zoo, a small tram will take you on a 50-minute journey through the 680 acres of forest, meadows, and marshland to discover elk, moose, deer, and bighorn sheep. Education and exhibits (including children's zoos) go hand in hand.

There are many ways, and places, at a zoo to reach the minds and focus the attention of young adults. The Cheney Discovery Center at Northwest Trek Wildlife Park is small but has a most effective, compact, show-and-tell-and-feel education facility in a log cabin in the woods for children of any age eager to learn about local Washington state wildlife. Skulls, bones, and skins are there to touch and identify. Benches and chairs offer a comfortable break. Northwest Trek is a soul-moving educational experience. Although not a zoo in the usual urban or urban-perimeter sense, it well deserves to be an AAZPA-accredited zoo.

➤ POINT DEFIANCE ZOO AND AQUARIUM

5400 North Pearl Street
Tacoma, Washington 98407
(206) 591-5337

Open: 10–7; call for winter hours

Best for: Pinnipeds; sea otters; musk oxen

Year opened: 1905

Acres: 27

Animal population: 5,390 (1,038 fish, 3,551 invertebrates); 314 species

Director: Tom Otten

Getting there: From I-5 (Highway 16) take Exit 132 to Sixth Avenue. Turn left, then right onto Pearl, which leads to Point Defiance Park. Go slowly to enjoy the magnificent trees.

Conservation: Survival center for the red wolf, North America's most endangered land animal. Golden lion tamarin and red wolf are among a number of SSP species exhibited.

Education: Evident throughout the zoo that education has a top priority. Classes, lectures, intern program, delightful nature walks.

Special attractions: Aquatic exhibits; World of Adaptations.

Gift shop: Pacific Rim Gift Shop carries posters, jewelry, books, and animal souvenirs.

Food: Snacks. Many good picnic spots.

The BBC ranked Point Defiance as one of the top five zoos in the world, and William Conway, president of the New York Zoological Society, claims this superb zoo and aquarium is his favorite. Its aquatic exhibits are tops, highlighting Pacific Rim wildlife with close encounters of the natural kind.

Be sure to check the animal program schedule immediately on arrival. There are performances from Memorial Day through

Labor Day, weather permitting. An innovative approach is used in getting the word out. A Macintosh computer near the entrance to the zoo provides information in an apparently handwritten script on the day's highlights and performances. Bird shows are at 3:00 P.M. daily, except Wednesday (birds' day off). Elephants may be found in their new $2.2 million barn, with two exercise yards, a state-of-the-art hydraulic restraint device, and two-story viewing from three sides of the exhibit. Elephant rides are available from 11:30 A.M. At other times, watch whales jump and blow and polar bears dive for their dinner. Staff members are available to answer questions about marine mammals from 11:00 A.M. until 4:00 P.M. at the Rocky Shore Complex.

Do not miss the South Pacific aquarium, Discovery Reef Nature Preserve, tide pool, and Rocky Shores exhibits, where you can see white whales, Alaska sea otters (who indulge themselves from an expensive menu of clams, crabs, and shrimp), seals, sea lions, auklets, and puffins (dirt in the exhibit allows them to burrow). At the Arctic Tundra exhibit you can see musk oxen, the last living line of the Ice Age goat-antelope; at the Pacific Rim exhibit, 12 Magellanic penguins and an octopus. The polar bear exhibit, with an 11-foot-deep saltwater pond, won an AAZPA award in 1982. The pinnipeds—seals and walruses—are the director's favorite exhibit.

The World of Adaptations is educational and entertaining. It is a joy to see how animals adjust to their environment, by the use of vegetation to camouflage their presence, or through an acute sense of smell, sight, or hearing. The 31 examples of animal adaptation include saw-whet owls, burrowing owls, golden lion tamarins, aardvarks, ocelots, bats, pythons, and tropical fish. The keeper offers demonstrations of animal diet preparation during the summer and on weekends in the winter.

➤ **SEATTLE AQUARIUM**

1483 Alaska Way
Pier 59, Waterfront Park

Seattle, Washington 98101
(206) 386-4300

Open: 10–7; call for winter hours

Best for: Salmon; sea otters

Year opened: 1977

Acres: 3.73

Animal population: 21,050; 393 species

Director: Cindi Shiota

Membership: Seattle Aquarium Society, (206) 682-3474

Getting there: By foot from downtown, or take a cab. Parking difficult.

Conservation: Focus on Puget Sound and North Pacific aquatic systems.

Education: Considered leader in working with handicapped population, using hands-on activities. Director Shiota particularly interested in interactive exhibitions.

Special attractions: Underwater Dome.

Gift shop: Fair.

Food: Snack at entrance. Better to go to one of many nearby eateries.

I found the Seattle Aquarium rather interesting once I got past the boardwalk entrance with its penny arcade atmosphere. I particularly liked the salmon ladder exhibit, which includes an overhead circular tank of baby coho salmon, back-lit by daylight. It is innovative and effective.

The Underwater Dome room is the aquarium's most popular exhibit, and certainly my favorite. The room is a hemisphere of 130 windows (110 are acrylic and 20 are laminated tempered glass) that protrudes up into the open waters of Puget Sound. Children and adults may sit on a carpeted, staired floor to look straight forward, up, or around to observe the aquatic life of Puget Sound that surrounds them—hundreds of fish, including the spiny dogfish and a school of herring.

The Seattle Aquarium, which is owned by the city and managed by the Seattle Department of Parks and Recreation, places considerable emphasis on education through its numerous exhibits and programs. In the main building demonstrations are given at street level, and a touch tank with sea stars, featherduster worms, and sea anemones provides a first-hand experience, as does a "Get Wet" hands-on program geared for children and also used with the handicapped. Lectures and field trips to explore Puget Sound are an opportunity to examine environmental issues.

♀ WOODLAND PARK ZOOLOGICAL GARDENS

5500 Phinney Avenue North
Seattle, Washington 98103
(206) 684-4880

Open: 9:30–6; call for winter hours

Best for: Gorillas; Asian elephants; gila monsters

Year opened: 1900

Acres: 90

Animal population: 3,991; 246 species

Director: David Towne

Membership: Woodland Park Zoological Society
(206) 789-6000

Getting there: Take Interstate 5 to 50th Street exit. Follow 50th Street west to zoo.

Conservation: Numerous SSP species, with emphasis on Asian elephant and lion-tailed macaque.

Education: Activities and Resources Center with strong education programs and Discovery Room.

Special attractions: Rain Forest.

Gift shop: Especially good.

Food: Snacks; restaurant planned.

Woodland Park Zoological Gardens has an outdoor African Savannah exhibit on three acres that most effectively creates an illusion of space. The animals are skillfully arranged in separated exhibits on a raised plain so as to appear all together, with excellent viewing opportunities. The result is a really superb display of Africa's horizon-to-horizon plains on the equivalent of the geographic head of a pin. Director David Towne's objective is to intrigue people, to get them to care and make an emotional commitment to saving the African plains.

Woodland has one of the best facilities—if not the best—for

Asian elephants. The elephants have a 4.6-acre forest with a winding stream, and the public may see them from eight different viewpoints. The 8,500-square-foot elephant barn, designed in Thai architectural style, has a rubberized floor to protect the elephants' feet and knee joints, and radiant heat, produced at a low cost, thereby allowing the doors to be left open. In a shady outside area, educational presentations are made to the public on elephants and their use as beasts of burden in Asia.

In the 2.5-acre, $9.2 million tropical Rain Forest, which opened in September 1992, visitors stroll along a boardwalk surrounded by 700 plant species, past emerald tree boas and red-billed toucans to a treetop observatory from which free-flying birds may be observed.

The Asian tropical forest exhibit is modeled after the Bronx Zoo's Jungle World, and has tigers, siamangs, orangutans, and lion-tailed macaques.

The zoo's Nocturnal and Tropical House is very effective: An elevated wooden catwalk passes through the dark (almost too dark) exhibit, and visitors can catch glimpses of nocturnal animals, including slowly shuffling lorises and porcupines.

The zoo has started implementing its $31 million master plan, which includes a Northern Trail, with Kodiak bears, gray wolves, river otters, bald eagles, and snowy owls; the Steppe Zone, with bison, pronghorn cattle, prairie dogs, llamas, rheas, and maned wolves; an indoor Desert Zone, with small mammals, birds, and reptiles; and a Temperate Deciduous Forest, with New England swamps and marshes.

As an integral part of its education program, Woodland Park Zoo has an attractive family-oriented Discovery Room located close to the zoo entrance with hands-on opportunities and also has a farm with domestic animals (Director David Towne strongly believes domestic animals should be part of a zoo).

One quarter of the food supply at the zoo is organically grown. Reptiles are given mouse embryos. As in a number of other zoos, at Woodland polar bears are given large blocks of ice to play with; the blocks have a special reward of a fish or an apple in the center that the bears can eat when the ice melts. Activity relieves boredom.

Woodland's gorilla exhibit is one of the best. Seattle has provided privacy for the gorillas while still giving the public an opportunity to see them. The breeding of endangered species is a main reason zoo experts give for having animals in captivity, and privacy, particular for births, is important to gorillas. "One day in October, 1983," a zoo report recounts, "a lowland gorilla (named Zuri) was born at the Woodland Park Zoo. But unlike any other captive gorilla births in the country, the event happened in a wild place where a mother could seek privacy from other troop members and give birth in dignity among the brush in a naturalistic gorilla exhibit designed by Jones & Jones Architects." The exhibit, which currently contains six gorillas, looks natural to the visitors and, presumably, to the gorillas. It isn't West Africa, but it is close, with fallen logs, places to hide, and real vegetation. Four different viewing areas allow the visitor to observe the gorillas from different angles. Another area adjacent to the present gorilla exhibit, formerly tenanted by bears, has been included as an extension for additional gorillas, including a male from the Phoenix Zoo.

Some facts on gorillas: There are three races of gorillas. The Western lowland gorilla, the smallest race, inhabits parts of the forest between western Cameroon and the Congo River. Eastern lowland gorillas are found in parts of the lowland forest of eastern Zaire and in some of the nearby highland areas. The Eastern lowland gorilla, not the mountain gorilla, has the honor of being the largest primate in the world, weighing an average of 363 pounds as compared to 343 pounds for the mountain gorilla. The mountain gorilla inhabits the Virunga volcano range in Zaire's Parc National des Virungas, in Rwanda's Parc National des Volcans, and Uganda's Gahinga Forest Reserve. Mountain gorillas may appear larger because of their thick hair, which they need to protect them not only from virtually continuous dampness but also from the cold at altitudes of 9,200 to 11,000 feet.

The major focus by zoos has been on the Western lowland

gorilla; there are essentially no mountain gorillas in zoos. There are about 600 gorillas in captivity; in the wild the estimates for the Western lowland gorilla are vague, ranging between 10,000 and 40,000. Mountain gorillas were "discovered" in 1903 when the scientific world was informed by a German colonial officer, Von Bereng, that he had seen what later was called *Gorilla berengei*. As recently as 1959 there were estimated to be 5,000 to 10,000 mountain gorillas. The mountain gorilla population that was 239 in 1981 is somewhat on the increase, now numbering about 310.

⟨ BARABOO ZOO

Ochsner Park
Baraboo, Wisconsin 53913
(608) 356-6319

Open: 9–4

Best for: Prairie dogs; timber wolves; llamas

Year opened: 1926

Acres: 2

Animal population: 67; 14 species

Director: Tom Stephany (director of Baraboo Parks and Recreation Department)

Getting there: Baraboo is north of Madison. Ochsner Park is in residential section of Baraboo.

Conservation: Involvement with the Wisconsin timber wolf reintroduction program. AAZPA membership as goal.

Education: Newsletters have educational content. Programs planned.

Special attractions: Unusual small community zoo.

Gift shop: No

Food: No.

I went to Baraboo to visit the International Crane Foundation (see profile) and the circus and found a little surprise, the Baraboo Zoo. Of the perhaps 600 to 750 zoos in the United States, 163 are accredited by the AAZPA. Of those that are not, some don't deserve to be—but others, like Baraboo, while neither large nor rich enough to apply and be accepted for AAZPA membership, are nevertheless little community treasures.

The Baraboo Zoo, an owl hoot away from residential houses, started with one white-tailed deer in 1926. A local citizen had a deer, didn't know what to do with it, and put it in the park; another Baraboo-ite followed the first citizen's lead and added a second deer. A year later the parks commission asked the city council for $300 to build a fence to protect the two deer. Two black bear cubs were added to the collection. The collection grew and so did local interest. In 1984 The Friends of Baraboo Zoo was formed. One of their ideas was to see that the money collected from downtown parking meters went to the zoo. In 1984, $282 was received as revenue.

Today Baraboo Zoo has a population of nearly 70 animals—not including local squirrels, birds, and invertebrates.

In October 1993 the zoo collection included 1 pair of timber wolves, 1 pair of black bears, 1 capuchin monkey, 1 great horned owl, 25 prairie dogs, 1 mute swan, 1 pair of bobcats, 1 pair of foxes, 1 raccoon, 3 adult deer, mallard ducks, and 2 llamas, Dr. Pepper and Lolita.

Sica, the timber wolf, was born in captivity to a breeder who sold the wolf to an individual. It is illegal for an individual to own a wolf, so Sica was confiscated and sent to the McKenzie Environmental Center, then to the Baraboo Zoo. Tom Stephany likes the story: from cage to park. I do, too. In 1986 Sica received a new home at the zoo, an 80-×-120-foot area. It has good natural landscaping and is easily viewable from a boardwalk platform.

The zoo has no pretensions, no expectation nor wish for an elephant. It offers a collection of wildlife in a quiet, attractive setting on a rise of land shaded by tall trees and punctuated by bushes and flowers. The zoo has good signs and provides an opportunity for a close look at its animals. Equally important, it instills an interest. You leave the zoo caring.

CIRCUS WORLD MUSEUM

426 Water Street   (608) 356-8341 (general)
Baraboo, Wisconsin 53913-2597   (608) 356-0800 (information)

Everyone loves the circus. For many it is a reminder of childhood, when one was younger and life was better. It is the magic
of laughter at the clowns in their droll costumes and painted
faces. It is the excitement and suspense of watching the acrobats
and high-wire performers, teetering at great heights under the
canopy. And it is the animals. Along with everything else that a
circus is, it *is* a traveling zoo.

There are a number of traveling circuses in the United States.
You can wait until the Big Top comes to town, or if the circus
doesn't come to you, you can go to it in Baraboo, Wisconsin,
where you will find the Circus World Museum and can see a Big
Top show, daily at 11:00 A.M. and 3:00 P.M. There is no backstage;
you are on stage. The preshow animal lineup is in full public
view, as I found when I brushed by the side of an elephant on my
way to find a seat. You can watch Zoppe-Hayes's horses circling
the ring; Jorge Barreda's cat act, which makes the big animals
seem as docile as house cats; and Lou Ann Jacobs's performing
elephants. There are even elephant rides.

An educational look at circus history can be found in the
Wagon Pavilion, with 150 antique circus wagons, and the Exhibit
Hall, which shows the movie *The Man and Legend*, about
Gunther Gebel-Williams, superstar wild animal trainer with the
Ringling Brothers and Barnum & Bailey Circus for over 20 years.
There is no denying that circuses are entertaining and fun, nor is
there any denying that the animals are a large part of the entertainment. It also can't be denied, however, that there is very little
that is educational in a circus; that is all it is—entertainment. But
if you think that I am going to state that animals should not
appear in circuses, you are wrong, for I, too, like to see a circus.

♠ HENRY VILAS ZOO

702 South Randall Avenue
Madison, Wisconsin 53715
(608) 266-4732
Open: 9:30–4:45
Best for: Primates
Year opened: 1911
Acres: 27

Animal population: 706;
174 species
Director: David Hall
Membership: Henry Vilas
Zoological Society
(608) 258-1460

Getting there: From Route 151/14 (Beltline Highway) turn north on Park Street to Regent. Turn left on Regent and left again on Randall to zoo.

Conservation: Participates in SSP programs, but needs a bit of tidying-up in its own backyard.

Education: Zoomobile, classes, Discovery Center/Herpetarium.

Gift shop: Inadequate.

Food: Small snacks and refreshments.

In 1904 Colonel and Mrs. William Vilas, in memory of their son, donated the land on the north shore of Lake Wingra where the Henry Vilas Zoo is located. In 1914 the Henry Vilas Zoological Society was organized to provide support for the zoo. Today, the zoo needs a face-lift; Bruce Behler, director of the Milwaukee Zoo, commented, "It is trying to update itself, but it needs money." This probably means it needs community support.

The zoo opened with five deer, and its appearance suggests that it has been struggling ever since. When I visited the zoo there was no seal in the seal exhibit, the penguins had too much sun, and there was no otter in the otter exhibit, where a rock pond was thick with leaves.

The zoo should concentrate on one or two projects—the children's zoo would be a good one—and sell or transfer all the other animals. The small island on which the children's zoo is located is thick with trees and bushes—messily so, not magically—but with creative design thinking it could become a major zoo attraction. The bird building, built in 1915, is passably good. A selection of existing exhibits should be highlighted, renovated, and made year-round, specifically, the Primate Center, the children's zoo, the otter exhibit, and the bird building.

The University of Wisconsin's Primate Center Zoo is, in fact, a circular exhibit of six cages thick with active monkeys exercising and playing on modern-art mobiles, wheels, and other fun shapes. They appear to be enjoying themselves, therefore visitors do too—especially children. The Henry Vilas Zoo deserves credit for its Discovery Center/Herpetarium, opened in April 1992, an interactive educational facility. The exhibit, which includes live animals, describes what has happened to animals of the world. The signage is good, and the composition of the exhibit is such as to provide a feeling of exploration. Hopefully the zoo is succeeding in its search for community spirit and funds.

✦ INTERNATIONAL CRANE FOUNDATION

E-11376 Shady Lane Road
Baraboo, Wisconsin 53913
(608) 356-9462-3-4

Open: 9–5; closed Nov. 1–April 30

Best for: Cranes

Year opened: 1973

Acres: 160

Animal population: 122; 15 species

Director: George Archibald

Getting there: From Route 12, north of junction with Route 33, exit to Shady Lane Road at "International Crane Foundation" sign just before Exit 92.

Conservation: Cranes, cranes, cranes!

Education: Publications; special programs; internships. Good film at start of educational tour (tour schedule: daily 10:00, 1:00, 3:00; call for summer, weekend, and holiday schedule).

Special attractions: Wisconsin Prairie Trails; Johnson Exhibit Pod.

Gift shop: Excellent. Good selection of publications on birds, especially cranes. (Particularly recommended: *Reflections: The Story of Cranes,* by Gretchen Holstein Schoff, and *Cranes, Cranes, Cranes.*)
Food: No.

Cranes, which are found on all continents except South America and Antarctica and are closely related to coots and rails, have been on our planet for 60 million years. The Sandhill crane dates from 9 million years ago and is the oldest living species of bird. Seven of the world's 15 species of cranes are endangered: the red-crowned, white-naped, wattled, Siberian, hooded, whooping (only about 230 birds, including those in captivity), and black-necked cranes (there are 10 in U.S. zoos).

The message of the International Crane Foundation (ICF) is important. The foundation, started in 1904, is "dedicated to the protection of cranes and their wetland homes, all around the world. Our story is about people of many countries, who love the cranes and work together in spite of political tensions . . . to make the world safer for cranes . . . and safer for people too." In a sense the foundation sets the cranes up as aerial ambassadors with a mission to improve conditions on our planet. All ICF members receive the foundation's publications, *The ICF Bugle.*

Cranes are traditional symbols of peace, happiness, and longevity. When you arrive at the foundation, deep in Wisconsin country, your tour starts with a film, followed by a walk past crown cranes in a Wisconsin prairie setting. The air is fresh and clear. You are already uplifted. A tour leader takes you to the Johnson Exhibit Pod, containing 13 species: red-crowned, demoiselle, blue, white-naped, Siberian, common, black-necked, whooping, sandhill, hooded, wattled, brolga, and Indian sarus. The Pod is a pie-shaped structure of fences, simply and well done, though a bit shadeless. The guide gives an outstanding narration on each of the species as the distant cry of cranes is heard from Crane Village some distance away (not open to the public), where crane breeding takes place. The tour ends with a visit to a chick hatching location. Take a walk to explore the countryside and listen to the cry of cranes mixing with the song of local birds.

Conservation is a primary activity of the ICF. In 1992, 28 whooping cranes were captive-raised. In 1990, ICF hatched an endangered black-necked crane, a first for North America. In cooperation with the Russians, expeditions have been mounted to study the endangered Siberian crane. The expedition tagged three common cranes with transmitters in order to study migration patterns. ICF has a strong wetlands conservation program, including the Tram Chim wetland project along the Mekong River in Vietnam. Protecting cranes means protecting their wetland habitat.

ᠺᠵ MILWAUKEE COUNTY ZOOLOGICAL GARDENS

10001 West Bluemound Road
Milwaukee, Wisconsin 53226
(414) 771-5500

Open: 9–4:30; Sun./holidays 9–6; call for winter hours

Best for: Sea lions; bonobos

Year opened: 1904

Acres: 194

Animal population: 5,590; 380 species

Director: Charles Wikenhauser

Membership: Zoological Society of Milwaukee County (414) 258-2333

Getting there: Take Route 94 (East West Freeway), going west from downtown Milwaukee. After crossing Route 894/45 look for zoo on left, on West Bluemound Road.

Conservation: Endangered species exhibited: Humboldt penguin, trumpeter swan, Siberian tiger, African kudu, bonobo.

Education: Workshops; day camps; guided and self-guided tours.

Special attractions: Sea lion show (May–Oct.); zoomobile; miniature zoo train; behind-the-scenes ride through the zoo (May–Oct.); Raptory Theater (birds of prey in free flight).

Gift shop: Posters, jewelry, books, and much more . . .

Food: Snacks abound; Flamingo Café.

The Primate Center complex is impressive for its efficient labyrinth of holding enclosures, with skylights and very high ceilings, containing trees and habitat furnishings. The center houses up to 28 gorillas, as well as Milwaukee's four bonobos. Bonobos, pygmy chimpanzees, are found in central and western Zaire, where eight percent of the species' range is still forested. Bonobos are the most intelligent species after humans. The bonobo population in the wild is about 15,000, with about 40 in captivity. Bonobos are in zoos in San Diego's Wild Animal Park, and in the Columbus and Cincinnati, Ohio, zoos.

Milwaukee has a modified local-release program. Tamarins are released into an unrestricted wooded area near the zoo's aquarium. To make sure no greater territory is reached by exploring tamarins, an attendant is on duty at all times, and the tamarins are radio-collared.

Deputy Zoo Director Bruce Behler showed me the zoo's hospital, which looked pretty good, although he informed me that he hopes the zoo will get a bigger and better one. The one they already have has X-ray and operating rooms and labs for blood and other sorts of tests. As we walked through the lab, Dr. Andrew Teare was examining penguin blood under a microscope, looking for malaria. Dr. Teare created the MEDARKS (Medical Animal Records Keeping System) program of ISIS (International Species Inventory System), and Cyd Mayer, also at work in the lab, created its computer software program, which is being used by 125 zoos worldwide. Medical research cannot be accomplished in a vacuum by one zoo. Sharing of knowledge is necessary.

Director Charles Wikenhauser said that the Zoo Society, not the zoo, manages the education program, which targets third- to sixth-graders, and zoo graphics, although both organizations work together and have unrestricted funds within the budget. He would like to see a component in the master plan for graphics and more focus at the zoo on conservation for the general public. The 1985 master plan made provision for several impressive new exhibits, including Wolf Woods; the polar bear exhibit with underwater viewing; a Dairy Complex (a cow barn with six varieties of dairy cattle, a learning center, and a dairy store); the Taylor Family Humboldt penguin exhibit; the three-acre Stackner Heritage Farm; and the Education Center (sponsored by the Dairy Council Wisconsin and formerly known as the children's zoo). Also, don't miss the Africa exhibit, where predator and prey (ostriches, African lions, hyenas, zebras, and cheetahs) appear to be in the same exhibit but are safely separated.

🐾 RACINE ZOOLOGICAL GARDEN

2131 North Main Street
Racine, Wisconsin 53402
(414) 636-9189
Open: 9–8; call for winter hours
Best for: White tiger; orangutan; kangaroo

Year opened: 1923
Acres: 35
Animal population: 281; 101 species
Director: Thomas Torhorst

Getting there: Racine is south of Milwaukee on Lake Michigan. From I-94 take Exit 333 east onto Route 20 (Washington Avenue) to downtown Racine. Just before lake, turn north on Main Street for about 15 blocks.

Conservation: SSP participation for golden lion tamarin, snow leopard; hopefully, in the future, tigers.

Education: An interpretive center will be located in the renovated main building.

Special attractions: Public park on lake.

Gift shop: Usual stuff.

Food: Small snack stand, in summer.

During my visit to the Racine Zoological Garden in 1990, Yvonne Strode, then keeper and now general curator, gave me a tour of the zoo, which is located on attractive grounds on the shore of Lake Michigan. In the summer people come to picnic or attend a concert at the Kiwanis Monorail Amphitheater, which juts out into the lake. I was impressed with the high spirits of all the zoo staff I met as I toured the zoo with Strode, who came to Racine from Peoria, Illinois.

Strode told me some of the zoo's history, a sad one: It had been inadequately managed by the city until 1990, when it was taken over by the Racine Zoological Society. Zoo employees were union members, some of whom had starting jobs on garbage trucks, and were delighted with a transfer to zoo jobs, which had a higher rating. They were not trained zoo personnel. When the society took over all zoo management, all of its union employees were replaced, resulting in a more efficient, dedicated staff.

By 1990, some renovation had taken place, with name bricks on the ground to thank those who gave in 1988, but much more was obviously needed. Strode told me of plans to renovate the main building, a very nice piece of architecture.

In October 1992 a $3 million proposal for capital improvement was submitted by the zoo to the board of directors of the society for their approval. The proposal was approved and is being implemented with a planned completion date of April/May 1994. The basement of the main building has been gutted and is being turned into an animal holding facility. In its rejuvenated form the main building will be divided into two sections: one for large cats and the other for a rain forest. There will be barriers, but no bars and plenty of trees.

Near the Sertoma Children's Petting Farm is a pleasant, minute building that serves as the nursery (and is therefore an educational stop for children) and contains an owl and newly born mice. The mice had a future, but a mighty short one: They were to be lunch for the snakes.

The main attractions of the zoo today are the white tiger and the orangutan. The zoo's elephant had been sent on a well-deserved vacation to a zoo in Ontario, Canada, with the hope that she would breed. Even though breeding was not accomplished, she has returned to the Racine Zoo. Her area is now twice the size it was when she left and has a big addition: a swimming pool.

Appendixes

APPENDIX A

High- and Low-Profile Animals

The author's assessment of the relative popularity of animal exhibits is based on research for this book. "Old Faithfuls" are perennial favorites ("I wanna see the elephant, Ma"). "Animals of the Moment" are those that are gaining special attention for new or upgraded exhibits because of their status as the targets of a Species Survival Plan (SSP) or as endangered or threatened species, or because of growing popularity. "Up and Coming" are animals that have proved difficult to exhibit in the past, or that simply have not received the attention they deserve, or on which an educational focus can be particularly productive. "Waiting to Be Appreciated" are animals that are receiving greater attention from zoologists but that have not yet found a place on the public's popularity list.

Old Faithfuls

Asian elephant	black rhinoceros
African lion	sea lion
shark	dolphin
giraffe	chimpanzee
Siberian tiger	bison
camel	penguin
flamingo	American alligator

Animals of the Moment

lowland gorilla	Grevy's zebra
orangutan	snow leopard
Bali mynah	Mexican wolf
Arabian oryx	Przewalski's horse

clouded leopard
white rhinoceros
giant panda
killer whale
ring-tailed, black, and
  ruffed lemur
Chinese alligator
Dall sheep
polar bear
Sumatran (hairy)
  rhinoceros
bongo

maned wolf
lion-tailed macaque
river and sea otters
Andean condor
golden lion tamarin
koala
cheetah
spectacled bear
okapi
sloth bear
gaur

Up and Coming

red kangaroo
wallaby
red panda
California condor
bats
giant anteater
hippopotamus
lemurs (all 36 species)
platypus

hummingbirds
snow monkey
radiated tortoise
invertebrates:
  butterflies, leaf-cutter
  ant, and other insects
jellyfish
coral reefs
octopus

Waiting to Be Appreciated

bonobo
Guam rail
gerenuk
elephant seal
sloth, two-toed and
  three-toed
St. Vincent parrot
aye-aye

Aruba Island rattlesnake
snub-nosed langur
black-footed ferret
giant anteater
tunafish
manatee (Amazonian,
  Caribbean, West African)

Director's Choice: Zoo and Aquarium Directors' (and Some Former Directors'*) Favorite Exhibits

CALIFORNIA
Monterey Bay Aquarium
   Kelp Forest—Nicholas Brown (National Aquarium, Baltimore), Tom Otten (Point Defiance Zoo and Aquarium), John Prescott (New England Aquarium), Chris Wemmer (National Zoological Park), David Towne (Woodland Park Zoo)
San Diego Wild Animal Park
   Monorail—Robert Yokel (Miami Metrozoo)

DISTRICT OF COLUMBIA
National Zoological Park
   Reptile House—Mark Reed (Sedgewick County Zoo and Botanical Garden)

ILLINOIS
Chicago Zoological Park, Brookfield
   Rain Forest—Robert Reece (The Wilds)
   Night Cats—Richard Lattis (city zoos of New York))

INDIANA
Fort Wayne Children's Zoo
   Bat exhibit—L. Patricia Simmons (Akron Zoological Park)

*An asterisk indicates a former director.

LOUISIANA
Audubon Park and Zoological Garden, New Orleans
Louisiana Swamp—Clayton Freiheit (Denver Zoo), Douglas
Myers (San Diego Zoo)

MISSOURI
St. Louis Zoo
Bird House—Stephen Wylie (Oklahoma City Zoological Park)
Cats—Johnny Martinez (Potawatomi Zoo)

NEBRASKA
Omaha's Henry Doorly Zoo
Lied Jungle—William Foster (Louisville Zoological Garden)

NEW YORK
Bronx Zoo (International Wildlife Conservation Park)
Himalayan exhibit—Chris Wemmer (National Zoological
Park), Warren Thomas* (Los Angeles Zoo)
Jungle World—William Dennler (Toledo Zoological Gardens), Lester Fischer* (Lincoln Park Zoological Gardens),
Robert Fry* (North Carolina Zoological Park), Palmer Krantz
(Riverbanks Zoological Park), Terry Maple (Zoo Atlanta), Edward Maruska (Cincinnati Zoo and Botanical Garden), Tom
Otten (Point Defiance Zoo and Aquarium), Robert Reece (The
Wilds), Khadejah Shelby* (Detroit Zoological Park), Warren
Thomas* (Los Angeles Zoo), Steve Taylor (Cleveland Metroparks Zoological Park), David Towne (Woodland Park Zoological Gardens), David Zucconi (Tulsa Zoo and Living
Museum) *Jungle World, Mangrove exhibit*—George Rabb
(Chicago Zoological Park)

OHIO
Cincinnati Zoo and Botanical Garden
Planting and red panda—L. Patricia Simmons (Akron Zoological Park)
Insect World—Hayes Caldwell (Caldwell Zoo), Palmer Krantz
(Riverbanks Zoological Park)

Cleveland Metroparks Zoological Park
  Rain Forest—Robert Reece (The Wilds)
Toledo Zoological Gardens
  Hippopotamus exhibit—Ted A. Beattie (Shedd Aquarium),
  Terry Maple (Zoo Atlanta), Earl Wells (Fort Wayne Children's
  Zoo)

TEXAS
Dallas Zoo
  African Plains—Jack Hanna* (Columbus Zoo)

WASHINGTON
Point Defiance Zoo and Aquarium, Tacoma
  Beluga whale exhibit—John Moore* (Rio Grande Zoological
  Park)
  Shark exhibit—Cindi Shiota (Seattle Aquarium)
  Polar bear exhibit—William Dennler (Toledo Zoological Gardens)
  dens)
Woodland Park Zoological Gardens
  Gorilla exhibit—Palmer Krantz (Riverbanks Zoological Park)

WISCONSIN
Milwaukee County Zoological Society
  African Predator/Prey—Johnny Martinez (Potawatomi Zoo)

The New York Zoological
Society's Education Programs—
A Sampler

Zoo Camp

Annette Berkovits, the dean of the education department of
NYZS The Wildlife Conservation Society, knew no English when
she arrived in New York as a young girl of fifteen. She was born
in Russia, near the Chinese border, then moved to Poland, where
she grew up. When she was twelve her family went to Israel for
two and a half years and then moved to New York City, where she
graduated from the Bronx High School of Science. Berkovits
initiated a program for the school on Animal Behavior when she
started to work at the Bronx Zoo. She also created the first
overnight program (Zoo Camp) in any U.S. zoo.

One day I dropped in on a Zoo Camp session about the Lost
Legend of the Gharial, held in the education building at the
Bronx Zoo. A man rushes into the room, to the astonishment of
students gathered in a semicircle on the floor. They are wide-eyed
at the sight of the hat, an immediate giveaway of the stranger's
identity: It is Indiana Jones. Indy moves rapidly around the
room. He is on the hunt for the skull of a gharial (a crocodilian
species). He leaves in the same mysterious whirlwind that surrounded his entry onto the scene. The instructor brings out large
tablets (like those in the Lost Ark?) and reads the story of Indiana
searching for the gharial—but animal names are missing from the
tablet, and the teacher calls on the children to help fill them in,
according to clues in the text. The class is divided into two teams,
each with a chance to guess names. When the tablets have been

read, the teacher then says that she cannot either bring back Indiana or the lost gharial, but she can bring them a live baby alligator. The children are thrilled. Holding the alligator before the class, the teacher asks the students conservation questions related to the alligator and its habitat. Conservation education can be exciting.

The NYZS's education department produces programs for parents, children, teachers and students. Three of the NYZS's programs are being used by other zoos and by schools, both nationally and internationally. Thirty-two zoos, and schools in 47 states in the U.S., are using NYZS's education programs.

Early Education—Pablo Python

Pablo Python Looks at Animals is for children in kindergarten through grade three. An introductory life sciences curriculum, it was validated in 1991 by the U.S. Department of Education's Program Effectiveness Panel as an exemplary science program worthy of dissemination to schools and other institutions. Pablo Python enhances the early childhood curriculum in other areas besides science, including reading, vocabulary, observation, writing, and mathematical skills. Pablo Python, which has lessons ranging from 30 to 90 minutes, may be conducted in the classroom throughout the year and schedules two to six zoo visits in the course of a year. Prior to teaching Pablo Python, teachers attend 12 hours of workshop training over a two-day period, and the course also involves parents. At the Bronx Zoo, Pablo Python is held in the Africa Lab, which is part of the Gelada Baboon exhibit. A large glass window in the classroom lets people look at the baboons, who look back.

For High School Students—WIZE

Wildlife Inquiry through Zoo Education (WIZE), for seventh grade and up, was a breakthrough program in conservation education. In 1981 the National Science Foundation (NSF) certified and funded the program, establishing the desirability of teaching about zoos in schools. It was the first time a zoo had been funded by the NSF. The program was actually implemented in 1988 in 10 states, involving 2,180 students, and by 1992 it had spread to 34 states with 73,663 students participating. WIZE was developed by the Bronx Zoo in cooperation with the Philadelphia Zoo, the Topeka Zoo in Kansas, and the Riverbanks Zoo in Columbia, South Carolina. It is an innovative interactive package of life science materials that coordinates the classroom curriculum, field work, and hands-on exhibits. Each classroom unit culminates in a well-planned zoo trip. WIZE materials, unlike most textbooks, provide the most up-to-date, scientifically accurate information prepared by professional zoologists, teachers, scientists, zoo educators, curriculum specialists, and administrators. WIZE gives students and teachers a feeling of involvement in a worldwide concern—helping wildlife survive. It cost about $750,000 to develop and test the WIZE program in the 1980's. Fortunately, the program has been adaptable to a wide variety of zoo and school settings.

Survival Strategies, one of the courses in the WIZE program, poses the question: Will wildlife as we know it survive through the twenty-first century? The program emphasizes the long-range concern for conservation by fostering appreciation for the central issues in conservation biology and introduces the role of zoos in conservation biology in a three-day lesson called "Hope for the Future: Zoos." The students are asked which animals zoos should attempt to save from extinction. Students are asked to select an animal they would choose to save, and to say why they have chosen that animal. They learn that zoos must also make such decisions, taking into account animals' needs, available space, budget, status of the animal in the wild, and even an animal's public appeal. Students are asked to list five animals that are popular and five that are unpopular at their local zoo. After a visit to the local zoo the student's pre-zoo-visit list is compared with what he or she observed at the zoo. On the basis of material they are shown, including a filmstrip, students are asked questions such as, Why did the keepers remove eggs from the condor? Why did the scientist give the gaur hormones? Why do zoos exchange animals? The students receive instruction on zoo techniques aimed at improving the survival of certain species into the twenty-first century, such as embryo transfers, artificial insemination, frozen-sperm banks, surrogate parents, rearing techniques to avoid imprinting by humans, techniques used to stimulate clutches or litters, exchanges of animals or genetic material to avoid inbreeding, and analysis of blood serum. Students learn that there is more to a zoo than simply the number of species on exhibit.

Teacher Training—HELP

The Habitat Ecology Learning Program (HELP) is expected to be available in 1994, and is targeted at teachers of grades four through six. Six zoos are working with NYZS The Wildlife Conservation Society on HELP as Partners in Progress: Dallas, Kansas City, Grassmere (Tennessee), Brookfield (Chicago), Lowry (Florida), and Fresno (California). The project calls for teachers and students to create "biome boxes," which will include flora, fauna, and cultural material. Schools will exchange boxes with other participating schools, and the students will be asked to identify the biome in the boxes, including the cultural items. The program calls for videotaping the students when the boxes are prepared and when they are opened, with a critiqued playback.

Career Assistance

The NYZS offers a course on Wildlife Careers for Women whereby members of the Girl Scouts are exposed to role models in various professional fields at the Bronx Zoo. One Girl Scout claimed at the end of the course, "Now I know what I want to do with the rest of my life!" Another career assistance program in Animal Care and Management was first given in 1992 for one month; during the last two weeks students applied what they had learned by designing an exhibit, taking the animals' and the public's needs into account.

Habitat: At the Center of Zoo Education

The keys to conservation education are immersion and habitat. To understand wildlife students must go *to* the exhibits, with as much direct observation as possible. From such study develops an appreciation for habitat conservation.

The NYZS's education department has plans for a $15 million Environment Education Center at the Bronx Zoo. The center will be within the $16 million Congo Forest habitat exhibit. At the heart of the center will be a Teacher's Training Complex that will contain an international teaching center, training workshops, a multimedia resource library, and a conference center. Also at the center will be the Early Childhood Learning Lab (the home for the Pablo Python program), the Primate Behavior Observatory, and the treetop Habitat Ecology Workshop from which mandrills, guenons, canopy-dwelling birds, and gorillas may be observed and case studies prepared. A lab will have aquariums, bird cages, and small-rodent exhibits, demonstrating the concepts of migration, hibernation, food storage, and life cycles based on seasonal changes.

Most important, the center will have an Endangered Species Lab, which will pose questions such as "What is a species?," suggest answers, and explain the causes of species' endangerment.

Traveling to See Animals

Eco-education

The United States has about 9,000 adventure travel organizations, and more than 300 tour operators who promote environmentally oriented tours. The following is a selection of representative nature-oriented organizations that offer eco-educational trips combining learning and pleasure.

Sven-Olof Lindblad's Special Expeditions
720 Fifth Avenue
New York, New York 10019
(800) 762-0003

Special Expeditions' *Sea Bird* (built in the United States in 1981; 152 feet long, 99.7 gross tons) is my preference for a visit to Baja California and the Sea of Cortés. I spent 10 days on it in 1993 with outstanding marine-sighting results: a pod of nearly 2,000 common dolphins, porpoises, bottle-nosed dolphins, 119 gray whales, a small number of humpback whales, blue and fin whales—all up close. There are few frills aboard the *Sea Bird*. The decor is plain, the staterooms functional though comfortable (of special merit are Category I staterooms on the bridge deck, opening directly onto the covered deck). The background to the fun of sightseeing was a serious concentration on animal behavior, habitat, and conservation. At the end of the trip naturalists made a plea for the passengers to take home with them an image in their mind's eye of what they had seen and to remember it from time to time.

The *Sea Bird* schedules a number of trips, including five 11-day Baja trips a season (late January to early March). Zodiacs are used for wet and dry landings as well as to gain a closer look at whales, dolphins, and seals. Naturalists with specialized experience give lectures daily and are available throughout the day and sometimes at night to answer questions and lead small groups ashore to see chuckwalla and blue-footed boobies or to identify cactus. Special Expeditions' worldwide itineraries are exceptionally well organized and managed. Their interest *is* environmental.

The American Museum of Natural History
Central Park West at 79th Street
New York, New York 10024
(800) 462-8687 or (212) 769-5700

The American Museum of Natural History has been conducting tours since 1953. They are currently administered by Special Expeditions. Lecturers accompany all tours, such as the Amazon and Orinoco tour with an anthropologist, ornithologist, and mammalogist aboard the vessel *Polaris*. Northwest Passage is a voyage aboard the 59-cabin icebreaker *Kapitan Khlebnikov* from Provideniya Bukhta (Providence Bay), Russia, through the Beaufort Sea, crossing the Bering Sea to Resolute, Alaska. The 69-cabin *World Discoverer* charts a course to Alaska's Katmai Peninsula, the Aleutian and Pribilof islands, and Providence Bay. On the *Polaris* you can also go to the Norwegian fjords, Bear Island, and Spitsbergen, and see the Arctic flora and fauna of the Lofoten Islands; polar bears, walruses, seals, reindeer, Arctic foxes, orcas, sperm whales, and numerous species of birds are sighted. Advertised as "family adventures," the museum conducts trips to Costa Rica to explore the Monteverde Cloud Reserve (monkeys, armadillos, coatimundis, anteaters, toucans, macaws, quetzels, motmots, storks) and Australia (kangaroos, koalas, bandicoots, platypuses, crocodiles, bowerbirds, parrots, and the marine life of the Great Barrier Reef).

Field Guides
P.O. Box 160723
Austin, Texas 88716-0723
(512) 327-4953

Field Guides specializes in birds. Their brochure is thick and informative, giving the kinds of details on the area to be visited that you want to know. It is a treat just to read it, with its descriptions of fjords, islands, deserts, and rain forests in inviting detail, and thorough listings of bird life (and incidentally other animals) in their habitat. The preface to the brochure states that there is "reason to lament what mankind is making of nature and [that Field Guides is] committed to the position that the Earth's natural resources should be shared and conserved with non-human creatures in mind." Field Guides funds and otherwise supports a variety of carefully selected conservation foundations, projects, and special needs. Is it not only natural that worldwide birding and worldwide conservation travel hand in hand? Field Guides has given recent attention to the 103,238-acre Cuyabeno Reserve lowland rain forest on Lagunas de Cuyabeno in Amazonian Ecuador. Although the reserve was created in 1979, only recently has a lodge been built, where during a six-day stay one can see numerous species of birds, including 36 species of antbirds. An equally exciting and rewarding trip is offered to Papua New Guinea.

Natural Habitat Wildlife Adventures
1 Sussex Station, Suite #110
Sussex, New Jersey 07461
(800) 543-8917 or (201) 702-1525

Offers the following tours:

Polar bear watch in Churchill, Manitoba: harp and hooded seals.

Seal watch around the Magdalen Islands (belonging to Quebec, located north of Prince Edward Island, to the east of New Brunswick and west of Newfoundland).

Baja whale watch in Magdelena Bay, aboard the vessel *Don Jose.*

Brown bears of Katmai, Alaska, viewed from platforms. Moose, bald eagles, and red-necked grebes are also among species seen.

Dolphins, a week-long opportunity to swim with the dolphins from the west end of Grand Bahama Island, Bahamas, on *Bottom Time II*. Swimmers are advised, "We will spend as much time in the dolphin area as the animals and weather allow. . . . Encounters last from minutes to hours depending on their level of interest in us."

Victor Emanuel Nature Tours
P.O. Box 33008
Austin, Texas 78764
(800) 328-VENT

VENT's tour schedule is neatly arranged according to the month. February, March, and April have the most tours, although each month offers a variety of destinations, from Churchill, Manitoba (polar bears), to Madagascar (lemurs); from Texas (whooping cranes) to Tobago (oilbirds). While the Caribbean, Africa, South America, the Far East, and India are listed, there are many trips in the United States. VENT gets high marks for coming up with new nature tours, both in the U.S. and abroad, and has a solid staff of naturalists as well as tour leaders on call. The company has established a special relationship with five lodges that they consider of especially unusual quality. Customized tour packages may be organized for groups of four or more wishing to visit: Cassowary House, Australia; Chan Chich Lodge, Belize; La Selva Lodge, Ecuador; Many Lodge, Peru; and Hato Piñero, Venezuela.

The Galápagos, which belongs to Ecuador, deserves special attention. Dozens of ships are now permitted by the Ecuadorian government to visit the Galápagos. At times ships will cluster about a cove when there is an exciting animal event. The 90-passenger *Santa Cruz*, a converted ferry owned by the government of Ecuador and leased to the Metropolitan Touring Company (Av. Amazonas 239, P.O. Box 2542, Quito, Ecuador, tel. 560 550), is simple, rustic, superb. The in-depth week-long itinerary included stops at 11 islands when I made the trip in 1988. We saw bottle-nosed dolphins; California sea lions; Galápagos fur seals; 72 (of the 125) species of birds on the islands, including blue-footed, masked, and red-footed boobies, the Humboldt penguin, the flightless cormorant, the magnificent frigate bird (rare), the lava gull, and 13 species of finches; as well as six species of reptiles (sea turtles, giant tortoises, and iguanas), and Sally lightfoot crabs. There is also the 20-cabin *Isabela II*, for a more intimate visit.

The government of Ecuador is ignoring the question of how long the Galápagos will survive in anywhere near their natural state. The government has set an absolute limit of 90 people to be on any one island at the same time and has also set a limit of 25,000 for the total number of Galápagos visitors per annum. In 1990 there were 50,000 visitors. In 1930, when Vincent Astor took his ship, the *Nourmahal*, to the Galápagos on a New York Zoological Society expedition, Charles Haskins Townsend went on the voyage as the New York Aquarium's representative. He wrote up the trip in the July–August 1930 *Bulletin* of the NYZS, stating that there were only "two small settlements of natives of Ecuador on [the Galápagos] islands a hundred miles apart" and that "the tourist would find little of interest in these islands, so difficult to penetrate, aside from views of vast lava fields, forbidding cliffs, wild anchorages in half-submerged craters and other volcanic phenomena. . . . The attractive features of the Galápagos Islands are those connected with a peculiar animal [the tortoise] and plant life living there." In 1980 the islands' population was 5,000; in 1990, there were 14,000, increasing at 12 percent annually, nearly all to care for tourists, not nature.

Ecotourism

The following are examples of organizations dedicated to ecotourism, involving participation by the tourist, to the benefit of the local population: The Audubon Society, Earthwatch, ACEER (Amazon Center for Environmental Education and Research) Foundation, El Refugio, Bio Tours, Conservation International, Conservation Tourism Ltd., the Smithsonian Institution, and the World Wildlife Fund.

The National Audubon Society
700 Broadway
New York, New York 10003
(212) 979-3066

The National Audubon Society's tours are accompanied by experts from their own staff or associated specialists. Tours go to the Amazon, the Pacific Northwest, Greenland, Iceland, Hudson's Bay, and the North Atlantic. National Audubon has also used the *Polaris* for shore bird-sighting trips from Spitsbergen to Bergen, Norway. North Atlantic cruises are on the 100-passenger *Nantucket Clipper*, and voyages to Alaska to see humpback whales and glaciers are on the *Sea Lion*. National Audubon's ecology work camps and workshops for teachers are attended by more than 1,000 annually. National Audubon has a presence in Guatemala, Mexico, Belize, Panama, Costa Rica, and Venezuela. Use the following telephone numbers to call for further information: travel and tours, (212) 979-3066; wildlife nature centers and sanctuaries, (203) 364-0048; education programs, (203) 364-0520; scientific reports and information, (212) 979-3074; ecology camps and workshops, (203) 869-2017.

Earthwatch
P.O. Box 403
680 Mount Auburn Street
Watertown, Massachusetts 02272-9104
(800) 776-0188 or (617) 926-8200

The mission of Earthwatch, founded in 1972, is to save fragile lands, monitor change on our planet, and conserve endangered species. With Earthwatch the objective is conservation, not commercialism. Earthwatch attracts about 3,000 people annually who are willing to work with scientists on their vacations and also pay for the privilege; this money supports about 120 projects annually worldwide (to date, 1,523 projects in 111 countries).

Earthwatch's approach is question-problem-solution–oriented. For example, the question is asked: Do copper mines and agricultural development threaten one of the world's largest artificial lakes, Kariba, in Zimbabwe? Four teams are organized to spend two weeks each in Zimbabwe to find out. Teams rotate between a research station and camping on a research vessel. They collect water, sediment, and plankton samples from the lake; monitor water temperature, and other factors; and perform simple lab tasks. Total cost, $63,800; individual cost, $1,595. *Question:* Can forest architecture teach us about species survival? Four teams go to Costa Rica, and four to Venezuela to try to find answers by laying out transects, studying plots, and mapping understory plants. Cost per person, $1,295. *Question:* How can we protect Brazil's remnants of coastal rain forest? Less than 5 percent of the original Atlantic tropical rain forest still stands. Teams will capture, collar, and radio-track the bizarre water possum and the endangered broad-nosed caiman; catch and release turtles and amphibians; describe and map habitats; and study biological control of the Queensland cane toad. Cost, $1,545 per person. Other general subjects for which specific answers are sought by Earthwatch include:

"Strategies for Survival"—animal behavior, species in danger, captive breeding, web of life, studying such diverse animals as mountain deer in Patagonia, lemurs in Madagascar, sloth bears in Nepal, and the platypus.

"The Human Factor"—"the first environmental crisis," in Bodrum, Turkey: Himalayan village life.

"Managing the Planet"—the impact of wolves and hunters on Poland's red deer population, and the wolves' survival prospects.

"Saving America's Forests."

"British Organic Farming."

ACEER—Amazon Center for Environmental Education and Research
One Environs Park
Helena, Alabama 35080
(800) 633-4734

International Expeditions
(same address as ACEER)
(800) 633-4734 or (205) 428-1700

ACEER is a nonprofit organization created in 1991 by International Expeditions. Its work is in Iquitos*, northeastern Peru, where it has constructed a 1,700-foot suspended canopy walkway adjacent to the Sucusari River, which flows through the 250,000-acre Amazon Biosphere Reserve. The site possibly has the world's record for tree diversity, a gauge used to assess overall biological diversity. The walkway brings in ecodollars from tourists and also provides a useful site for tropical-rain-forest research. Nearly one third of the world's 8,600 species of birds can be found in the Amazon Basin. Two thirds of the forest's living matter is in its canopy, nearer sunlight, and scientists have arrived at the conclusion that the forest's canopy may be more important than its floor.

ACEER can provide accommodations at Explorama Lodge for 10 researchers and 20 visitors, who arrive on a palm-thatched riverboat; it conducts international rain-forest workshops at Iquitos and in Costa Rica at the Montverde Cloud Forest and Tortuguero National Park. Workshops, open to public participation, provide opportunities to learn about the forest *in the forest* from rain-forest experts. Site visits lasting from one to several days are also possible, providing an unforgettable experience in the rain-forest canopy.

International Expeditions, founded in 1980, organizes tours to the rain forests in Costa Rica (1,500 species of trees, 850 species of wildlife, and 6,000 species of flowering plants), Ecuador, Belize and Guatemala (a 10-day trip into the jungle, to Tikal, and to the marine reefs), the Peruvian Amazon, and Venezuela, as well as trips to Africa, India, Australia, Nepal, China, Thailand, and Malaysia. Working with the World Wildlife Fund, the Smithsonian Institution, and the Nature Conservancy, International

*See *National Geographic Traveler*, November/December 1993, p. 9f.

Expeditions hopes to expand the present Amazon Biosphere Reserve to 1,000,000 acres.

El Refugio
Mr. Randolph Brooks
"El Refugio"
Casilla de Correo Nro. 2111
Santa Cruz de la Sierra, Bolivia
Tel. 425 263, fax 427 773

or

Mr. Ian Phillips, London, (81) 995-6892; Greencastle, Pennsylvania, (717) 328-3409

El Refugio is dedicated to the preservation of the diverse ecosystem areas of the 125,000-acre El Refugio and 1,745,000-acre Noel Kempff Mercado National Park in Bolivia. El Refugio differs from the ACEER Foundation, which organizes workshops and provides facilities for tourists' visits, and from Bio Tours (see below), which is a commercial adjunct to a philanthropically supported effort. El Refugio seeks 300 private investors at a $12,500 "membership" fee. A membership, which extends to spouse and children, may be sold or bequeathed. Membership rights allow one to visit El Refugio (best time is August–December), where a lodge is being built. A member's contribution is recognized by the Bolivian government as representing a concern for environmental issues. Research to date has identified many endemic species of flora and fauna, including over 500 bird species and 24 palm and 29 orchid species. The endangered species include the pampas deer, black caiman, and South American river turtle, as well as a number of vulnerable species such as the jaguar, giant otter, giant anteater, and bush dog. It is quite possible that entirely unknown species may be found, particularly invertebrates.

Bio Tours
Poba International # 156
P.O. Box 52-1308
Miami, Florida 33152-1308

In Venezuela:
Torre Diamen
Piso 1, Oficina 19
Av. La Estancia
Chuao, Apartado 64597
Caracas, Venezuela
Tel. 916965

Bio Tours provides "a paradise for nature lovers and bird watchers" at Hato Piñero, Venezuela, a private reserve situated from 300 to 1,800 feet above sea level and including wetlands, a dry plateau forest, semideciduous to evergreen forests, medium-high deciduous forests, and gallery forests. Some of the animal species that may be seen at Hato Piñero include jaguars, pumas, two species of peccaries (piglike animals), and tapirs (shy ungulates closely related to horses and rhinoceroses), as well as foxes, capybaras (the world's largest rodent), bats, tayras (a furry creature that resembles the weasel), red howler monkeys, capuchin monkeys, giant and lesser anteaters, and caimans, iguanas, and snakes (including the anaconda, the world's largest water snake), plus 340 species of birds. A biological station has been established by the Branger Foundation to conduct scientific research as well as behavioral and ecological studies, including artificial insemination of local cattle, the development of forage seed production, evaluation of the first commercial crop of babas (a crocodilian) and of the effect of agricultural exploitation on the area, to avoid a negative impact on the area's ecology. Additional goals are recovery of species in danger of extinction, such as the jaguar, puma, and yellow-knobbed curassow; protection of wetlands; and increased introduction of fruit trees into the region.

Conservation Tourism Ltd.
65 Walnut Street, Suite 301
Wellesley, Massachusetts 02181
Tel. (617) 239-3626, fax (617) 239-3610

Chairman of Conservation Tourism Ltd.: Norman Fast

In Costa Rica:
The Rain Forest Aerial Tram
Apartado 592-2100
San Jose, Costa Rica
Tel. and fax (506) 25-88-69

Located on 338 acres in a rain forest one hour from San Jose, the Rain Forest Aerial Tram is still in the development stage, although plans are firm and financing is being obtained. A 90-minute, 1.7-kilometer noiseless aerial tram ride will take a maximum of six scientists and tourists (who will be charged $40–$45) at a time for rain-forest-canopy exploration.

At the halfway mark will be a stop at the Center for Canopy Exploration, where a research and educational facility and visitor's center will be located, teaching students and tourists the "value of maintaining the world's tropical rain forests." From the center, visitors will be able to take guided walks along trails near the Corinto River. At the visitor's center lectures will be given on tropical biology and conservation. The center will also have a small guest lodge, a restaurant, and a gift shop with materials on the rain forest. The tram's ecotouristic impact will be seen in its economic success, proving that there are more profitable uses for the rain forest than clearing it for short-lived agricultural production; the tram's minimal impact on the surrounding ecosystems will serve as a model for future developments.

Conservation International
1015 18th Street, N.W.
Washington, D.C. 20036
(202) 429-5660

Conservation International's primary focus in Africa is on Madagascar and, in South America, on Brazil; CI has led nature travel expeditions to Costa Rica and the Brazilian Amazon. In Madagascar, the fourth-largest island in the world, tour participants experience encounters with a number of the 35 species of lemurs, 300 endemic birds, and numerous flora. CI has organized a workshop on the sustainable use of tropical rain forests in Panama, introduced a program in Japan to direct Japanese political and financial resources to support ecosystems, worked with the U.S. Agency for International Development on a Natural Resources Management Project in Botswana, and worked with Domestic Technology International, Inc., an ecotouristic firm. CI established Ecotrust in 1990 to "conserve representative examples of North American temperate rain forest ecosystems." For information on Ecotrust: 1200 N.W. Front Avenue, #470, Portland, Oregon 97200, (503) 227-6225.

The Sierra Club
730 Polk Street
San Francisco, California 94109
(415) 923-5630

The Sierra Club was founded in 1892 and is dedicated to the preservation of nature, especially of forests. The Sierra Club created the Sierra Club Legal Defense Fund to act in defense of our environment, and now also offers more than 300 trips, with the number of participants limited to 15 persons. Ninety percent of the trips take place in the United States, such as the trip to the Four Peaks Wilderness of Arizona to work on the Chillicut Trail, although the club conducts international trips to 23 countries. A recent trip to the Sardar Sarovar Dam Project in India focused on the dam's contribution to deforestation and wildlife depletion in Rajasthan. About 70 of the Sierra Club's trips include a conservation task, such as clearing new trails.

The Smithsonian Institution
1100 Jefferson Drive, S.W.
Washington, D.C. 20560
(202) 357-4700

For research expeditions:

490 L'Enfant Plaza, S.W.
Washington, D.C. 20560
(202) 287-3210

A catalog on foreign land tours is issued in March. To request a tour and seminar brochure, call (202) 357-4700.

The Smithsonian offers about 150 tours, half of them international, and the majority leaning toward education and culture, such as an ecotouristic trip to the tropical forests of Yucatan, Mexico, to survey the effect of hurricanes on birds and vegetation; or an expedition to monitor an active volcano in Costa Rica. Tours are categorized as foreign study tours, domestic study tours, Smithsonian seminars, or research expeditions.

The World Wildlife Fund (WWF)
1250 24th Street, N.W.
Washington, D.C. 20037
(202) 293-4800

Since its inception in 1963 WWF has been a growing force in conservation, organizing, and supervising research and conservation projects in the field. WWF's mandate is to help save the Amazon rain forest, protect endangered parrots from international trade, preserve the habitats of Madagascar, reverse the loss of wetlands in the United States and around the world, and end the degradation of the Great Lakes. WWF "is the largest private organization working to protect endangered wildlife and wild lands," with one million members in the United States. WWF trips often involve looking at a project they support. Tourists may participate in WWF's involvement with the local population in the Annapurna Conservation Area, Nepal, where a tourist, forestry, and agriculture program has been established that combines habitat protection with sustainable development.

The Ecotourism Society
801 Devon Place
Alexandria, Virginia 22314

The Society's interest lies in the impact of tourism on natural areas. If you wish to check on organizations with a stated interest in ecotourism, contact the society, which is currently preparing ecotourism guidelines.

Publications

A useful guide is *The Buzzworm Magazine Guide to ECO-TRAVEL* (1993) with 100 worldwide adventures, available from Buzzworm Books, 2305 Canyon Boulevard, Suite 206, Boulder, Colorado 80302, (303) 442-1969. A good introductory chapter on ecotourism by Lisa Jones, *Buzzworm* magazine editor, deals with the question "How do we know that our money will go toward protecting the place to which we travel?" The book is extremely well organized with detailed information and maps, and "eco-interpretation" and "ecofocus" comments on each tour. I highly recommend the book and *Buzzworm* magazine.

A nice little book is *Eco-Vacations: Enjoy Yourself and Save the Earth* (1991), by Evelyn Kaye, available from Blue Penguin, 147 Sylvan Avenue, Leonia, New Jersey 07605. The title hits the nail on the head. The book is divided into two sections, one providing "Program Topics," which lists ideas, subjects, and organizations, and the second, a very helpful list of "every organization" offering eco-vacations. This list ranges from the American Horticultural Society, which offers trips (including cruises) in the $4,000 price range, to American Youth Hostels, whose travel packages go for as low as $250. The book describes raft trips down the Colorado River, or in Utah and California, or with the Canyon Field Institute in Colorado; expeditions to look for plants in Venezuela; in Alaska, canoeing on Wonder Lake in Denali

National Park or spotting caribous, moose, and grizzly bears; and even living for a while in a lodge or a four-bedded hogan (a hut) analyzing tree rings and pollen cores in Crow Canyon, Colorado. I recommend it as a reference guide for eco-education.

Another eco-education reference related to ecotourism is *The Adventure Vacation* (1987), by Andy Alpine and Steen Hanse, copublishers, Fireside Books Division of Simon & Schuster, New York. Particularly useful is the section "Nature Expeditions," listing tour, safari, and outfitter organizations as well as clubs and accommodations according to geographic location. Those that I find of particular appeal include:

Camp Denali, P.O. Box 67, Denali National Park, Alaska 99755, (907) 683-2302 (winter); (907) 683-2290 (summer). This camp is a "Shangri-La for the naturalist." Wood cabins with woodstoves sleep two to six. June–September. Caribous migrate in and out of Denali during the whole June–September period.

Colonel Sam Hogan, Safaris, Casilla A-122, Quito, Ecuador 450242. An exploration deep into the jungle along the Amazon River Basin.

GEO Expeditions, P.O. Box 27136-STB, Oakland, California 94602, (415) 530-4146. Organizes trips to northern Australia, for its marsupials and spectacular birds. A 14-day safari into the Kimberly Plateau.

Zoo/Aquarium Ecotravel Programs

You may wish to call your local zoo and inquire whether they have a travel program. Some zoos and aquariums offer specialized or unique tours not offered by others. All trips are usually accompanied by lecturers and qualified tour guides (usually with a specialized field of interest such as biology, ornithology, mammalogy), and most often briefing materials are provided. The following is a list of some zoos and aquariums that have travel programs, and gives a sampling of the types of trips offered.

Akron (Ohio) Zoo, (216) 434-8645. Annual tours to Belize, Costa Rica, the Amazon, Alaska.

Arizona–Sonora Desert Museum, Tucson, (602) 883-1380, Mary Erickson. A variety of one- to 10-day trips are offered into Arizona's Sonora Desert with a stress on biology and geology.

Baltimore Aquarium, (410) 576-3875, Christie Korbeck. Argentina (seven days, May), encounter whales, penguins, and elephant seals at Tierra del Fuego and Patagonia. Iceland (seven days, July), work along with aquarium researchers on the study of Icelandic puffins at a location three hours by boat off the town of Heimay on the Westman Islands. Florida (seven days, July), at Dolphin Research Center at Grassy Key, assist in the training of dolphins, swimming with them.

Buffalo Zoological Garden, (716) 837-5172, Denise Moll. Costa Rica (11 days, February 1994; expected to be offered in 1995), organized by Park East Tours. Tortuguero National Park, for iguanas, river turtles, three-toed sloths, river otters, and monkeys (howler, spider and white-faced). Santa Rosa National Park, for peccaries, white-tailed deer, and over 250 species of birds. At Tamarindo, observe leatherback turtles laying their eggs on the beach. The Monteverde Cloud Forest, where 300 species of birds, including the long-tailed quetzal, may be seen.

Chicago Zoological Park, Brookfield (708) 485-0263, ext. 307, Gay Kuester. Fifteen days in April–May on the vessel *Coral*, hosted by the director of herpetology, Ray Pawley. South Africa (September). Tasmania and South Australia (18 days, October). Seattle (six days, July) to Olympic Peninsula, Point Defiance Zoo and Aquarium in Tacoma, Seattle Zoo, Seattle Aquarium, and Mount Ranier. Guatemala (16 days, February), Cultural Discovery Tour: Minerva Zoo for birds of prey, Rio Dulce for bird life, turtle project at Canal de los Inglesas, Project ARCAS (Association for the Rescue and Conservation of Wild Animals) where injured or rehabilitated birds reside, plus Mayan ruins at Tikal, with an abundance of wildlife. Galápagos. Kenya (16 days, February), "Kenya Under Canvas" (tented safari), for wildlife plus visits to schools in Kenya.

Cincinnati Zoo and Botanical Garden, (513) 281-4701. First U.S. zoo to have an exotic travel program. Botswana (14 days, October). Australia outback (14 days; call for dates). Kenya (14 days, June). Borneo, Bali (17 days, fall), to see orangutans, bird life. Tanzania (12 days, July). Ecuadorian Amazon (12 days, fall).

Cleveland Metroparks Zoo, (216) 661-6500. Ontario, Lake Erie (four days, September), bird of prey migration along lake, by motorcoach from Cleveland to Sandusky, and return to Cleveland.

Columbus (Ohio) Zoological Gardens, (614) 645-3400, Travel Program. Australia (two weeks, October–November), with an optional trip to New Zealand. Guatemala (visit to ARCAS species rehabilitation program). Kenya and Tanzania.

Dallas Zoo. Dallas Zoological Society runs the tours. (214) 943-2771, Karen Hamilton. Kenya (13 days, July). Amazon: Peru, Brazil (10 days, March), headwaters of the Amazon with naturalists and a zoo staff member. Sail from Iquitos, Peru; disembark in Manaus, Brazil. Texas (5 days, February 1995), coastal birdwatching with visit to whooping crane winter grounds by boat; to Rockport out of Corpus Christi.

Denver Zoological Gardens, (303) 331-5806, Anne Pinfield. Costa Rica (11 days, April). Namibia and Botswana (18 days, April). Kenya (16 days, September), to Sweetwater tented camp, near Mount Kenya Safari Club; Samburu Game Park (gerenuk, reticulated giraffe and Grevy's zebra), Nakuru Lake (flamingo), the Ark lodge (bongo), and Maasai Mara (plains animals). Denver Zoo tours uses Fun Safaris, a members of AAZPA whose staff specialize in zoo safaris. Colorado (eight days, summer), a trip to the San Juan Mountains for people 50 years and over. Future tour plans include Mexico's Baja California (six days, January–February), scuba diving in the Sea of Cortés; Zimbabwe; and Australia.

International Crane Foundation, Baraboo, Michigan, (608) 356-9462, David Thompson or Jim Harris. Southeast Russia (18 days, early summer), in the Muravyovka Nature Park, the first private reserve established since the Tsarist revolution, close to the Amur River, on the Russian side of the Russian-Chinese border, to observe red-crowned and white-naped cranes. Trip may be tax-deductible as it is a work trip. Southwest China (18 days, February), working trip to observe feeding habitats of black-necked cranes.

Jacksonville (Florida) Zoological Park, (904) 757-4463. Kenya (16 days, April). Namibia, Botswana, Zimbabwe (16 days, August), Etosha Pan, Okavango Delta, Victoria Falls. Kenya, Tanzania, South Africa (January 1995), Natal, Transvaal parks. Zambia, Zimbabwe, Botswana Elephant Back Safari (July 1994), five days riding elephants and swimming with baby elephants, also visiting Zimbabwe. Jacksonville Zoo works with Fun Safaris, Inc., of Bloomingdale, Illinois, whom they consider outstanding.

Kansas City (Missouri) Zoological Gardens, (816) 333-7406, Marci Jones. Africa.

Lincoln Park (Chicago) Zoological Gardens, (312) 294-4662. The Lincoln Park Zoological Society runs the tours, (312) 935-6700. Antarctica (two weeks, winter). Thailand, Indonesia (two weeks, fall). Costa Rica (1995). Ask about tours to East Africa organized by Park East Tours, (800) 223-6078. Desert and Delta Safari by Explorers World Travel, (800) 672-3274 or (708) 295-7770. Southern Africa (Namibia, Botswana, Etosha Pan National Park, Victoria Falls, Chobe National Park, Moremi Wildlife Reserve).

Los Angeles Zoo, (213) 664-1100. Asia (November), Singapore, Thailand, Borneo, led by the zoo director. Africa (August), to Zambia, Zimbabwe, Botswana, led by the general curator. The Los Angeles Zoo is particularly anxious to renew its tours to Rwanda to see the mountain gorillas.

Minnesota Zoological Garden, Apple Valley, (612) 431-9200, Julie Lee. Bahamas (one week, fall), scuba diving, swimming with dolphins (zoo has a dolphin program at the zoo). Minnesota (one day, summer), Lake Petin for bald eagle watch (sightings of 45 and upwards are the norm). Future: Kenya (10 days, February 1994, probably available in 1995), plus Tanzania (7 days), with pre-trip classes offered at the zoo on wildlife and culture. Galápagos (12 days, March). Australia (sometime in the next two years).

National Zoological Park, Washington, D.C. Friends of the National Zoo runs tours, (202) 673-4961, Kate Cresswell. Kenya (two weeks, May). Alaska (one week, August), inland waterways on the *Sea Bird.* Namibia (10 days, September). Peruvian Amazon (10 people, call for dates), plus pretrip workshop. Brazilian Amazon (call for dates). Also trips to: Costa Rica and Belize, Ecuador and the Galápagos, and a five-day trip starting in Portland, Maine, and traveling by bus up the Maine coast with a naturalist for bird watching, a lecture at the College of the Atlantic on Mount Desert Island, and whale watching.

New England Aquarium, Boston, (617) 973-5210. Papua New Guinea (19 days, April), John Prescott, aquarium director, and Sylvia Earl, scientist and ocean explorer (now associated with Deep Ocean Engineering), will lead a diving and snorkeling tour, with three days spent on the Sepik River and diving to explore World War II shipwrecks and sea life off Medang.

NYZS The Wildlife Conservation Society International. *For domestic travel,* (718) 220-5085. Great Swamp National Wildlife Reserve, a day trip to 7,000 acres and 222 species of birds, just 26 miles from New York City. Whale Watching from Plymouth, Massachusetts, two days of humpbacks, finbacks, minkes. Hudson Sail: Hudson River history while observing shore birds. Jamaica Bay Bird Walk, a wilderness of 9,000 acres on New York City's doorstep. Alaska by Land (summer) with Richard Lattis.

For international travel, (212) 879-2588 or (908) 362-7744. Call for dates. Brazil, visit the Pantanal and parks of Iguacu Falls. See hundreds of species of animals, including six members of the toucan family, Hyacinth macaw, crab-eating fox, coati, jaguar, black-capped capuchin, white-eared opossum, and the endangered tegu lizard. Botswana, the Okavango Delta, visit Machaba, Pom Pom, and Shinde Island. See elephants, lions, zebras, giraffes, bush babies, genets, and jackals as well as sitatungas on Shinde Island. Costa Rica, Belize, Guatemala, Panama: WCSI has a number of travel opportunities to these countries, which are all a part of the Paseo Pandera Project to preserve biological diversity, enhance wildlands set aside for conservation, and restore sections of the corridor that comprises the Central American isthmus. Ecotouristic emphasis. Family Safari in Kenya (summer) with Richard Lattis.

North Carolina Zoological Park, Asheboro. The North Carolina Zoological Society runs tours, (919) 879-7270, Sally Steel. Caribbean cruise on the vessel *Nantucket* to St. Thomas, Virgin Gorda, and Tortola for snorkeling and exploration of islands with naturalists. Not a regular tourist trip. South Africa, Zimbabwe, Botswana safari (14 days, March), includes four days riding elephants in the bush and swimming with baby elephants at Abu Camp. South Africa, and Zimbabwe, visits to zoos in Pretoria and Johannesburg.

Oklahoma City Zoological Park. The Oklahoma Zoological Society runs tours, (405) 427-2461, Betsy Allie. Oklahoma (two days, October), annual tour of Tall Grass Prairie Preserve and Sutton Avian Research Center. East Africa (two weeks, January–February 1995), Serengeti, Maasai Mara.

Philadelphia Zoological Garden, (215) 243-1100, Jean Segal Gaughan, director, Interpretive Services. Kenya (11 days, October–November). Also planned: Guatemala (visiting the Mayan ruins of Tikal), New Guinea, Antarctica, Galápagos, and Botswana (wild-dog study). Emphasis on work of scientists in the field.

The Phoenix Zoo, (602) 273-1341, ext. 7331, Mary Ashley. Kenya (two weeks, June) with extension to Zimbabwe or Zambia. Australia (two weeks, May or August), coastal areas. Ecuador (12 days,) Galápagos and mainland. California (overnight in San Diego, annually, in January), whale watching for eight hours off

San Diego at Mexico's Los Coronados Islands. Baja California (one week, January).

St. Louis Zoo. Tours run by Friends of the Zoo, (314) 647-8210, ext. 370, Eileen Johnson. Costa Rica, Darien Jungle, Panama Canal (11 days, April). The Amazon (eight days, July), rain forest and Incas, Machu Picchu extension of seven days; Kenya, (14 days, depart September 12). India (16 days, departs October 22), Nepal extension seven days.

San Diego Zoo. Tours run by Zoological Society, (800) 541-0077 or (619) 295-1080. In 1995: Two annual safaris to Kenya and Tanzania (January and February) to view the great migration of the wildebeest and zebras. Also Baja California (April 1 to 9, 1994), Zimbabwe and Botswana (September), New Zealand (November).

San Francisco Zoological Gardens, (415) 753-7171, ask for travel program. Kenya (14 days, June). Aberderes a highlight; also Maasai Mara, Nakuru. Madagascar (18 days, October), tour organized by International Expeditions to look for the indri (the largest of prosimians) in tropical rain forest; visit the semiarid and arid southern part of the island, including Berenty Reserve, where ring-tail and other lemur species will be seen; visit the northwestern part of Madagascar, the island of Nosy Be, for more lemurs.

Santa Barbara Zoological Gardens, (805) 962-5339, Kris. California (one day, April) 10:00 A.M. to 2:30 P.M., whale watching from the zoo's hilltop, then on the zoo vessel, *Condor*.

Seattle Aquarium, (206) 386-4353, Janet Criscola. Tours in Washington State:

In the Puget Sound by kayak to see sea lions breed and bask (one day, spring).

Shore birds migrating in protective lagoons (one day, spring).

Overnight camping in Potholes (a lake with islands) to observe Western grebes courting and "dancing" on the water (two days, May).

Gray whale watching, out of Westport (three-hour cruise, March–April).

Orca whale watching, 85 to 90 percent chance of sighting Orca (one day, June–August).

Canoe paddles on the Nisqually Delta. Eagles, osprey (one day, July–August).

Cedar River to watch salmon spawning upstream (one day, October).

Skagit River on a float trip to observe as many as 200 bald eagles feeding off carcasses of dead salmon (three hours, January–February 1995).

Sunset Zoological Park, Manhattan, Kansas, (913) 587-2737. Kenya (12 days, October) led by zoo director Don Wixom. Amazon. Future tours to Galápagos (12 days, March 1995; a probable repeat of 1994, led by General Curator Mike Quick). Alaska, Australia, and The Zoos of Europe (including several in Germany, Antwerp, Amsterdam, Rotterdam, London, and perhaps the island of Jersey) led by Research Director Bob Klemm (10 days).

Woodland Park Zoological Gardens, Seattle, Washington, (206) 646-7677, Kumi Kilburn. Belize (10 days, April), rain forest, savannah, mangrove swamps, the world's second-longest barrier reef, 500 species of birds; visit the Bermudian Landing Community Baboon Sanctuary (ecotourism), the Cockscomb Jaguar Reserve, and Belize Zoo. Zimbabwe, Zambia, Botswana (19 days, August), lakes and woodlands of Zambia for puku, Thornycroft giraffe, and leopards; camp next to the Zambezi River, canoeing close to hippos; explore the Kalahari Desert; a night at Victoria Falls. India (22 days, November), for tigers, elephants, and birds. Amazon (eight days, December–January) study of the rain forest (25,000 species of exotic plants, one third of the world's 8,600 species of birds); a visit to the canopy walkway of ACEER—Amazon Center for Environmental Education and Research; optional extension to Machu Picchu. Mexico, to the Sierra Madre to witness the monarch butterflies that have migrated from the Great Lakes and New England; visit the new zoo, Selva Mágica. Australia (15 days, March), snorkel off the Great Barrier Reef or board a submersible vessel; in sanctuaries, see koala, emu, kangaroo, potoroo, and duckbill platypus; penguins on Phillip Island; rain forests of Cape Tribulation; Lamington National Park for the satin and regent bowerbirds; visit Taronga Park Zoo and Healesville Sanctuary.

Zoo Atlanta, (404) 642-1983, Suzanne Ballew. Kenya (annually, two weeks in July, limited to 18 persons). Galápagos and Ecuadorian Amazon (two weeks in July, five on board a ship). Also planned: Thailand (fall 1994). Possible: Botswana, Zimbabwe, South Africa. Future trips: Baja California (seven days, expected to be offered in 1995), on the *Sea Bird*.

ZooMontana, (406) 652-8100, Jim Duncan, administrator. Zoo Montana is a new $4½ million, 70-acre zoo in Billings, grand opening in 1994. Only northern hemisphere animals, including Siberian tiger, river otters. Zoo Montana has been offering tours (Kenya, Australia, Costa Rica, and Panama Canal, Tanzania) since 1989 with a dual purpose: to acquaint people of Montana with non-Northern Hemisphere wildlife *and* to build up an interest in the zoo. Call for program.

Tour Operators Accredited by the AAZPA

Baja Expeditions, Inc., 2625 Garnet Avenue, San Diego, California 92109, (619) 581-3311.

Fun Safaris, Inc., P.O. Box 178, 231 Lakeshore Drive, Bloomingdale, Illinois 60108, (800) 323-8020. Fun Safaris has provided one or more tours to 70 percent of the AAZPA-accredited zoos and aquariums. Specialties: Australia, Alaska, Argentina, and Africa (in Botswana, an elephant-riding safari and a swim with baby elephants).

Harmsafari, 2150 West Washington Street, Suite 501, San Diego, California 92110, (800) 541-0077. Specialty: Africa.

International Expeditions, Inc., One Environs Park, Helena, Alabama 35080, (800) 633-4734 or (205) 428-1700. Specialty: Natural history programs.

Lemur Tours, Inc., 2562 Noriega Street, #203–204, San Francisco, California 94122, (800) 735-3687. Specialty: Madagascar, Mauritius, Kenya, Tanzania.

Park East Tours, Inc., 1841 Broadway, Suite 900, New York, New York 10023, (800) 223-6078 or (212) 765-4870. Specialties: East Africa (Kenya, Tanzania), southern Africa (Botswana, Zimbabwe, Zambia), central Africa (Rwanda, Zaire), Galápagos, Ecuador, Costa Rica, Belize, Guatemala, Alaska, India, Australia, New Zealand, China.

Princess Tours, 2815 Second Avenue, Suite 400, Seattle, Washington 98121, (800) 421-4725 or (206) 728-4202. Specialty: Alaska (Prudhoe Bay Wildlife Tour).

Wildlife Safari Pty., 346 Rheem Boulevard, Suite 107, Moranga, California 94556, (800) 221-8118. Specialty: Africa.

Zoo Life, 11661 San Vicente Boulevard, Los Angeles, California 90049, (310) 820-8841. Specialty: Diving and safaris (Africa). Publishers of *Zoo Life* magazine.

List of Zoos and Aquariums by State

WISCONSIN

Index

ABOUT THE TYPE

This book was set in Bodoni Book, a typeface named after
Giambattista Bodoni, an Italian printer and type designer of
the late eighteenth and early nineteenth century. It is not
actually one of Bodoni's fonts but a modern version based
on his style and manner and is distinguished by a marked
contrast between the thick and thin elements of the letters.